"LIBERTY OR DEATH!"

THE NORTHERN CAMPAIGNS IN THE

AMERICAN REVOLUTIONARY WAR

by
Gregory T. Edgar

Gregory T. Edgar
July 26, 1995

Published 1994 By
HERITAGE BOOKS, INC.
1540-E Pointer Ridge Place, Bowie, Md., 20716
(301) 390-7709

ISBN 0-7884-0023-1

DEDICATION

This book is dedicated to all those who have given their lives so that others may be free. And also to David George Edgar and Fay Ashton Reed, who taught this author to love American History. They are both dearly missed.

ACKNOWLEDGEMENT

The author is grateful to Mr. Donald Walcott for reading the manuscript and offering very helpful suggestions and encouragement.

CONTENTS

v

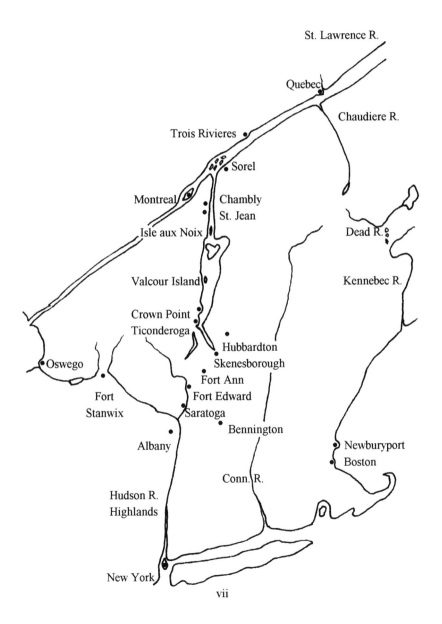

THE NORTHERN CAMPAIGNS
IN THE AMERICAN
REVOLUTIONARY WAR
1775 - 1777

St. Lawrence R.

Quebec

Chaudiere R.

Trois Rivieres

Sorel

Montreal

Chambly
St. Jean

Isle aux Noix

Dead R.

Valcour Island

Kennebec R.

Crown Point
Ticonderoga

Hubbardton

Oswego

Skenesborough

Fort Ann

Fort
Stanwix

Fort Edward

Saratoga

Bennington

Albany

Newburyport
Boston

Conn. R.

Hudson R.
Highlands

New York

INTRODUCTION

The Northern Campaigns

Though the American Revolutionary War (1775-1783) started in the Boston area, the theater of operations for the main British and American armies shifted in 1776 to New York, and again in 1777 to Philadelphia. But during the first three years of the war, there were also other, smaller armies engaging each other on the northern frontier: upstate New York, northern New England, and parts of Canada. What came to be known as the Northern Department of the Continental Army, and the armies that opposed it, are the focus of this book.

Why did these armies operate so far from the main armies and the population centers? The answer lies in the strategic importance of the Hudson River. Originating in the Adirondack Mountains of northeastern New York, the Hudson flowed due south, close to New England's western border, until it emptied into New York's harbor and the Atlantic Ocean. If the British could control traffic on the Hudson, they could effectively isolate New England from the other colonies and, more importantly, cut off an important supply line to Washington's main army.

The administration in London knew this, and so did the Continental Congress. Both sides were determined to gain control of the south-north waterway that ran from New York to Quebec, starting with the Hudson and continuing north through Lakes George and Champlain, then along the Canadian Rivers Richelieu and St. Lawrence. This route had been used just one generation earlier, during the French and Indian War, when a British-American army successfully attacked the French colony of Canada and ended the war. Now Canada was a British colony, and a potential staging ground for an invasion of the rebellious colonies to the south.

To prevent this, two American armies were sent north in 1775. One went via the Hudson River and the other went up Maine's Kennebec.

If they could capture the strongholds of St. Jean, on the Richelieu, and Quebec, on the St. Lawrence, they would take away this threat of invasion. Possession of Canada would also give the Congress an important bargaining chip in the expected peace negotiations. (In 1775, most Americans expected a very short war and a reconciliation with the mother country; desire for independence was still a year away.)

However, the American armies achieved only partial success. To accomplish more would have required substantial assistance from the Canadians. But they had no desire to be "liberated" from what was a just British rule, especially since Parliament's recent Quebec Act had guaranteed them the right to practice Roman Catholicism. When the Protestant Yankees arrived, they were met with indifference and distrust. Their request for men, and their attempts to purchase food with paper "continentals," were refused.

Most of the Americans' short term enlistments were due to expire on January 1, 1776, and Quebec still had not been taken. So, during a blinding snowstorm on New Year's Eve, the American commanders, Richard Montgomery and Benedict Arnold, launched a desperate assault on the fabled fortress. After coming close to victory, the attack ended in disaster. Montgomery was killed, Arnold wounded, and several hundred others were taken prisoner. Arnold, though, kept up his blockade of the city throughout the bitter winter, hoping for reinforcements in the spring.

In May, 1776, the first breakup of the ice brought the arrival from London of a new British army, augmented by German mercenaries. They overwhelmed the smallpox-ridden American northern army, which fell back to Lake Champlain's Fort Ticonderoga. There Arnold led the frantic construction of gunboats and other small warships. This forced the slower British to spend the valuable summer months building a superior fleet, so they could eliminate this obstacle and transport their army and supplies southward. They intended to reach Albany by the fall. Arnold commanded the tiny "mosquito fleet" in a three day battle (the first major U.S. naval engagement). His fleet was destroyed but he had delayed the British. When they reached Ticonderoga, it was too well defended to risk an assault, and it was too late in the season to begin breaking ground for time-consuming siege tactics. The frustrated British Army returned to Canada for the winter.

By the summer of 1777, the Congress was convinced that the British Army in Canada would sail down the Atlantic to attack Charleston or Philadelphia, and not make another attempt on Ticonderoga. Therefore, fewer resources were allocated to the northern army. But Congress had guessed wrong, and the British returned. Ticonderoga fell, the northern army was scattered, and it looked like the British, led by the charismatic "Gentleman Johnny" Burgoyne, would reach Albany. However, his army became bogged down while making the long overland portage between Lake Champlain and the Hudson. Tadeusz Kosciuszko, a volunteer military engineer from Poland, led one thousand Americans with picks, shovels and axes in a delaying action, felling trees and damning up streams to flood the road.

It took Burgoyne twenty-three days to move his army the twenty-three miles to the upper Hudson. This gave the northern army time to regroup along the Hudson. And for Washington to send north reinforcements, including Daniel Morgan's rifle corps, expert woods fighters. Burgoyne would later term them "the finest regiment of rangers in the world." The tide was definitely turning in the Americans' favor. Victories near Bennington, Vermont, and Fort Stanwix, New York, clipped off Burgoyne's left and right wings. News of these victories brought thousands more Americans to the Hudson as, now that prospects appeared brighter, farmers and others all across New England and New York now found the courage to "meet the British."

Though running out of men, food and time, Burgoyne ruled out a retreat to Canada. Instead, he gambled on his ability to force his way through the American lines, which Kosciuszko had established on a hillside above the Hudson. After two unsuccessful battles, Burgoyne could not even reach those lines, as Arnold and Morgan led wave after wave of men out of the woods to attack his advancing army. Defeated, Burgoyne surrendered his entire army at the riverside village of Saratoga.

Saratoga may be considered the turning point of the war, as Benjamin Franklin and Silas Deane used the shocking news to finally persuade the French to join the United States in an open military alliance. Four years later, a French fleet and a combined French-- American army would force another British army to surrender at Yorktown, Virginia, effectively ending the war.

This book concludes with a chapter on prisoners of war. The treatment of Burgoyne's defeated army is examined, as well as other prisoners of war on both sides. First-hand accounts by prisoners who survived captivity provide especially compelling reading.

Images of the Revolution

Ask a few Americans what they can recall about the American Revolutionary War, and what will they tell you? One may describe an image of Thomas Jefferson and other men in a large room, each waiting his turn to sign the Declaration of Independence. Another might picture George Washington standing in the bow of a small boat on a snowy evening, being rowed across the Delaware River.

These are not the only images we should have of our nation's founding years. Politicians and generals alone do not make a revolution. Our heroes should include the common people, as well - the men and women who endured those hard times and bore the brunt of sacrifice. Let us have images of them, too.

So how do we learn about these people? By letting them tell us their stories. Though a few wrote memoirs after the war, most of the first-hand accounts that have survived are diaries and letters. These people probably did not intend for us to read them, but that is what we must do if we are going to come to know these people, to learn from them, and appreciate them and what they did for us.

The writings used in this book, from Americans, British and Germans, reflect the wonderment they felt when they encountered new places, people and customs. The rare big event, such as a battle, is usually described in detail, but we can also learn from their other words. We see their opinions of the events and people that impacted their lives in personal and powerful ways. But we come to know them best when they record occasional moments of humor, and when their pens vent their feelings of joy, sadness, homesickness, despair, rage and fear.

Read their writings, let them speak to us, and we will truly learn our history. For history is not a series of events, but the stories of people.

CHAPTER ONE
LIFE IN "THE GRAND AMERICAN ARMY"
APRIL - AUGUST 1775

"Where the principles of democracy so universally prevail, either no discipline can be established, or he who attempts it becomes odious and detestable, a position which no one will choose."

> - *General George Washington's secretary, writing home to his wife in Pennsylvania about the Yankees of New England.*

After the April 19, 1775 British raid on the patriot supply depot at Concord, they marched back to Boston. Within two days, they found themselves surrounded by nearly 20,000 angry citizen-soldiers. Untrained in warfare, these "Yankee" (New England) militia were scorned by the professional British soldiers as a "rabble in arms." The bloody return march from Concord and Lexington had been a hit and run affair, but the British officers predicted that, if it came to a pitched battle, the Yankees would never stand their ground and fight.

Eight weeks later, however, they found out the Yankees would indeed fight. On June 17, the British once again ventured out of Boston to attack the rebels, this time on Breed's and Bunker's Hills above nearby Charlestown. It took three suicidal frontal assaults against their entrenched foe, before the British finally reached the Yankee earthworks and forced them to flee back to their main camp. By then the Yankees had run out of ammunition. The British had won the battle, but it was a hollow victory, for they had suffered over one thousand casualties. One British officer wrote home, saying, "Three more such victories and we will no longer have an army."

1

The British learned some hard lessons at the Battle of Bunker Hill. They had underestimated the Americans' will to fight. They would not easily be taken, unless they could somehow be forced into fighting in the open, without the protection of stone walls or earthworks. General Thomas Gage wrote home, confidentially, to his friend, Lord Barrington.

> [The Americans are] not the despicable rabble too many have supposed them to be. These people shew a spirit and conduct against us they never shewed against the French, and every body has judged of them from their former appearance and behaviour, when joyned with the Kings forces in the last war, which has led many into great mistakes. They are now spirited up by a rage and enthousiasm as great as ever a people were possessed of.

In England, the press expressed similar shock at the news of Bunker Hill. Typical was the comment, "We expected to find them a cowardly rabble who would lie quietly at our feet, and they have disappointed us."

The American countryside, with its hills, forests and creeks, made impractical the normal tactics and strategies of the British Army, developed for fighting on the open plains of Europe. Lord Germain, the new Secretary of War, clearly stated the dilemma when he declared, "the manner of opposing an enemy that avoids facing you in the open field is totally different from what young officers learn from the common discipline of the army." But, instead of adapting to the conditions in America, and learning the Indian style of woods fighting, British generals would strive throughout the war to force the rebels to fight in the open. General Sir Henry Clinton explained, in 1779, that this would put the armies "upon terms tolerably equal," which was "the object of every campaign during this war."

Knowing those conditions would favor the better trained British

2

Army, American generals avoided being drawn into battles on open ground. General George Washington told Congress, in 1776, that the war should be defensive, concentrating on skirmishing, harassing the enemy, and cutting off their supply lines. He wrote, "we should on all occasions avoid a general action, and never be drawn into a necessity to put anything to risk." He knew that he could not risk the capture of his army in a large scale battle that could only favor his better equipped foe. Despite pressure from the Congress and the press to act offensively, Washington would only attack when he had an advantage. He continued to stress a defensive posture throughout most of the war, "remaining quiet in a secure, fortified camp, disciplining and arranging the Army, till the enemy begin their operations, and then to govern ourselves accordingly."

To maintain that "secure, fortified camp" meant almost endless intrenching, throwing up walls of earth. What success the Americans achieved at Bunker Hill was due mainly to their skillful and rapid intrenching the night before the battle. Throughout the war, they would rely on intrenching as their primary defensive strategy. It would be an appropriate and successful one, allowing their superior marksmanship to bring devastating results. Like other European armies of the period, the British Army placed little or no value on this defensive measure, preferring to shoot it out in the open and rely on mass volleying followed by a bayonet charge.

The British, and their German allies, had too much contempt for Americans to hide behind intrenchments when the "despicable rabble" dared to attack them. In General Howe's narrative describing how he conducted the war, he stated his belief that works of that kind were "apt to induce an opinion of inferiority," whereas he wished always to create "the impression of superiority."

The British had won the Battle of Bunker Hill, and now controlled the two small peninsulas of Boston and Charlestown. But they would not venture out against the rebels again. As General Percy said, "We cannot afford another victory."

* * * * *

The colonial troops soon overcame the depression caused by the retreat from Charlestown. Instead of being discouraged, they correctly attributed their defeat to the shortage of gunpowder and bullets. Now, as the siege dragged on, they used their Yankee ingenuity to find ways of procuring small amounts of powder from the British. Private Isaac Greenwood recalled the many bombs which frequently came from British cannon: "falling on marshy land they would bury themselves from ten to twelve feet in it, whereupon the wet ground having extinguished the fusee, the Yankees would dig them up to get the powder out."

In August, Private Elkanah Watson visited the powder house at the patriot army's headquarters in Cambridge.

> I observed to the officer, "Sir, I am happy to see so many barrels of powder here." He whispered a secret in my ear, with an indiscretion that marked the novice in military affairs. "These barrels are filled with sand." "And wherefore?" I inquired. "To deceive the enemy," he replied, "should any spy by chance look in."

The American generals knew they must also accumulate a large supply of cannon balls, so that if they ever acquired enough cannon and powder they would be able to force the British to either fight or quit Boston. A newspaper in September published the following article:

> General Putnam, by his ingenious invention and incredible courage, having nearly expended his cannon balls before the king's schooner, took this method to get more from the *Somerset* in Boston harbor: He ordered parties consisting of about two or three of his men to show themselves on top of a certain sandy hill, near the place of action, in sight of the man-of-war, but at a great

4

distance, in hopes that the captain would be fool enough to fire at them. It had the desired effect, and so heavy a fire ensued from this ship and others, that the country round Boston thought the town was attacked. By this he obtained severeral hundred balls, which were easily taken out of the sand.

Private John Trumbull, who had celebrated his nineteenth birthday soon after reaching camp at Roxbury, recorded in his journal some of the lessons learned in the first few weeks of the siege:

> The enemy occasionally fired upon our working parties, whenever they approached too nigh to their works; and in order to familiarize our raw soldiers to this exposure, a small reward was offered in general orders for every ball fired by the enemy which should be picked up and brought to headquarters. This soon produced a very unfortunate result, for when the soldiers saw a ball, after having struck and rebounded from the ground several times roll sluggishly along, they would run and place a foot before it to stop it, not aware that a heavy ball long retains sufficient impetus to overcome such an obstacle. The consequence was that several brave lads lost their feet, which were crushed.

Chasing after cannon balls was not the only way the Yankees amused themselves while waiting for the redcoats to venture out of Boston. Private David How, of Methuen, Mass., recorded in his journal these entries for three days within the same week:

> This day tow men in Cambridge got a bantering who wodd drink the most and they drinkd so much that one of them died in about one hour or two after. ...
> There was two women drumd out of camp this fore

noon. That man was buried that killed himself drinking.
...
There was a man found dead in a room with a woman this morning. It is not known what killed him.

The influence of the clergy can be seen in the many general orders admonishing against swearing, gambling and other vices. One order addressed prostitution:

That all possible care be taken that no lewd women come into the camp; and all persons are ordered to give information of such persons, if there be, that proper measures be taken to bring them to condign punishment, and rid the camp of all such nuisances.

Despite efforts to dictate the army's morals, neither the clergy nor the generals could stop the soldiers from having their frolics. It was observed in Cambridge that "many men lost to all sense of decency & common modesty are running about naked upon ye bridge whilst passengers and even ladys of ye first fashion in the neighborhood are passing over it." The bathing men seemed "to glory in their shame." At least these men bothered to bathe themselves, showing more concern about personal hygiene than many did. One soldier noted the "great neglect of people repairing to the necessaries" (outhouses). Instead of walking the short distance to the necessaries, many soldiers dropped their "excrament about the fields pernishously," greatly endangering health in the camps.

Benjamin Thompson, of Woburn, Mass., outwardly was a soldier in the army, but secretly was a spy supplying the British high command with information. He wrote to General Gage that the army was "as dirty a set of mortals as ever disgraced the name of a soldier." Unlike the British generals, Washington would not allow wives and other camp followers to accompany the soldiers.

They have no women in the camp to do washing for the men, and they in general not being used to doing things of this sort and thinking it rather a disparagement to them, choose rather to let their linen rot upon their backs than to be at the trouble of cleaning 'em themselves.

The camp itself had a motley appearance, as described by the Reverend William Emerson in a letter to his wife back home in Concord:

Tis also very diverting to walk among the camps. They are as different in their form as the owners are in their dress; and every tent is a portraiture of the temper and taste of the persons that encamp in it. Some are made of boards, some of sailcloth, and some partly of one and partly of the other. Others are made of stone and turf, and others again of birch and brush. Some are your proper tents and marquees and look like the regular camp of the enemy.

In July, the newly arrived Virginian generals, George Washington, Charles Lee and Horatio Gates, were not favorably impressed with the New England army. Washington found them to be far less vigilant than he would have liked, with the British Army only a few miles away: "It is among the most difficult tasks I ever undertook in my life to induce these people to believe that there is, or can be, danger till the bayonet is pushed at their breasts."

What disturbed Washington most was the Yankee social custom of "levelling." He soon attempted to put a stop to it. Reverend Emerson wrote home again, after the Virginians' arrival:

New lords, new laws. The Generals Washington and Lee are upon the lines every day. New orders from his Excellency are read to the respective regiments every morning after prayers. The strictest government is taking place and great distinction is made between officers and soldiers. Everyone is made to know his place and keep in it, or receive thirty or forty lashes according to his crime.

But the spirit of levelling was too strong. Washington's secretary, Joseph Reed, wrote home to his wife in Pennsylvania:

> Where the principles of democracy so universally prevail, either no discipline can be established, or he who attempts it must become odious and detestable, a position which no one will choose. You may form some notion of it when I tell you that yesterday morning a captain of horse, who attends the general from Connecticut, was seen shaving one of his men.

The general from Connecticut was Israel Putnam. It is not surprising that one of his captains was found shaving a private, for Old Put himself was known to occasionally cook dinner at the campfire, and find other ways to ensure that his men were well taken care of. Unlike the aristocratic Washington, Putnam believed officers should not hold themselves above their men. Jacob Francis, a New Jersey free Negro, was helping to build a breastwork at Lechemere Point, in Cambridge, when he first saw the Yankee general.

> The men were at work digging, about five hundred men on the fatigue at once. General Putnam came riding along to look at the work. They had dug up a pretty large stone which lay on the side of the ditch. The general spoke to the corporal, who was standing looking at the men at work, and said to him, "My lad, throw that stone up on the middle of the breastwork."
>
> The corporal, touching his hat with his hand, said to

the general, "Sir, I am a corporal."

"Oh," said the general, "I ask your pardon, sir," and immediately got off his horse and took up the stone and threw it up on the breastwork himself and then mounted his horse and rode on.

The levelling spirit hampered Washington's efforts to achieve proper subordination in the army. Benjamin Thompson, the spy, explained it in his letters to the British authorities.

> The very spirit which induced the common people to take up arms and resist the authority of Great Britain should induce them to resist the authority of their officers, and by that means effectually prevent their making good soldiers. ... [It is due to the] great degree of equality as to birth, fortune and education that prevails upon them. For men cannot bear to be commanded by others that are their superiors in nothing but in having had the good fortune to get a superior commission, for which perhaps they stood equally fair. The officers and men are most commonly neighbours and acquaintances, and as such can with less patience submit to that degree of absolute submission and subordination which is necessary to form a well-disciplined corps.

General Washington expressed his own opinion confidentially in a letter to his nephew back in Virginia:

> These New England men are so defective in materials for officers that it must require time to make a real good army out of 'em.
>
> Their officers, generally speaking, are the most indifferent kind of people I ever saw. I have already broke one Colonel and five Captains for cowardice and for

drawing more pay and provisions than they had men in their companies. They are by no means such troops, in any respect, as you are led to believe of them from the accts. which are published. I dare say the men would fight very well, if properly officered, although they are an exceeding dirty and nasty people.

There has been so many errors and abuses to rectify - so many examples to make - and so little inclination in the officers of inferior rank to contribute their aid to accomplish this work, that my life has been nothing else but one continued round of annoyance and fatigue.

Soon Washington realized that "they will not be drove," they "must be disciplined by degrees." He instructed one colonel to be strict in his discipline, but to require nothing unreasonable of his men. He should listen to their complaints, and redress them if well founded. But he should avoid too great a familiarity with his men and subordinate officers, lest he lose the respect necessary for effective command. Above all, he should "impress upon the mind of every man the importance of the cause, and what it is they are contending for." Knowledge and morale, in Washington's mind, were essential to proper subordination.

* * * * *

In late July and early August, 1430 riflemen from Virginia, Maryland and Pennsylvania arrived in camp at Cambridge, with their buckskin clothes, coonskin caps, long beards, and seven-foot "rifle-guns." So hardy were these men that they came the whole four to seven hundred miles - "a pleasant march" - in about three weeks without a single recorded loss of a man to illness.

Like the Yankees, these backwoodsmen "chose our officers" before setting out from home. In some places, too many men had turned out, more than could be supplied and fed. One captain tried to be objective in choosing who could enlist.

He took a board a foot square and with chalk drew the shape of a moderate nose in the center and nailed it up to a tree at one hundred and fifty yards distance, and those who came nighest the mark with a single ball was to go. But by the first forty or fifty that fired, the nose was blown out of the board.

On their way north, the rifle companies created a sensation wherever they stopped long enough to give shooting and tomahawk throwing demonstrations. One rifleman recorded in his journal that, in passing through Litchfield, Conn., they "took a girl out of jail, and they tarred and feathered another Tory near Hartford, who [had] said when they marched by that he was sorry to see so many men going to fight the king." Another rifleman was impressed with "the populousness of New England, the unfair number of fine ladies, the stones and walls of stones."

Because of their long journey, the riflemen were, at first, excused from normal camp duties. Zealous and bored, and eager to "meet the British," they often snuck away from camp without orders, to shoot at the British sentries, who quickly learned the danger of exposing themselves. Soon after their arrival in camp, Washington issued orders to stop the unauthorized practice, but the orders were ignored. He then declared that anyone wishing "to pass down to the out centinels nearest the enemy" would require a pass from one of the major-generals. He explained his annoyance at the riflemen, in his general orders to the army:

Contrary to all order, straggling soldiers do still pass the guards, and fire at a distance where there is not the least probability of hurting the enemy, and where no other end is answered but to waste their ammunition, expose themselves to the ridicule of the enemy, and keep their own camps harassed by frequent and continual

11

alarms, to the hurt and detriment of every good soldier, who is thereby disturbed of his natural rest, and at length will never be able to distinguish between a real and false alarm.

These backwoodsmen, not used to a sedentary life, were even less suited to the boring camp life than the New Englanders. Where there was an abundance of rum and hard cider, fights were inevitable. One such fight, between Virginians and Yankees, was recalled many years later by Israel Trask, who claimed to have seen General Washington gallop to the scene. "He threw the bridle of his own horse into the servant's hands, sprang from his seat, rushed into the thickest of the melee, seized two tall brawny riflemen by the throat, keeping them at arm's length, talking to and shaking them."

Washington soon tired of his fellow southerners. Their insubordination reached a climax on September 10. Jesse Lukens, himself a "rifleman" from Virginia, but one of the majority of them who were orderly, described the action in a letter home:

> We were excused from all working parties, camp guards, and camp duty. This indulgence, together with the remissness of discipline and care in our young officers, had rendered the men rather insolent for good soldiers. They had twice before broke open our guard house and released their companions who were confined there for small crimes, and once when an offender was brought to the post to be whipped it was with the utmost difficulty they were kept from rescuing him in the presence of all their officers - they openly damned them and behaved with great insolence. However, the colonel was pleased to pardon the man and all remained quiet.
> But on Sunday last, the adjutant having confined a sergeant for neglect of duty and murmuring, the men began again and threatened to take him out. The adjutant,

being a man of spirit, seized the principal mutineer, and ordered a guard to take him to Cambridge at the Main Guard, which was done without any violent opposition. But in about 20 minutes 32 of Captain Ross's company with their loaded rifles swore by God they would go to the Main Guard and release the man or lose their lives, and set off as hard as they could run - it was in vain to attempt stopping them.

We stayed in camp and kept the others quiet - sent word to General Washington, who reinforced the guard to 500 men with fixed bayonets and loaded pieces. Generals Washington, Lee and Greene came immediately, and our 32 mutineers who had gone about half a mile towards Cambridge and taken possession of a hill and woods, beginning to be frightened at their proceedings, were not so hardened, but upon the General's ordering them to ground their arms they did it immediately. The General then ordered another of our companys to surround them with their loaded guns, which was immediately done.

You cannot conceive what disgrace we are all in and how much the General is chagrined that only one regiment should come from the South and that set so infamous an example: and in order that idleness shall not be a further bane to us, the general orders on Monday were "That Col. Thompson's regiment shall be upon all parties of fatigue and do all other camp duty, with any other regiment."

The men have since been tried by a general court martial and convicted of mutiny and were only fined 20s each, too small a punishment for so base a crime and mitigated no doubt on account of their having come so far to serve the cause.

Soon after this incident, a Massachusetts general was happy to write, "They do not boast so much of the riflemen as heretofore, General Washington has said he wished they had never come; General Lee has damned them and wished them all in Boston." Indeed, some of the riflemen, recent Scotch-Irish immigrants, defected to the British, having been disillusioned with life in "The Grand American Army." These rugged frontiersmen were not in their element in a siege - they were men of action, as they would later prove in the expedition to Quebec, and at Saratoga and elsewhere. When it came to endurance under extreme hardships, and courage and skill in woods fighting, they were unsurpassed. The riflemen from the southern mountains epitomized the kind of extreme individualism that had helped bring on the war, and the determination that would allow Washington to hold together a nucleus of his army long enough to eventually win the war.

By September, Washington learned that the British Army was building barracks and importing coal. He read these signs as meaning they planned to stay put in Boston until reinforcements arrived the next spring. Reassured, he felt secure enough to detach some of the restless riflemen and Yankees from the army. He would send them north, through the wilderness of Maine and beyond, on a secret expedition to conquer Canada.

CHAPTER TWO
AMERICA TAKES THE OFFENSIVE
AUGUST - NOVEMBER 1775

"Don't let it trouble you about our going to St. Johns, for it is our duty to go. The cause is just and I make no doubt we shall have success."

- Private Rozzle Fellows, writing home to
  Canaan, Conn., from Crown Point, N. Y.

Before following the riflemen and Yankee militia on their trek from Washington's camp in Cambridge, Mass., through the Maine wilderness to Quebec, let's turn our attention a few hundred miles west to Lake Champlain.

On May 10, Connecticut's Benedict Arnold had accompanied Ethan Allen and his "Green Mountain Boys" of the Hampshire Grants (present day Vermont) in attacking Ticonderoga and Crown Point. The British commanders at those Lake Champlain forts had not yet heard the war had started, so they were caught completely by surprise, and the forts were taken without a shot being fired. The next day, Allen had used a ship stolen from a local "Tory" (loyalist) to sail north to Canada. There, on the Richelieu River, he had also surprised the British garrison in the fort at St. Jean (St. Johns), and captured the soldiers and another ship. By then, news of the invasion had reached the Canadian Governor, General Guy Carleton, who quickly dispatched a large party of Canadian militia to march to St. Jean. The Americans wisely took their spoils back to Ticonderoga.

All this had happened without the knowledge or consent of the Continental Congress, which was shocked when it heard the news. Not wanting to further antagonize Parliament with hostile acts, Congress at first voted to give the forts and prisoners back to the British. Within days, an express rider arrived from Connecticut with the message Congressman Silas Deane had requested. He stood up and announced that that colony was ready to defy the Congress and send its own militia to the lake, to prevent Congressional troops from giving the forts back. Congress backed down, and appointed one of its own, New York's General Philip Schuyler, to oversee the lake's defenses. Schuyler was the first commander of what would become known as the Northern Department of the Continental Army.

After the British attack on Bunker Hill, Congress was more willing to take aggressive actions. On June 27, it authorized Schuyler to lead an army of New York and New England troops to "take possession of St. Johns, Montreal, and any other parts of the country, and pursue any other measures in Canada which may have a tendency to promote the peace and security of these colonies." John Adams and others in Congress knew that possession of Canada was vital to the safety of the northern colonies. They would not allow "our enemies to pour down Regulars, Canadians and Indians" from the north, as France had during the old French wars. Possession of Canada would also be a very good bargaining tool when representatives of Congress and Parliament sat down to negotiate American liberties. Some even predicted that the conquest of Canada would result in the ouster of the hard liners in the King's administration, opening the way for more peaceful measures and a speedy reconciliation.

Philip Schuyler spent the summer struggling with committees and merchants to provide him with the men, equipment and food supplies he would need for the planned invasion of Canada. He also had to contend with the prejudices and distrust that the colonists had for one another. The Yankees blamed all the delays on the "Yorkers." One man wrote to Connecticut's Governor Trumbull, reminding him that New York's legislature has "scarcely a majority who are sound friends to the cause." He thought that "our not being in better preparations here is owing to the negligence of New York." A Pennsylvania officer observed that the aristocratic Schuyler made no effort to "conceal the extreme contempt he felt" for Yankee officers, the "pumpkin gentry."

The men and supplies finally arrived, but the invasion of Canada was delayed several more days in late August, as Schuyler had to attend an Indian conference in Albany. He convinced the Iroquois sachems, at least for the present campaign, to "bury the hatchet" and "not take any part" in this "family quarrel."

In Montreal, Governor Guy Carleton was also attending an Indian conference. The Canadian Indians offered to lay waste the enemy's frontier settlements from New York to Maine. But Carleton took just a few dozen of the Indians, and only for scouting duties. They "were somewhat disgusted at their offer being rejected." The humanitarian Carleton, so unlike other British generals, explained his decision in a letter to his superior, General Gage, in Boston: "What is or can be expected of them, farther than cutting off a few unfortunate families, whose destruction will be of little avail towards a decision of the present contest?"

By the end of August, Schuyler's army of 1200 had sailed and rowed its way north to Isle aux Noix (Nut Island), where Lake Champlain empties into Canada's Richelieu River. By now, the British commander at St. Jean, twenty miles downriver, had learned of the invasion. His Indian scouts had brought in the head of a Green Mountain Boy, Remember Baker, on the end of a pole, as well as a paper Baker had been carrying that described St. Jean's defenses.

From Isle aux Noix, Schuyler dispatched Ethan Allen and John Brown to enlist Canadians and Indians. In his address, which Allen and Brown carried to the Canadians, Schuyler stated that "the Grand Congress" had ordered him to expel the British troops, who wished "to enslave their countrymen." The Congress "could not conceive that anything but the force of necessity could induce you tamely to bear the insult and ignominy that is daily imposed on you, or that you could calmly sit by and see those chains forging which are intended to bind you, your posterity, and ours, in one common and eternal slavery."

Ethan Allen had already made an attempt at Indian diplomacy back on May 24, two weeks after taking Ticonderoga, when he had sent a letter to the Caughnawagas of Canada:

> We hope as Indians are good and honest men you will not fight for King George against us as we have done you no wrong and would chuse to live as brothers. I always love Indians and have hunted a great deal with them. I know how to shute and ambush just like Indian and want your warriors to come and see me and help me fight Regulars. You know how they stand all along close together rank and file and my men fight so as Indian do and I want your warriors to join with me and my warriors like brothers and ambush the Regulars. If you will I will give you money blankits tomehawks knives and paint and the like as much as you say because they first killed our men when it was peace time and try to kill us all.

After pitching their tents at Isle aux Noix, the Americans fired three cannon shots, the signal for the Canadians to come forth to join the "army of liberation." There was no response.

* * * * *

Why was there no multitude of Canadians waiting for that signal, like the minutemen of Massachusetts back in April? The answer lies in the makeup of the population and the treatment they received under British rule. Canada had been a French colony until Wolfe defeated Montcalm on the Plains of Abraham, outside Quebec, in 1759. Since then, Canada had been ruled by a British governor, who was advised by a set of appointed Councillors. With the French defeat, most of the bureaucrats and the aristocratic landed gentry, or "seigneurs," left for France. Going with them were almost all of the Roman Catholic bishops and monks, leaving behind only the local parish priests. Collection of tithes, the mainstay of the Church, was forbidden by the new government. The seigneurs were no longer allowed to impose tithes and other taxes on the peasants, or "habitants," who composed almost the entire population of Canada.

Those seigneurs who chose to remain now lived on the relatively meagre rents they could legally collect from their habitant tenants. The seigneurs, frightened by republican ideas spreading from the south, and hoping to obtain government posts, became loyal supporters of the British governor. Not surprisingly, from this tiny aristocratic segment of Canadian society Carleton chose almost all his Council members.

There was one more segment of Canadian society - Protestants from England and the southern colonies, mostly fur traders or merchants located in Montreal and Quebec and along the Richelieu River. Despite the fact that there were, according to Carleton, only "about three hundred and sixty [Protestants] besides women and children in the whole colony of Canada," they controlled "seven-eighths" of the colony's trade. They referred to themselves as "Old Subjects," because they had been subjects of the English King longer than the French Canadians, or "New Subjects."

With settlement of the French War in 1763 came a promise from the King and Parliament that eventually Canada would have a representative government. The Old Subjects felt they should have a dominant part in the government. They agitated, and in some localities, such as Montreal, demanded political privilege. By 1770, Governor Carleton realized the only way to effectively govern the former French colony was to allow the French New Subjects equal rights. His primary motive was to win the allegiance of the New Subjects, in case France should attempt to retake Canada.

So Carleton asked for a leave of absence and returned to England. There he lobbied for four years, until Parliament finally enacted the Quebec Act. Its passage, in 1774, guaranteed the habitants freedom of religion, opportunities to fill government posts, and freedom from persecution by the Old Subjects. It also put to rest all thoughts of representative government. This was the "insult" that Congress and Schuyler repeatedly referred to in their addresses to the Canadians. The intelligence that Congress and its generals had been given by their agents in Canada had been based solely on contact with Old Subjects. John Brown had misled them into believing that "the Canadians will join us. There is a great defection amongst them."

But these Old Subjects were only a few hundred. The 75,000 habitants were content with the mild rule of Governor Carleton. For fifteen years, they had enjoyed the luxury of not being forced to perform military service, unlike their former life under French rule. And they lived a more prosperous existence now, without the heavy taxes formerly imposed by the seigneurs and the Church. They had had no Stamp Crisis, no Boston Massacre to arouse them. Agents and propaganda sent by Congress and the Boston Committee of Correspondence had failed. The French Canadians, entirely Catholic, were not about to pay much attention to rhetoric about liberty from men who, in their protest against the Quebec Act, had openly voiced their hatred of Roman Catholics. And the English-speaking Protestant trader-merchant community had balked at overtures from a Congress which would have forced them to stop trading with Britain. To make such a commitment, they said, would be "bringing down ruin upon our own heads."

Like the American general, Governor Carleton, too, experienced disappointing results from his recruiters. Listening to the advice of his Council, he appointed seigneurs to be the officers in his reactivated militia. However, the seigneurs could not persuade the habitants, who might have been willing to serve under officers of their own choosing. The seigneurs, without the former feudal laws of the French rule, were now nearly powerless and universally despised by the habitants. Their efforts at recruiting were resisted, particularly those of the more odious seigneurs who commissioned their own relatives as subordinate officers.

In one village, after an attempt by an ambitious seigneur to force 100% enlistment, instead of the customary 15 men per village, the people signed an oath to never take up arms against Americans, to burn the house and barn of anyone in the village who did, and to meet force with force should Carleton try to coerce them. In another village, the recruiting seigneur struck one farmer who refused to enlist. The wrath of the villagers was such that the haughty young seigneur had to make a hasty departure. But on leaving, he threatened to return with British Regulars to make things smart for their disobedience. The enraged habitants gathered their guns and pitchforks, and marched, 350 strong, to meet the Regulars. Fortunately, Carleton sent a representative to defuse the crisis.

So Governor Carleton again went to Bishop Briand, of Quebec, for help. The bishop had earlier issued a statement praising the English King for the Quebec Act, and urging the Canadians to ignore republican propaganda. This time he urged enlistment, but his message went unheeded. Then he issued a warning that any Catholic in Canada who disobeyed would risk denial of the sacraments. The vicar of Montreal added to this the denial of burial in consecrated ground. Leading French Canadians responded to the bishop's call to arms by accusing him of selling out to the English government. Thirty songs and fifty broadsides sprang up, lampooning the bishop. Many of them made much of the fact that he had been given a 200 pound per year pension by the governor. One popular song ended this way:

> Then let's die, so dear Briand -
> Clever head he wears - may get
> From our courage and our blood
> Bigger gifts and pensions yet.

Bishop Briand defended himself in his private correspondence:

> They say of me that I am English. It is true, I am
> English; as you should be, and as they should be, since
> that is what they have sworn to be. I preach not war,
> but obedience and respect for authority, and the fidelity

they have promised to their oath and their king.

Governor Carleton, becoming desperate, offered commissions to three Old Subject merchants in Montreal. However, they refused Carleton's offer, for they were not willing "to be ordered out away from their families and affairs upon every false alarm." The Old Subjects generally agreed only to promise to defend their own town, should it be attacked by the Americans. Otherwise, they would stay put. One Englishman wrote in July, from Quebec, to a friend in London: "It is certain that all winter the people of our Colonies have been corresponding with the Canadians and English people settled here and I am apt to think that is the cause of the present coolness." Carleton was especially incensed at the Old Subjects' indifference and blamed it on those "damn'd committees that had thrown the province into its present state and prevented the Canadians from taking arms." He must have had a hollow laugh when he read a letter from Lord Dartmouth instructing him to raise 3000 Canadians to support the King's forces in Boston.

The only recruiting success Carleton had was not due to his own efforts, but to those of a retired captain named Alan Maclean. Back in his native Scotland, Maclean had foreseen the war in America and offered to raise Highlander recruits among the recent emigrants living in America and Canada, many of them former soldiers of the British Army. The King accepted the plan on April 3, 1775, and Maclean, now a Lieutentant-Colonel, sailed for Boston. There he received the blessings of General Gage, sent recruiters to North Carolina and Newfoundland, and set out himself for New York's Mohawk Valley. When he arrived in New York City he was arrested, but released for lack of evidence. Maclean enlisted 400 Scots in the Mohawk Valley but, with Schuyler's army forming at Ticonderoga, they chose to stay home to protect their families and wait for a safer time to organize. Maclean then headed north and arrived in Quebec with a letter of introduction from General Gage. Although Carleton welcomed the help, he wrote to Gage, "in this Province he seems to have little chance of success."

But, to the governor's surprise, Maclean was able to recruit enough Scots in Nova Scotia and Montreal to form a Royal Highland Emigrants regiment.

* * * * *

Back at Isle aux Noix, Schuyler was left with about 1000 troops, after having sent 200 men to accompany Ethan Allen and John Brown in their recruiting and patrolling efforts. Leaving a small contingent at Isle aux Noix with most of the supplies, Schuyler pressed on toward St. Jean, twenty miles downriver. About a mile short of it, the men landed their assortment of small boats, came ashore in "a close, deep swamp," and began marching to the fort "in grounds marshy and covered with woods."

St. Jean's fort was still in the final stage of being rebuilt by 530 Regulars, 70 Royal Highland Emigrants, 90 Canadian militia, and 100 Indians, all under the direction of Major Charles Preston.

The Indians and Canadians went into the woods to wait in ambush for the approaching "Bostonaises." Major Preston chose to remain with all his Regulars and Highlanders within the protective walls of the fort. If he had gone out with the Canadians and Indians, he could have observed the practical use of "Indian style" woods fighting. The habitants had used this style effectively in past wars, but British officers disdained it as barbaric.

Portions of a Connecticut regiment led the advance, a short distance ahead and to the left of the rest, eager to be the first to "reconnoitre the fortress." While wading across a deep stream with a muddy bottom, they were greeted with a surprising blast of close musket fire. Sixteen men dropped down, eight of them dead. Those still standing returned the fire and then quickly moved to the left into dense thickets. For a half hour, irregular bush fighting went on, until the bulk of the Americans reached the stream, forcing the outnumbered Canadians and Indians to return to the fort. As General Schuyler put it, "our troops gallantly pressing on them, they soon gave way and left us the

23

ground." Rather than press hastily on, the general ordered the men to start digging intrenchments for defensive purposes, while he took the necessary time to plan how the fort should be taken, perhaps the next morning.

That evening in St. Jean, Monsieur Belestre, who had led the Canadian militia, was seen with mug in hand loudly and frequently boasting how he stopped the American "pumpkins." As for the Indians, they were furious that Preston had kept his soldiers inside the fort, instead of joining the fight.

Late that night, a muffled voice came from the woods, and General Schuyler went out to have a conference with Moses Hazen, an Old Subject informer. Hazen was the one who, the previous May, had rushed to Governor Carleton to warn him of the attack on St. Jean after Ticonderoga had fallen. Hazen now told the American general that the fort was "complete and strong, and plentifully furnished with cannon." And one of the vessels, "to carry sixteen guns," would be ready to sail in three days. He also predicted that, not "one Canadian" was likely to join the Americans. In conclusion, Schuyler wrote, Hazen "judged it would be imprudent to attack St. John's, and advised us to send some parties among the inhabitants and [for] the remainder of the Army to retire to Isle aux Noix, from whence we might have intercourse with LaPrairie" to the west (where Allen and Brown were recruiting).

In council the next morning, Schuyler expressed the opinion that it was "absolutely necessary" to retire to Isle aux Noix. The majority of his officers agreed, being haunted by the thought of the British schooner reaching Lake Champlain and cutting off their supply line - and, if need be, their route of retreat. Once back at that island in the Richelieu, they would be able "to take measures for preventing her entrance to the lake." There they would await "intelligence touching the intentions of the Canadians" and, when reinforced, march by land against Montreal, "should the Canadians favor such a design." Schuyler sent off a letter to Congress: "Should we not be able to do anything decisively in Canada, I shall judge it best to move from this place, a very wet and unhealthy part of the country, unless I receive orders to the contrary." The British could not have asked for a better turn of events.

The retreat to Isle aux Noix was a propaganda victory for the British, as it convinced many Canadians that the ultimate victor of the campaign would be the British, and it would be wise to either join the British side or stay home. It also gave Major Preston time to complete the strengthening of his fort and construction of his schooner. However, he was soon left without his Indian allies. They went home, annoyed with him for keeping his Regulars in the fort during the swamp fight.

Other factors had influenced the Indians to desert the British at St. Jean. One was the death of their interpreter in the skirmish with the Americans. Another was their respect for Ethan Allen, the conqueror of Ticonderoga. Allen had sent a messenger to the Caughnawaga chief, demanding to know why some from their tribe "had taken up arms against the United Colonies." The answer was soon brought to Allen by two humble high warriors: "contrary to the will of the chiefs," the warriors assisting the British had been under the influence of British rum, "but we have sent runners and ordered them to depart from St. Johns."

Three days after the American retreat to Isle aux Noix, 400 more New Yorkers and 300 Connecticut men arrived to bolster the army. Among them was Captain John Lamb's respected and "indispensably necessary" New York City artillerists. That same day, Schuyler received a letter from James Livingston, an Old Subject merchant of Chambly, a small town between St. Jean and Montreal. He promised that a "considerable party" of Canadians would join the American Army if it placed a sizable force between St. Jean and Chambly.

So Schuyler ordered General Montgomery to take 800 men and march around to the west of St. Jean and eventually come out on the road to Chambly. Mostly the "sweepings of the streets" of New York City, they lacked military or woods experience. They drifted downstream and landed their bateaux. Montgomery stayed on the riverbank with 300 men, while Colonel Ritzema led his 500 New Yorkers into the dark night woods.

Thoughts of Indians waiting in another ambush were hard to suppress. The flanking party, unable to see its way through the thick woods, and fearful of becoming lost, decided to fall back to find the main column of the detachment. As they approached it, they were mistaken for Indians and fired upon. It was not very many moments later when the entire detachment stampeded out of the woods, and collided with Connecticut troops that General Montgomery had just sent to provide cover for them. The enraged and embarassed Colonel Ritzema slowly walked out of the woods alone, his entire regiment having left him.

Montgomery gave them a tongue lashing, exhorted them "to act like men," and sent them back into the woods. One quarter mile in, shells and grapeshot from a British bateau in the river crashed and rattled through the trees. This time only about 250 of the 500 men panicked and ran. The others pressed on, led by Ritzema. They encountered a British outpost, and skirmished with them. By now it was 3 a.m., so Ritzema decided - or perhaps was persuaded - to return to the boats to catch some sleep, rather than press on with half his force missing.

At the request of "some of the officers," Montgomery held another council, where it was decided to make a third try, but first "the troops should declare whether they were ready to march." With daylight to provide them relative safety, they voted to try it again. Just then, someone shouted that the British schooner was coming up the river "completely equipped" for battle. Again, a few officers requested a council of war. This time, "the majority of voices" favored a retreat to rejoin the rest of the army at Isle aux Noix.

After retreating a few miles, Montgomery, not content with such a disgraceful result, abruptly ordered the boats to shore. He then went ashore with only the officers, so as to face the men in the boats. He offered to lead them in an immediate march against St. Jean, which might be caught by surprise, since the Americans had been seen retreating upriver. Before the men came to a decision on his offer, one of them called out that the schooner was again in sight. That settled the question: "The troops were hardly restrained from pushing off without their officers." Back at Isle aux Noix, the returning troops, mostly Yorkers, were viciously jeered and sneered at by the Yankees who had spent a peaceful night in camp.

A few days later, September 16, Schuyler returned to Ticonderoga, his fever and pains having returned "with double violence, every prospect of a speedy recovery vanished." Command of the army fell to his second, Brigadier-General Montgomery, who was encouraged later that day by the arrival of Seth Warner and 170 of his Green Mountain Boys, "able bodied, stout, active fellows, used to the woods." Also, from New Hampshire, came a company of volunteers, many of them students from Dartmouth College, as well as 100 Rangers under Timothy Bedel. And finally, a handful of Chambly men that James Livingston and Jeremiah Duggan had recruited made their way to the American camp. Montgomery's force was now over 2000 men, with a respectable train of artillery. Soon Schuyler would be forwarding even more. Montgomery also could now command the entrance to Lake Champlain, after the arrival of a schooner, a sloop, two row-galleys and ten bateaux, all built at the mill of the Tory, Philip Skene, south of Ticonderoga.

The energetic Montgomery did not waste any time in returning to assault St. Jean. Schuyler had been gone less than 24 hours when Montgomery brought forward all his effectives, and had them intrench as near to the fort as safety would allow. He began bombarding its earthen walls, but with little effect. By now, the troops were in a fighting spirit after being chastised by their officers for their conduct in the woods the other night, and especially now that they had learned the Indians had dug up the graves of the dead Americans and "mangled them in the most shocking manner."

The night after Montgomery's arrival, there was action outside the other side of the fort. Major John Brown and 120 of his recruiting force had captured a train of 20 wagons carrying artillery supplies, winter clothes, and rum destined for the fort. Acting quickly, Brown's men left the wagons as a roadblock, and hid the cargo in the nearby woods, then began intrenching next to the wagons. At dawn, Major Preston sent out 100 Regulars, covered by two light field pieces, to disperse Brown's men and bring in the supplies. The Regulars fired upon Brown's men, who stopped their digging and scurried for cover. "The grape shot and musket balls flew very thick," recalled one of them. The famed bayonet charge of the Regulars sent Brown's men retreating slowly to the woods, shooting as they went. Several minutes of musket fire ensued, the British behind the wagons and partially built breastwork, the Massachusetts men behind trees.

Montgomery, hearing it, led the New Hampshire Rangers and Green Mountain Boys through the woods to the other side of the fort, to assist Brown. The smaller British detachment heard him coming and returned to the fort, taking with them the captured Moses Hazen. That night, an Indian still loyal to Major Preston slipped out of St. Jean and past the Americans to carry a request for help to the governor at Montreal.

Montgomery quickly called a council of war to set strategy. This new roadblock, between the fort and Chambly, would be improved and manned by Bedel's Rangers. Seth Warner and John Brown were to take their men and roam the area between St. Jean and the St. Lawrence River. They should intercept Governor Carleton, should he try to reach St. Jean with a relief force. Ethan Allen, also in that area, would continue his efforts to recruit Canadians. General Montgomery would go back to the other side of the fort to supervise the siege. Eventually, the troops and civilians within its walls would be starved into some action - either capitulating or coming out to fight.

* * * * *

A few miles to the northwest of Chambly, Ethan Allen had become bored with recruiting. The Indians persisted in their neutrality and, of the 250 habitants he had recruited, all but 80 had soon after deserted. He therefore decided to return to St. Jean. On the way, he came upon

Major Brown and his 200 Massachusetts men who had been patrolling the area, looking for the governor. Allen and Brown decided to combine their forces for an unauthorized attack on poorly defended Montreal. Before dawn, the two parties would cross the St. Lawrence and approach opposite ends of the walled city.

Within a few hours, however, Brown reconsidered the assault, considered it too risky, and aborted his part of it without crossing the river. By that time, Allen and his 80 Canadians had already crossed in canoes and were out of communication with Brown. Ethan Allen later wrote an account of the attempt on Montreal:

> We were most of the night [Sept. 24-25] crossing the river, as we had so few canoes that they had to pass and re-pass three times to carry my party across. Expecting Brown's party was landed on the other side of town, he having the day before agreed to give three huzzas with his men early in the morning, which signal I was to return, that we might each know that both parties were landed; but the sun by this time being near two hours high, and the sign failing [to be heard], I would have crossed the river back again, but as there could not more than one third of my troops cross at one time, the other two thirds would of course fall into [the enemy's] hands. I therefore concluded to maintain my ground.

News that "Ethan Allen, the notorious New Hampshire incendiary," was about to attack threw the town "into the utmost confusion." Some officials took refuge on ships in the river. Drums beat the alarm. According to the governor, only "the old gentlemen and better sort of citizens turned out under arms." Carleton sent out a force of 250, composed of Regulars, French and English militia, and Indians. Carleton and General Prescott both chose to stay within Montreal's walls, ready to flee downriver to Quebec, should the defensive force fail. Continuing with Ethan Allen's account:

The enemy began the attack from woodpiles, ditches, buildings, and such like places, at a considerable distance, and I returned the fire from a situation more than equally advantageous. I ordered a volunteer, Richard Young, with a detachment of nine men, under the cover of the bank of the river to the left of the main body.

The fire continued for some time on both sides; and I was confident that such a remote method of attack could not carry the ground. But near half the body of the enemy began to flank round to my right; upon which I ordered a volunteer, by the name of John Dugan, who had lived many years in Canada and understood the French language, to detach about fifty of the Canadians and post himself at an advantageous ditch on my right to prevent my being surrounded. He advanced with the detachment, but instead of occupying the post, made his escape, as did likewise Mr. Young upon the left with their detachments. I soon perceived that the enemy was in possession of the ground which Dugan should have occupied. At this time I had but forty-five men with me; some of whom were wounded. The enemy kept closing round me. Being almost entirely surrounded with such vast unequal numbers, I ordered a retreat, but found that those of the enemy who were of the country, and their Indians, could run as fast as my men, though the Regulars could not.

Thus I retreated near a mile, and some of the enemy, with the savages, kept flanking me, and others crowded hard in the rear. I expected in a very short time to try the world of the spirits; for I was apprehensive that no quarter would be given to me and therefore determined to sell my life as dear as I could. One of the enemy's officers, boldly pressing in the rear, discharged his fusee at me; the ball whistled near me, as did many others that day. I returned the salute and missed him, as running had put us both out of breath. I then saluted him with my tongue in a harsh manner, and told him that as his numbers were so far superior to mine, I would surrender, provided I could be treated with honor, and be assured of good quarter for myself and the men who were with me.

The officer I capitulated with then directed me and my party to advance towards him, which was done, I handed him my sword, and in half a minute after a savage came running to me with an incredible swiftness; he seemed to advance with more than mortal speed (as he approached near me, his Hellish visage was beyond all description, snakes eyes appear innocent in comparison of his) and in less than twelve feet in front of me, presented his firelock. I [placed] the officer to whom I gave my sword between me and the savage, but he flew round with great fury, trying to single me out to shoot me without killing the officer; but by this time I was near as nimble as he, keeping the officer in such a position that his danger was my defence. But in less than half a minute, I was attacked by just such another imp of Hell; then I made the officer fly around with incredible velocity, for a few seconds of time, when I perceived a Canadian taking my part against the savages; and in an instant an Irishman came to my assistance with a fixed bayonet, and drove away the fiends, swearing by Jasus he would kill them.

The Regular officers said that they were very happy to see Col. Allen. I answered them that I should rather chose to have seen them at Gen. Montgomery's camp. No abuse was offered me till I came to the barrack yard at Montreal, where I met Gen. Prescott, who asked me

31

my name, which I told him. He then asked me whether I was that Col. Allen who took Ticonderoga. I told him I was the very man; then he shook his cane over my head, calling many hard names, among which he frequently used the word "rebel," and put himself in a great rage. I told him he would do well not to cane me, for I was not accustomed to it, and shook my fist at him, telling him that that was the beetle of mortality for him if he offered to strike. Capt. M'Cloud of the British whispered to him that it was inconsistent with his honor to strike a prisoner. He made the following reply: "I will not execute you now, but you shall grace a halter at Tyburn, God damn ye."

So ended the military career of the famed leader of the Green Mountain Boys. Ethan Allen was quickly sent in irons to England. He never felt the hangman's halter around his neck, although he was exhibited for the curious to come see and speak to. Exchanged in 1778 for a captured British officer, Allen went immediately to see Washington at Valley Forge. The commander, perhaps with some reservations, recommended that Congress commission him a colonel in the army (he had been an unranked volunteer, the "Colonel" title a self-imposed one). Colonel Allen returned to Bennington to regain his health. He never returned to active duty, preferring to spend his time and energy harassing New York settlers still claiming title to Vermont land. As governor of the independent republic of Vermont, he tried in vain to persuade Congress to admit it as the fourteenth state. As a ploy to pressure Congress, Allen held negotiations with the British to set up Vermont as a neutral state, but nothing came of the attempt other than a blemish on Allen's reputation. New York's opposition blocked Vermont's admission into the union until 1791.

Ethan Allen's fame spread far and wide in 1779 with the publication of his memoirs. Eight editions were printed within the first two years. His exciting accounts of the capture of Ticonderoga, the Canadian campaign, and the persecution of American prisoners stirred readers to a patriotic zeal. It brought to the public's attention the plight of the thousands of Americans suffering and dying in the hulls of British prison ships and other makeshift prisons.

A few years later, with the publication of a theological treatise, Ethan Allen added "heretic" to the "treason" label his negotiations with the British had given him. The lengthy title began, *Reason, The Only Oracle of Man, Or a Compenduous System of Natural Religion* ... It was denounced in hundreds of pulpits and newspapers. When Allen's death in 1789 was published in the newspapers, the president of Yale noted the occasion in his diary, "Ethan Allen of Vermont died and went to Hell this day."

* * * * *

Meanwhile, back at the siege of St. Jean, progress was discouragingly slow. The American expedition to conquer Canada had turned into a stalemate. Just keeping their ground seemed to be all that the Connecticut troops were willing to do. Distrustful of their "Yorker" commander, they were unwilling to tighten the siege by building earthworks closer and be "drawn under the guns of the fort." Montgomery noticed that "the old story of treachery spread among the men as soon as we saw the enemy." The Yankees felt the New York general was secretly working toward an American defeat. At times, the Yankees boldly disobeyed his orders and did the opposite, prompting him to write down his famous comment, "the privates are all generals."

By early October, Montgomery realized that his heaviest guns were ineffective, not being within close range of the fort, which was located on the west side of the Richelieu River. The heavy American guns were behind earthworks on the east side of the river. From there, they had forced the British schooner Royal Savage to fall back downriver to a position harmless to the Americans. Eager to take the fort, the American general issued orders to move these batteries across the river and inland a few hundred yards to the left end of the American line, so as to face the fort's southwest (and most vulnerable) point. Men were set to work felling trees for a wooden "corduroy" road to bring the artillery through the swamp, and preparing fascines for the new breastworks.

But the apparent aim of the general - to bombard the wall's weakest point, then take the fortress by storm - did not set well with his subordinate officers. Samuel Mott looked upon the attempt as "dangerous," its prospects of success "dubious." The other officers agreed. Major Brown, who had gained Montgomery's confidence, was asked to talk to him about his recent change in strategy. Brown gave his report and, as usual, added his own opinion: "unless something [else] was undertaken, in a few days there would be a mutiny. The universal sense of the army" called for bombardment from the east side, where the fort sloped gently to the river and was quite open.

General Montgomery considered Brown's report and decided to submit himself to the humiliating democratic style of military planning so foreign to his prior European training. "To a man," his subordinate officers found his reasoning "insufficient," and he reluctantly dropped his plans. The New York general, a former British officer, was realizing that American militia "carry the spirit of freedom into the field, and think for themselves."

The continuous American shelling pounded away at the defenses and the spirit of the enemy. Major Preston's weariness was reflected in his journal entry for October 15th:

> The weather grew very cold, and as the windows of the house were all broke as many as cou'd find room in the cellars slept there. The rest, unable either to get a place or to bear the heat and disagreeable smell arising from such numbers being crowded together, slept above in cold and danger or walk'd about the greatest part of the night. Towards evening we were again saluted with shells; and, the night being cold and wet, it was thought proper to rouse us at midnight with a few shells and

shot.

The favorite dwelling place of the officers, a stone house in the northern half of the fort, was suddenly hit one morning while Major Preston sat drinking tea with some officers. A cannon ball passed through the wall, showering the table with debris, and driving the corner of a brick into Captain Strong's leg.

On another day, when the officers' quarters were demolished by a shell, everyone got out in time except a huge man named Salaberry, who was discovered with not a scratch on him after the dust blew away, supporting up what was left of the building on his broad shoulders. During the entire siege, less than twenty-five men inside the fort died from American muskets and cannon.

With no food coming in, Major Preston's 600 hungry soldiers by now were on half rations. And their clothes and shoes were wearing out. Most of the garrison had to "tear off the skirts of their coats to wrap around their feet." The Canadian militia, one by one, snuck away during the nights, and most of the Indians had long since gone. Sentry duty became a test of nerves. One night a sentry heard something in the brush outside the fort. His challenge not being answered, he ordered the artillery officer on duty to open fire. According to Lieutenant John Andre, the next "morning a horse was found dead; this was the enemy our sentry had seen and challeng'd."

As the siege dragged on, and the hoped for relief force did not appear, Canadian and Indian deserters trickled into the American camp. Samuel Mott wrote home to Connecticut that the Indians "and Canadians who join us, have all learned English enough to say 'Liberty' and 'Bostonian,' and call themselves Yankee. The Indians boast much of it, and will smite on their breasts, saying 'Me Yankee.'"

Outside the fort, the intrenched Americans were also suffering from the cold fall weather and the frequent heavy rains. October brought an unusually high number of heavy rainstorms. Soon, "upwards of six hundred" men were sent back to Isle aux Noix, too sick for duty. Learning of the army suffering from "fever and ague," one reader offered a "certain cure" in the <u>Connecticut Courant</u>: "Take of spiders webb sufficient for three pills, rolled well together, about the size of a large pea [and] drink them off in a gill of good old spirits as the chill commences."

Each day, the weather grew colder and the rains kept falling with hardly a break. Montgomery wrote, "We have been like half drowned rats crawling through the swamp." He was anxious to take St. Jean and move on to Montreal and possibly Quebec before the harsh Canadian winter set in. In one letter, he reflected upon the prospects of a "winter campaign in Canada! Posterity won't believe it!" The same men who, when approaching St. Jean several weeks earlier, had expected "in five days" to be "possessors of Montreal" now began to wonder if they would ever see it.

Although the purchase of produce from nearby habitants brought in some food, Schuyler's return to Ticonderoga proved the saving of the army. He discovered that, while he had been away, there had been "a scandalous want of subordination and inattention to my orders." In his first six days back at Fort Ti, the general sent forward as much food as had been shipped in the previous twenty-two. He wrote to Washington, "If I had not arrived here, even on the very day I did, as sure as God lives the army would have starved." Montgomery agreed, telling Schuyler that his return to Ticonderoga "enabled us to keep our ground."

While Montgomery was coping with an army of "citizen soldiers," his superior, General Schuyler, was doing likewise back at Fort Ti. Almost 400 additional Connecticut troops, under General Wooster, had arrived at the fort ahead of Wooster, and when Schuyler ordered them to move forward to St. Jean they chose not to obey. Schuyler expressed his exasperation in a letter to Washington, dated October 18: "Do not choose to move! Strange language in an army; but the irresistible force of necessity obliges me to put up with it." When Wooster, a major-general in the militia, arrived, he was reluctantly persuaded by Schuyler to put himself under Montgomery, only a brigadier-general in the Continental Army. Three days later, Schuyler again wrote to Washington:

> General Wooster's Regiment, detained here now for three days by violent gales and heavy rains, are now in doubt whether they will proceed to the Army at St. John's. The general's secretary and his chaplain inform me, that many of the officers and most of the men apprehend being detained in Canada all winter; that they may be prevented by frost from returning; that they will perish with cold or with sickness; that if the Army should be under the necessity of retreating from St. John's, many must fall a sacrifice to the enemy, as there will not be boats sufficient to bring them away (although we really have craft sufficient for a thousand more than the Army consists of); that none but the general, his secretary and chaplain have any inclination to proceed. The weather is now clearing, the wind favourable, and I wait in the most distressing anxiety for the morrow to see the event.

The next morning, a much relieved Schuyler was able to write:

> General Wooster's Regiment is just sailed. They are gone with the greatest reluctance. The parson has been indefatigable to persuade them to move. They consist of three hundred and thirty-five, officers included; ninetyeight having returned home, discharged between Albany and Fort George, and fifty-one sick and sham sick are left here.

While Montgomery's army was making slow progress at St. Jean, James Livingston and his fellow Canadians had started "a war" down-river at Chambly, where they were skirmishing with the Regulars of Fort Chambly, and seizing small craft along the river, so they could not be used for escape by the Regulars of either Chambly or St. Jean. Samuel Mott wrote home to Connecticut's Governor Trumbull on October 6, from the camp outside St. Jean:

> On the 3d instant there was a severe engagement between the French Whigs on one side, and the French Tories and Regulars on the other side, at Chambly. They lost several men on each side. In short, it is a melancholy prospect to see that all Canada is in one continued scene of war and bloodshed. If we don't carry our point we have brought Canada into the most deplorable situation possible to conceive, as those people who have taken arms in our favour, with their wives and children, will be left to cruelty without mercy.

On the night of October 13, Montgomery sent two bateaux filled with habitants and light cannon floating silently downriver, past the guns of the fort and the British schooner, then through the treacherous rapids. Hearing the waterfall above Chambly, they quickly maneuvered the bateaux to shore and disembarked. With James Livingston's force of 350 Canadians and Americans, they began laying siege to the castle-like fort at Chambly whose sixteen-foot high walls of stone protected 88 Regulars and plentiful military stores.

A few of the cannon balls crashed through the thin stone walls. Fearful that a cannon ball might ignite the large magazine within its walls, the British commander surrendered the fort, on October 18th, after only a four day siege. The captured supplies included 124 barrels of gunpowder, 150 muskets, 6500 cartridges, 138 barrels of edible provisions, etc. Clearly, Carleton had erred in leaving such supplies in a fort that could not be defended against light cannon. Elated, Montgomery wrote to Schuyler from outside St. Jean, "We have gotten six tons of powder which, with God's blessing, will finish our business here." Montgomery also sent a letter to Carleton, promising the "law of retaliation" would be exercised upon the Chambly prisoners, should he hear of Ethan Allen and his 38 fellow captives suffering.

The 88 captured Regulars and their 30 women and 51 children from Fort Chambly were marched to the American camp and paraded in front of the St. Jean fort. As they passed by, three of the women (whose husbands were inside Fort St. Jean) boldly broke out of line and walked toward the fort. The stunned American soldiers stood watching, waiting for an order to stop them. Along the fort walls, tense musketmen held their aim on the Americans. They, too, listened. As the women neared the fort, they quickened their pace, not daring to look behind them. No order came. The gate was quickly opened to admit the womem, and reunite them with their husbands inside the besieged fort.

In late October, an American cannon chanced to hit the *Royal Savage*, which had ventured too close to the American riverside batteries. With the feared schooner now out of action, Montgomery persuaded his men to move the biggest guns across the river to a point close to the fort's weak stockade fence. Once located there, the guns finally affected some damage. Several days later, a New York officer wrote home about the action:

> On Saturday, the 28th ultimo, the main body of the army decamped from the south, and marched to the north side of the fort, under the command of General Wooster. We were joined in the evening by General Montgomery, and the same night we began to throw up a breastwork on an eminence which entirely commanded the enemy's works, in order to erect a battery of cannon and mortars. This battery they kept continually pelting at with grapeshot and shells, but without doing us the least injury, until Wednesday morning, when we opened our battery, with which we kept an almost incessant blaze on them [the] great part of the day, and likewise from our battery on the east side of the river, which the enemy returned with the greatest spirit.

Late in the afternoon I received a message from General Montgomery, ordering me to cease firing till further orders; these orders were extremely disagreeable to me, when I saw some of my men bleeding before my eyes, and dying with the wounds which they had received. On our ceasing to fire, the General ordered a parley to be beat, and sent in an officer to demand a surrender of the fort. Two officers soon after returned with him, and were led blindfold through the camp to the General's tent, where a pretty long conference was held, and they promised the General an answer from the commanding officer next morning, which promise was complied with. The answer imported that if they should receive no relief within four days, he would then send in some proposals. The General replied that he must have an explicit answer next morning and the garrison must remain prisoners of war, at all events. This, though very unpalatable, they were at length obliged to digest, as you see by the capitulation.

The garrison, consisting of about six hundred men, marched out and grounded their arms and were immediately embarked in batteaus for Ticonderoga, Connecticut, or any other place which the Continental Congress may direct. This most fortunate event will be a fatal stab to the hellish machinations of the foes of freedom, as it will facilitate the reduction of Canada and secure the Canadians in our favour.

We have taken seventeen pieces of excellent brass artillery and a considerable number of iron cannon. There were in garrison about 500 regular troops; the rest were composed of Canadian volunteers, among whom are many of their noblesse; who, I believe, are (from appearance) on the stool of repentance.

Knowing his 500 Regulars were almost the entire British force to defend all of Canada, Major Preston had valiantly held off the rebel army for forty-five days. James Bellamy, a private from Cheshire, Conn., later recalled hearing the British commander speak to Montgomery: "'In obedience to what has been done, I lay down my arms, but of choice I had rather die by them,' and the tears ran down his cheeks, and he cried like a child."

Just a few hours earlier, a man had been captured trying to reach the fort. When taken, he was seen putting something in his mouth.

> The general compelled him to take physic. In about two hours after taking the physic, the prisoner discharged a ball, which on being examined was found to be of silver and went together with a screw, and on taking it apart it contained a small bit of paper on which was written these words: "Hold out and you shall be relieved."

The captured messenger had been sent by Carleton. After Ethan Allen's capture, the militia at Montreal swelled with about 900 new enlistments. But within the next few weeks most of them went home, tired of waiting for Carleton to act. He was reluctant to use the militia, since he felt he could not trust them. He had been waiting for a reinforcement of British Regulars. On September 25th, Lord Dartmouth had ordered five battalions to Canada, but wintry weather would blow them off course. In October, General Howe, at Boston, detached a battalion of marines for duty in Canada, but Admiral Graves refused to transport them to the St. Lawrence with the northern winter close at hand. So, after procrastinating until mid-October, Carleton sent for Col. Maclean to come up from Quebec with all the recruits he could muster.

Just four days before Major Preston would capitulate at St. Jean, Carleton had finally set out to rescue the besieged fort. He brought with him 800 men - a mixed force of militia, Royal Highland Emigrants, and a handful of Regulars and Indians. Carleton led most of them as they started across the St. Lawrence River at Montreal to the town of Longeuil in hopes of reaching St. Jean. Maclean led the remainder in an attempt to cross farther upriver.

Seth Warner and his Green Mountain Boys, with a company of New Yorkers, perhaps 350 men altogether, were hiding on the Longeuil shore. As Carleton's force neared the shore, the Americans opened up a thunderous fire of grapeshot and musket balls. Reportedly, fifty men were killed in the bateaux, which quickly turned around and returned to Montreal. No Americans received as much as a scratch. "What shall I do?" asked the Frenchman in charge of the one light cannon that Carleton had brought along in one of the boats. "Go and have supper in town," replied the governor in disgust. Upriver, Maclean's detachment was also badly savaged by Major Brown's men, mainly because many of the Scots refused to fight. Carleton gave up the rescue mission. It was too little, too late.

Now that St. Jean and Chambly had fallen, the next step would, of course, be Montreal. However, the Connecticut troops voiced their unwillingness to proceed. General Montgomery had "to coax them," promising to discharge them as soon as Montreal was occupied. Many of them seemed to have started the expedition with the belief that their services would no longer be needed once St. Jean was taken. Typical was the attitude expressed in a letter home to Canaan, Conn., from Private Rozzle Fellows. On September 2, at Crown Point, he had written to his father, "I cannot wish to set out for home till I have seen our army at St. Johns." That done, it was time to go home.

The Connecticut troops were not the only ones Montgomery found to be less than enthusiastic about proceeding on to Montreal. The New York troops, by now in rags, almost mutinied when he insisted on allowing the Regulars to take their summer and winter clothing with them on their trip to Connecticut, where they would reside while in captivity. Montgomery wrote, "there was no driving it into their noddles, that the clothing was really the property of the soldier, that he had paid for it. I wish some method could be fallen upon of engaging

<u>gentlemen</u> to serve."

The march from St. Jean to Montreal began on November 5, and was most difficult, as Benjamin Trumbull, chaplain of a Connecticut regiment, noted in his journal:

> I marched the whole of the day in mud and water sometimes midleg high and in general over shoe. The whole day was stormy; it rained and snowed till about sunset, when the snow and rain ceased and the wind blew up raw and cold at north west. Under our feet was snow and ice and water, over our heads clouds, snow and rain; before us the mountains appeared all white with snow and ice. It was remarkable to see the Americans after almost infinite fatigues and hardships marching on at this advanced season, badly clothed and badly provided for, to Montreal, pressing on to new sieges and conquests.

The Indians and most of the Canadian recruits once again deserted. Montreal's stockade walls, so thin that they "could only turn musketry," would not deter the approaching Americans. Carleton knew he could not hold the town. "It is obvious," he wrote to Gage, "that as soon as the rebels appear outside the town in force, the townspeople will give up on the best terms they can procure." He sent Maclean and some of his Highlanders to Quebec, then busied himself destroying what supplies he could not carry onto the eleven ships of various sizes anchored nearby in the St. Lawrence. Finally, with Montgomery's army at the city gates, Carleton set sail down the St. Lawrence to establish Canada's last defense at Quebec.

His retreat downriver was halted by a change in wind direction, preventing his little fleet from running a gauntlet past the American artillery onshore at the Sorel narrows. For several anxious days, Carleton waited in vain for the wind to shift.

At last, he decided he could wait no longer; he must reach Quebec and organize its defenses. On the evening of November 16, "dressed like a man of the people," the governor climbed into a whale-boat to be commanded by a merchant ship's captain known as "La Tourte" (the pigeon), owing to his reputation for fast sailing. With muffled oars, and silent hand touch signals, Carleton, La Tourte, and a few oarsmen pushed off toward the narrows of Sorel. Blazing fires on both shores lit up large areas of the river. The oarsmen stopped rowing and crouched down, drifting with the current. From shore, in the dark, the whale-boat resembled one of the large drifting logs so common in the St. Lawrence. For nine miles they drifted through the narrows, holding their position in mid-stream by paddling with their hands, and hearing the barking dogs and talking sentries of the spread out American camp.

When safely past the Americans, the exhausted governor came ashore and had a quick dinner then fell sound asleep at the home of a seigneur who lived nearby. He was awakened in the morning by the voices of American soldiers demanding lodging at the house. With the only exit being the front door, the governor, wearing his habitant clothes and relying on his fluent French, elbowed his way through several Americans crowded into the front hall. When he reached the street, he rejoined his oarsmen and continued rowing downstream until he was picked up by a larger vessel and taken safely to Quebec, where he was welcomed by the salute of the fort's big guns.

But the eleven ships Carleton left behind above Sorel, carrying almost 100 fighting men and valuable supplies, did not have such good luck. The Americans' Major John Brown, carrying a white flag, boarded one of the ships and told General Prescott, who Carleton had left in charge of the fleet, that the Americans had a battery of 32-pounders at Sorel. Brown even offered to show them to anyone Prescott chose to send with Brown. Brown showed Prescott's man some light cannon nearby and told him, "If you should chance to escape this battery, which is my small battery, I have a grand battery at the mouth of the Sorel which will infallibly sink all your ships." The man believed Brown without asking to see the fictitious "grand battery" of 32-pounders. He reported back to Prescott, who immediately surrendered the fleet, its 100 men, and its cargoes (which included cannon, muskets, and 200 pairs of new shoes).

While Carleton and his fleet had been waiting above Sorel for the winds to shift, the citizens of Montreal had no soldiers to defend them. They offered no resistance to Montgomery, who occupied the town on November 13. When news of Montreal's "liberation" reached the Congress in Philadelphia, Thomas Jefferson declared that the success of American arms corresponded with the justice of the cause, and "In a short time, we have reason to hope, the delegates of Canada will join us in Congress, and complete the American union."

But the Canadians waited, to see if Montgomery could also take the stronghold of Quebec, where Governor-General Guy Carleton would be personally directing the defense of a fortress that, through all the colonial wars, had never been taken by storm.

Montgomery intended to remain in Montreal for the winter, most of his troops having finally set out for their homes. He wanted to wait for the good weather and reinforcements that spring would bring. But, just a few hours after he marched triumphantly into Montreal, he received word that another American army, having traversed the uncharted wilderness of Maine, was outside the gates of Quebec, waiting for him to join them for a combined assault on that fabled fortress.

"At evening we came in sight of a house, which was the first we had seen for the space of 31 days. Our cloathes were torn in pieces by the bushes and hung in strings, few of us had any shoes ... beards long and visages thin and meagre. I thought we much resembled the animals which inhabit New Spain, called the Ourang-Outang."

> *- Private Abner Stocking, on the Chaudiere River, after having marched through the wilderness.*

During the summer of 1775, General George Washington fretted over the chances of success that Schuyler's army might have in their expedition down the Richelieu and, hopefully, the St. Lawrence. The New York troops would be green, perhaps not to be counted on under fire. Washington was aware that New England militia were independent thinkers who elected their own officers, and that they distrusted "Yorkers." Would the Yankees, half of Schuyler's force, obey a New York general? Surely, the respected General Carleton would put up a stiff, well-organized resistance at St. Jean and, if necessary, at Quebec. That fabled fortress, atop a 300-foot cliff, during all the colonial wars had only been taken once - when, in 1759, its defenders ventured outside its protective walls to battle the enemy on an open plain.

Washington concluded that if Canada was to be taken, it would take more than Schuyler's force to do it. A second expedition should be sent, this one from the east, "to make a diversion which would distract Carleton, and facilitate" Schuyler's attack from the west. Carleton would have to abandon his defenses along the Richelieu, or risk the loss of Quebec, "in its present defenseless state an easy prey" to this second American army.

During the long summer evenings in Cambridge, Washington mulled over a published journal and map written by a British Army engineer, John Montresor, in 1761. He had traveled the wilderness of northwestern Maine with a handful of British Rangers and Indian guides. They had paddled and carried their canoes from Quebec to the New England coast and back to see if it was, as rumored to be, the best and shortest way to attack Canada." After Montresor returned, the man who sent him on the expedition, General James Murray, concluded the route was feasible for a few men in canoes, but was "impractical" for the passage of large numbers of troops.

George Washington came to a different conclusion. In Cambridge, he talked to some visiting Penobscot Indians, who told him of the many times their tribe had made the same trip on annual hunts. They offered to assist the expedition as guides and hunters. Washington was skeptical of their loyalty. Their talk lacked the caution so typical of Indians. They seemed almost eager for an American army to venture into their homeland. The general, ever distrustful of Indians, and careful not to become vulnerable to British spies, refused their offer.

A few white men from Maine were also consulted, though none could be found who had traveled the entire Indian route. It started with the Kennebec River, which would be followed from its mouth at the Atlantic Ocean up to a "Great Carrying Place" where the boats and supplies would have to be carried over a portage of twelve miles, to a gentler stream known as the Dead River. With the long and prominent Mount Bigelow as a landmark, and Montresor's map and journal providing directions, the portage to the Dead River would be easy enough. Four of those twelve miles would actually be over ponds. After rowing up the Dead River, the army would then have a carry of four miles over a mountain ridge known as the "Height of Land," which forms the border with Canada. It separates the waters that flow north to the St. Lawrence from those flowing south to the Atlantic.

This final portage would bring them to a stream which emptied into Lake Megantic, whose outlet, the Chaudiere River, flowed all the way to a point on the St. Lawrence a few miles from Quebec. Washington, seeing that nearly the entire distance was by water, convinced himself that "the land carriages of the route proposed" were "too inconsiderable to make an objection" in his decision to authorize the expedition.

Although Congress had formulated and authorized Schuyler's campaign, the Kennebec-Chaudiere expedition was conceived and authorized by Washington without consulting Congress. Suspecting some Congressmen were keeping the British abreast of its activities, Washington did not inform Congress until the expedition was on its way north. In Boston, General Gage did in fact learn of the expedition before it left Massachusetts, but he did not risk detaching part of his army to try to stop or harass it.

Washington knew he would need a forceful and proven leader, whom men from diverse colonies would follow. It would also help if the leader, unlike Schuyler, had a strong will, a healthy body, and some knowledge of Quebec and the French language. One man possessing all these qualities was Benedict Arnold. The former New Haven merchant and sea captain was familiar with Quebec, having sailed there many times to buy horses and other goods to sell in the Carribbean.

Back in May, Benedict Arnold had joined forces with Ethan Allen in the surprise capture of Ticonderoga. When Arnold returned to Cambridge in August, he went to see the Commander-in-Chief. He told Washington of his desire to still lead an expedition against Canada, as he had expressed in his letters to the Continental Congress. Convinced that Arnold was his man, Washington appointed him a colonel in the Continental Army. Both his commission and the expedition itself would have to await the endorsement of Philip Schuyler. Washington insisted on deferring to Schulyler, since he was head of the army's Northern Department. Three weeks passed before an aide returned from Ticonderoga with Schuyler's enthusiastic endorsement.

Washington's final instructions to Arnold included a reminder that he place himself under Schuyler if they should meet in Canada, and that a proclamation of goodwill, written by Washington, be distributed to the French Canadians. The soldiers should, under no circumstances, mistreat the Canadians because of their Roman Catholicism: "avoid all disrespect or contempt of the religion of the country and its ceremonies. Prudence, policy and a true Christian spirit will lead us to look with compassion upon their errors without insulting them." Washington knew that the cooperation of the Canadians would be crucial.

Now that he had found a commander for the expedition, Washington asked Ajutant-General Horatio Gates to raise 1000 to 1200 volunteers from among the 15,000 men in the Cambridge and Roxbury camps. A notice called for "active woodsmen well acquainted with batteaus" to present themselves. Every rifle company immediately volunteered to go. They were eager for action and tired of the drudgery of camp life. However, Washington felt he could only spare three of these sharpshooting companies, in case the British ventured out of Boston. Pennsylvania rifleman George Morison recalled:

> There were then in the camp at Cambridge eleven companies of Riflemen, the commanding officers of whom cast lots who should go on this expedition. The result was that three officers were chosen, viz. Capt. Daniel Morgan of Virginia, Capt. Matthew Smith and William Hendricks of Pennsylvania.

It was fortunate for the expedition that one of the winning lots was cast by Daniel Morgan. His leadership and fierce determination to continue in the face of terrible hardships would become indispensable on the long journey. Daniel Morgan was a frontiersman with grit. Once, fleeing from an Indian war party, he had made his escape by clinging, half-conscious, to his horse though his neck had been grazed by a bullet that tore through his cheek and took out half his teeth on that side of his mouth. Six feet tall and solidly muscled at 200 pounds, his bellow commanded respect from his men, as it was backed by his reputation as a wrestler and boxer. Morgan was famous in backwoods Virginia for taking on any comer, and challenging those who beat him until he finally was victorious.

Daniel Morgan had good reason for wanting to meet the British in battle. Like George Washington, he had been with General Braddock on his fateful expedition against the French and Indians at Fort Duquesne (Pittsburgh) in 1755. Morgan had gone as a nineteen-year-old teamster, driving a supply wagon. The brash young American struck a British officer, in a dispute over a personal injustice. Sentenced to 500 lashes, Morgan took his punishment without a murmur. Ever since then, he maintained that the scars totaled only 499, and he would invite anyone to inspect his back and see if their count agreed with his. He would explain:

> That is the doing of old King George. While I was in his service, upon a certain occasion, he promised me 500 lashes. But he failed in his promise and gave me but 499, so he has been owing me one ever since. While the drummer was laying the lashes on my back I heard him miscount one. I did not think it worthwhile to tell him of his mistake, and let it go.

Around camp, word quickly spread that the charismatic Benedict Arnold and the adventure-seeking riflemen would be leading the expedition. That was enough to attract plenty of Yankee farmboys who, like the riflemen, sought the glory and excitement of an active campaign, and were bored and disillusioned with the war so far. Most of the New England volunteers had little experience either with woods or with bateaux. The best suited New Englanders for the expedition were probably the Green Mountain Boys and New Hampshire Rangers, who unfortunately were already in Canada with Schuyler and Montgomery.

There were also several unattached persons with the rank of

51

"volunteer" signing up for the expedition. These included a few recent deserters from the British Army, two hardy women who were accompanying their husbands, and a brilliant nineteen-year-old named Aaron Burr. The adopted son of the president of the College of New Jersey (Princeton), Burr had graduated from that college at the age of fifteen, then studied theology and law. When the war started, he eagerly gave up the books for a military career.

In all, 1051 men set forth. Most of them were only enlisted until January 1, 1776, but they were confident they could take Quebec and return home by then. The three rifle companies left Cambridge on September 11, 1775, and marched, out of sight of the British, through back country towns to Newburyport. The eleven musket companies followed two days later. Their delay, according to Private Ephraim Squier, was caused by their refusal "to march till we had a month's pay." At Newburyport, all fourteen companies embarked on fishing ships to the mouth of the Kennebec River, on the Maine coastline.

From there, Arnold expected to reach Quebec after a march of 20 days but, as a precaution, he ordered 45 days worth of provisions. Judging from Montresor's journal, the distance from the mouth of the Kennebec to Quebec would consist of 180 miles of smooth rivers. The men would soon find that the Kennebec, Dead and Chaudiere Rivers were anything but smooth, and the trip would take more than twice as many days and almost twice the distance predicted.

At Newburyport, the citizens were given a "general review" with its "manual exercise." Connecticut's Private Abner Stocking, age twenty-two, thought the "spectators appeared much affected. They probably thought we had many hardships to encounter and many of us should never return to our parents and families." Private Joseph Ware, a Rhode Island farmer, echoed the same thoughts in his journal that night: "we had the praise of hundreds of spectators who were sorry to see so many brave fellows going to be sacrificed for their country." But certainly not all the soldiers had such dismal thoughts, as they set out for the north country. One rifleman pictured spending "the winter in joy and festivity among the sweet nuns" at Quebec.

The men embarked the next morning on eleven "sloops and schooners, containing, upon an average, 100 troops." New Hampshire's Dr. Isaac Senter, age twenty-two, reflected the morale of the army in his journal. "We were all in high spirits, intending to endure with fortitude all the fatigues and hardships that we might meet with in our march to Quebec." However, he soon recorded the effect of their first leg of the journey - a sea voyage to the mouth of the Kennebec River. It was not an auspicious way to start the trip: "heavy wind with considerable rain, this bringing on a swell, occasioned most of the troops to digorge themselves of their luxuries so plentifully laid in" at the send-off feast the night before. It probably did not help matters that most of the ships had a strong "smell of fish."

Reaching the Kennebec on September 20th, they dropped anchors at Georgetown, where the local minister came aboard one of the ships to pray for their success. One hour and forty-five minutes later, he finished his prayer and let the weary soldiers take their evening meal. The next day, they sailed up the river for fifty miles, to Fort Western (present day Augusta) and disembarked. Here they were supplemented by a company of local militia.

The locals gave the expedition a gala send-off at Fort Western, featuring a "three-bear barbicue," pumpkin pies, and rum. The chief attraction was Jacataqua, an Indian beauty, half French and half Abenaki, known as the "Queen with the golden thighs." She was so captivated by the young Aaron Burr that she went with him on the march.

Despite the gala send-off, Arnold could not feel very satisfied at Fort Western. Conspicuously absent were 100 barrels of flour, which Washington's commissary-general had been ordered to send to Fort Western. Arnold had included these 100 barrels in his calculations for provisioning the army. No time could be wasted sending back to Cambridge for the missing flour. The army would simply have to make do with the flour they brought with them on the ships.

In August, a Fort Western man named Reuben Colburn had been contracted to build more than 100 "bateaux" (oversized rowboats).

They would be used to transport the tents, barrels of food and gunpowder, chests of money, etc. Each bateau was worked by five men equipped with oars and poles. The poles were for pushing the boats upstream when the current was too strong to use the oars. Each pole was equipped with a hook at one end, to facilitate lifting the boat out of the water at the carrying places.

Over 500 men set out in the bateaux, and a handful, including Arnold, went in canoes. The remaining half of the army walked in single file along the riverbank. At first, Arnold divided the riflemen into small groups, as he and Washington had planned, to serve as flankers and scouts for the musket companies. But this caused discontentment among the independent-minded frontiersmen. Captain Daniel Morgan approached Arnold to inform him of this and remind him that when the riflemen had enlisted in the spring they had been promised that they would serve only under their own officers. This must have reminded Benedict Arnold of the similar problem he had faced back in May with Ethan Allen's Green Mountain Boys. Having learned from that experience, this time Arnold quickly came up with an arrangement to satisfy everyone. He would change the army's marching order, dividing the army into four divisions.

The first division, composed of the three rifle companies, and led by Daniel Morgan, would set out ahead of the others. Because these hardy frontiersmen were the toughest and most skilled in woodcraft, Arnold asssigned them the task of clearing a road wherever necessary along the riverbank and at the carrying places, to ease the movement of the rest of the army behind them. They would also serve as the army's first line of defense against ambush by Indians. They wore caps of raccoon fur, with the tail hanging down in the back, moccasins made of deerhide, and long shirts and leggins also made from deerhide, some with words painted on them: "LIBERTY OR DEATH." These were the "shirtmen" that a British officer in Boston had wrote home about, describing them as the world's worst "widow makers."

Ahead of the riflemen, Arnold sent a scouting party in two birch bark canoes. Pennsylvanian Lieutenant William Steele took eight men of his choice, plus two local guides. Steele's mission: "ascertaining and marking the paths, which were used by the Indians at the numerous carrying-places ... and ascertain the course of the river Chaudiere, which runs from the height of land towards Quebec." They were also ordered to find and kill the Abenaki Indian, Natanis, who Arnold had been falsely told was a British spy.

One of Steele's hand-picked men was sixteen-year-old John Joseph Henry. Two years before, John had returned, on foot, from Fort Detroit to his home near Lancaster, Pennsylvania. The trek through the wilderness was so difficult that his older guide had died on the way, leaving young John to find his way home alone. When the war broke out in April of 1775, John, "fired with an enthusiastic love of country," determined to join up with a rifle company then forming at Lancaster. His father, a military supplier, forbade him to go, saying he was too young. John's mother, knowing there was no keeping him, secretly made the hunting shirt he wore when he ran off to join the rifle corps while his father was away on business at Reading. The rifle corps happened to stop at Reading on the way north. As John nervously stood in line with the other riflemen, his father walked by the whole line without seeming to notice his son.

Years later, when he wrote his memoirs of the Quebec campaign, John Henry recalled the strange "moose-deer." And the trees, especially the "balsam fir," which

> yields a balsamic liquid much esteemed by the medical profession. The bark is smooth, except that there are a vast number of white and lucid protuberances upon it. Getchel, our guide, taught me its use. In the morning when we rose, placing the edge of a broad knife at the under side of the blister, and my lips at the opposite part, on the back of the knife, which was declined, the liquor flowed into my mouth freely. It was heating and cordial to the stomach, attended by an agreeable pungency. This practice, which we adopted, in all likelihood con-

tributed to the preservation of [our] health, though much wet weather ensued, and we lay often on low and damp ground.

While searching for "The Great Carrying Place" between the Kennebec and Dead Rivers, and "blazing the trees and snagging the bushes with our tomahawks," the scouts saw many "moose-deer." They reluctantly let the moose pass by, unmolested, lest the sound of their rifles alarm any hostile Indians nearby. They would have done well to shoot the moose, for by the time the bedraggled scouts returned to the main column they had nearly expired from starvation.

By October 8th, Henry and the other scouts, by now nearly out of food, had passed the Great Carrying Place and had travelled the length of the Dead River. They were now at the end of a chain of ponds which form the headwaters of the Dead River. Just beyond these ponds was an imposing ridge, which the army must cross to reach the Chaudiere River.

On this lake, we obtained a full view of those hills which were called the "Height of land." It made an impression upon us that was really more chilling than the air which surrounded us. We hurried ashore - drew out our canoes, and covered them with leaves and brushwood. This done, with our arms in our hands, and our provision in our pockets, we made a race across the mountain, by an Indian path ... [Lt. Steele] asked if any one could climb a tree, around the foot of which we stood? It was a pine of considerable height, without branches for forty feet. Robert Cunningham, a strong athletic man, about twenty-five years old, presented himself. In almost the twinkling of an eye, he climbed the tree. He fully discerned the meandering course of the river [the seven mile stream leading to Lake Megantic]. The country around and between us and the lake was flat. Looking westward, he observed smoke, intimating this to us from the tree where he sat. We plainly perceived it. Cunningham came down; the sun was setting seemingly in a clear sky.

Now our return commenced - It so occurred, that I was in the rear, next to Getchel, who brought it up. We ran in single file, and tried to stride into the footsteps of the leader. The race was urged, and became more rapid by the indications of a most severe storm of rain; we had scarcely more than gotten half way up the hill, when the shower came down in most tremendous torrents. The night became dark as pitch; we groped the way across the ridge, and in descending, relied on the accuracy of our leader; we continued with speed. The precipice was very steep; a root, a twig perhaps, caught the buckle of my shoe. Tripped, I came down head foremost, unconscious how far, but perhaps twenty or thirty feet. How my gun remained unbroken, it is impossible to say. When I recovered, it was in my hands.

Feeling for the path with my feet, my arrival at the canoe place was delayed till ten at night, an hour and more later than my friends. A wigwam was made in a hurry with forks and cross-poles, covered by the branches of fir. Sleep came to my eyes, notwithstanding the drippings of the pelting storm, through the humble roof.

The next day, the scouts headed back down the Dead River, by now a series of rapids, due to the swelling caused by the rain. Obstacles in the "quick water" badly ripped one of their birch canoes and tore the other one completely in half. To men much fatigued from their exertions, weak from hunger, and 100 miles from the army, these accidents were indeed discouraging. But Getchel, their guide from Fort Western, showed them how to repair the canoes, using bark from birch trees, turpentine from pine trees, stringy roots from cedar trees, and the fat-soaked burlap bag that formerly held their pork. When they reached the northern end of the Great Carrying Place, the designated rendezvous with the army, no one was there. The scouts began to think the army had returned to Cambridge, and they would "all die of mere debility in these wilds," since they were too weak "to bear the canoes across the twelve-mile carrying-place" to the Kennebec. "As a last effort to save our lives," the scouts abandoned the canoes, and set out on foot to "follow the army, which we were now assumed, had returned." On October 17, twenty-six days after starting their scouting trip from Fort Western, they met the army's advance corps, clearing a road across the Great Carrying Place.

While the scouts had been far ahead, the main column had been experiencing its own hardships. From Fort Western all the way to the Great Carrying Place, the men found the Kennebec to be "not even boatable." George Morison, the Pennsylvania riflemen, described it in his memoirs:

> The water was for the most part very shallow; insomuch that no use could be made of the oars. Could we have plied them, our employment would have been less toilsome; at least it would have varied our labour. Not once in the whole course of the Kennebeck was there an occasion for rowing.

To bypass the rapids and frequent falls, the men halted at numerous carrying places, some only a few yards, others a few miles. Here they unloaded the cargoes. Private Simon Fobes, of Bridgewater, Mass., explained in his journal how the portages were performed:

> The boats were turned bottom up, and four men would take one on their shoulders and march along, the edge of the boat, being somewhat sharp, pressing very painfully on the flesh. Each barrel of provision was carried by four men, being swung by ropes on two poles. It

58

was a fatiguing and painful task; but performed with much patience and fortitude, and without murmuring.

Each empty bateau weighed 400 pounds. The men would go back and forth over the portage until all the material had been carried. Officers worked side by side with their men, sharing their food, their toil, and their luck. After a long day of pushing, pulling and carrying, much of it while waist deep in water and mire, the men had to sleep on cold, often wet ground. On one such night, by the candlelight in his tent, Dr. Isaac Senter remarked in his journal, "wet and fatigued as we were, we had to encamp on the cold ground. It was at this time that we inclined to think of the comfortable accomodations we had left at home." Private Caleb Haskell, a farm boy from Newburyport, observed, "Now we are learning to be soldiers."

Hastily built of green pine, it was not long before the bateaux warped, causing infuriating leaks. And the rocky river bottom, with its sunken logs and tree roots, "soon ground out the bottoms" of the boats. If the boats could not hold up, the prospects of the army reaching Quebec were gloomy indeed. Arriving at Norridgewock Falls on October 5th, Senter observed the results of the first quarter of the trip:

> By this time, many of our batteaux were nothing but wrecks, some stove to pieces, &c. The carpenters were employed in repairing them, while the rest of the army were busy in carrying over the provisions, &c. The bread casks not being water-proof admitted the water in plenty, swelled the bread, burst the casks as well as soured the whole bread. The same fate attended a number of fine casks of peas. These with the others were condemned. We were now curtailed of a very valuable and large part of our provisions. Our fate was now reduced to salt pork and flour.
>
> Friday, 6th. Several of our army continued to be troubled with the dysentery, of which disease, capt. Wil-

liams, a gentleman from Connecticut, came nigh to lose his life. Continued getting over provisions, &c. Weather mostly cloudy and considerable reign.

Saturday, 7th. We were still at Norridgewalk, where was now most of the army. By a council of the officers, it was thought advisable to send letters into Quebec.

While still at the Great Carrying Place, Arnold despatched two Abenaki Indians, in a birch-bark canoe, with two letters - one addressed to General Schuyler, the other to an American-born merchant Arnold knew at Quebec. Instead, they brought the letters directly to the lieutenant-governor. Suspecting that the letters might be intercepted by the enemy, Arnold exaggeratingly claimed to have 2000 men and already be on the Dead River. And he added, "hope in a fortnight of having the pleasure of meeting you in Quebec." Arnold wanted to make it easier for Schuyler and Montgomery by scaring the governor into sending part of his forces at St. Jean back to Quebec.

Impressed with the pristine beauty of the wilderness, George Morison thought the army was trespassing on a place that "Nature appointed for the beasts of the forests and not for man. Surely such an invasion must be deemed flagitious, and an infringement on the ordination of God." Perhaps it was, for Arnold's troops were given an abundance of rainy, cold weather. For several days, virtually no progress could be made because of torrential rains.

When not wet from the rains, the men were soaked from wading the icy waters, pushing and pulling the boats. Waking one morning, an officer observed his wet clothes were "frozen a pane of glass thick." By now on half rations, the weary men found the ground on the Great Carrying Place was "extremely bad, being choked with roots which we could not clear." They came to a pond, which offered a break from the drudgery of eating nothing but salt pork and flour. There "taking eight or ten dozen" trout "in an hour's time" was the norm for a single man. At one place the men found a meadow of waist-high grass, which they cut and used for covering for the night, being short on tents and blankets.

After a third pond, the men had to carry the boats and supplies over a northeastern spur of the long landmark recognizable from Montresor's map as Mount Bigelow. From this high point they looked down and saw the Dead River, just beyond a mile's stretch of open, grassy plain. That "plain" turned out to be a spruce and cedar bog, and the "grass" a spongy moss that looked solid but wasn't. With each step a man took, he sank through this and the foot or more of mud beneath it, his foot finally settling among hiddden tree roots, exceedingly hard on the feet. George Morison described this last mile as "by far the most fatiguing movement that had yet befell us." But still the men tried to keep their sense of humor.

> The rains had rendered the earth a complete bog; insomuch that we were often half leg deep in the mud, stumbling over old fallen logs, one leg sinking deeper in the mire than the other, then down goes a boat and the carriers with it, a hearty laugh prevails. The irritated carriers at length get to their feet with their boat, plastered with mud from neck to heel, their comrades tauntingly asking them how they liked their washing and lodging; perhaps a few paces further, down they go, the laugh reverts upon them; the others, who just before met with a like misfortune, call out to them to come here and they would lift them.

Meagre rations, fatiguing exertions, drinking water that was "quite yellow," and working and sleeping in wet clothes with no protection from the cold and wind. It all combined to take a toll on the men, according to Dr. Senter's journal:

> Monday, 16th. - We now found it necessary to erect a building for the reception of our sick, who had now increased to a very formidable number. A block house

was erected and christened by the name of Arnold's Hospital, and no sooner finished than filled. A young gentleman by name Irwin was truly deplorable. When he came to wading in the water every day, then lodging on the ground at night, it kept him in the most violent rheumatism I ever saw, not able to help himself any more than a new born infant, every joint in his extremities inflexible and swelled to an enormous size.

Finally the men completed the long portage, and headed up the Dead River, a deep, meandering, "gentle and leisurely stream," leading them to those distant mountains called the Height of Land. Abner Stocking's journal entry for October 16 explains how it was named: "The river is so remarkably still and dead that it is difficult to determine which way it runs." George Morison: "On Dead River we found relief from our hardships, the water being deep and dead for many miles; we could now make use of oars, the easiest employment we had yet."

These relatively easy days did not last. Nature struck with what the U.S. Weather Bureau, 150 years later, concluded was a wayward Carribbean hurricane that drifted far up the Atlantic. Private Ephraim Squier, of Ashford, Connecticut, noted the weather:

> [October] 19th. This morning it begins to rain ...
> 20th. Last night it was very rainy and continues raining hard all day ...
> 21st. Last night likewise was very rainy and continues raining exceedingly hard all day. A windier and rainier day I never see. We went till almost night then went ashore to camp, and at length with utmost difficulty kindled us a fire, but could not take much comfort, the wind blowed so high and rained so hard till about 10 or 11 o'clock at night, when the river obliged us to retreat from our fire; the river raised, we judge, 12 feet; so

windy it was dangerous being in the woods.

By the next day, the responsibility of preserving the lives of over 1000 men must have weighed heavily upon the mind of Benedict Arnold, as he wrote in his journal:

> Sunday, October 22nd. This morning presented us a very disagreeable prospect, the country round entirely overflowed so that the course of the river, being crooked, could not be discovered, which with the rapidity of the current renders it almost impossible for the battoes to ascend the river, or the men to find their way by land or pass the small brooks.

Isaac Senter wryly wrote in his journal, "From a dead river it had now become live enough." Many of the men awoke to find their last barrel of flour or pork had floated away during the night. The majority of the men, now on foot, were forced far back from the original riverbed, the river having overflowed its banks and flooded the surrounding land for more than a mile on each side. Its many feeding brooks "were swelled to an enormous size," forcing "the land party to trace them up for many miles till a narrow part offered, and then could only cross by felling large trees over them." Some companies lost the way, and exhausted search parties in boats had to be sent out to find them and lead them back to the main column.

With the Height of Land still to be overcome, and provisions almost entirely gone, except for the well-stocked fourth division in the rear, Arnold ordered a council with those officers who were near him at the front of the army. Should we give up and go back to Cambridge, or go on to the formidable Height of Land and beyond? The vote was unanimous - go on, but only after sending back the sickest men and calling up provisions from the rear division. Soon Arnold was recording in his journal:

Sent back the sick, 26 in number, & ordered Col Green & Col Enos to send back as many of the poorest men of their detachment as would leave 15 days provision for the remainder. 50 men set out early for Chaudiere Pond, in order to forward on provisions from the French inhabitants.

Unfortunately for the starving army, these 50 men, under Captain Hanchet, of Suffield, Conn., after carrying their heavy bateaux over the snow-covered Height of Land, would become lost in the swamps near Chaudiere Pond (or Lake Megantic, as Montresor called it, after the Indian name Ammeguntick). From that day on, Hanchet held a grudge against Arnold, and would later be one of three officers who rebelled against him. Most of the other soldiers, though (judging by the several that kept diaries or wrote memoirs of the expedition), did admire Benedict Arnold's leadership. Private Abner Stocking was one:

> Our bold though inexperienced general discovered such firmness and zeal as inspired us with resolution. The hardship and fatigue he encountered he accounted as nothing in comparison with the salvation of his country.

Arnold sent back 90 men, in ten boats, to the rear division, with orders for Colonel Enos to divide his relatively plentiful food supplies, and send forward the portions to be allocated to the three divisions in the front - those of Morgan, Greene and Meigs. Those divisions had originally gone forward from Fort Western with light supplies, to be less encumbered, while the bulk of the provisions were brought up by Enos's rear division over the roads cleared by those in front.

Meigs's division (the third) was in the process of passing Greene's (the second). Dr. Senter noted the discouraging sight of the sick men returning from Morgan's and Greene's divisions:

Here we met several boats returning, loaded with invalids, and lamentable stories of the inaccessibleness of the river, and the impracticability of any further progress into the country. I was now exhorted in the most pathetic terms to return, on pain of famishing. Not far had I proceeded before I discovered several wrecks of batteaux belonging to the front division of riflemen. Two miles from thence I met Col. Greene's division waiting for the remainder of the army to come up, that they might get some provisions, ere they advanced any further. Upon enquiry I found them almost destitute of any eatable whatever, except a few <u>candles</u>, which were used by boiling them in water.

Wednesday 25th. A storm of snow had covered the ground nigh six inches deep, attended with very severe weather. We now awaited in anxious expectation for Col. Enos' division to come up, in order that we might have a recruit of provisions.

Colonel Greene found Colonel Enos and handed him Arnold's order to apportion the food and come forward "with all possible despatch." After reading it, Enos called a council of the officers, his own and those who brought the order. "The matter was debated upon the expediency of proceeding on for Quebec." Colonel Greene and his officers voted to go on, but the officers under Colonel Enos voted to return to Cambridge. Enos initially broke the tie by voting to proceed, "yet had undoubtedly preengaged to the contrary, as every action demonstrated."

Immediately after the voting, Enos let his subordinate officers talk him into joining them and returning to Cambridge with his entire fourth division. They had listened attentively to the tales told by the sick men Arnold had sent back, and were convinced that anyone who continued to follow Arnold would surely perish. As to the division of pork and flour, Enos replied that his men were out of his power, and that they had determined to keep their possessed quantity whether they went back or forward. They finally concluded to spare [us] 2 1/2 barrels of flour, if [we] determined to pursue our destination. We were left the alternative of accepting their small pittance and proceed, or return. The former was adopted, with a determined resolution to go through or die.

Gradually, the stunning news - that Enos had turned back with his 350 men and nearly the entire food supply - reached the starving, exhausted men spread out over twenty miles in the front. The men in boats, struggling against the current, and those on land, slipping on the snow and wet leaves and needles underfoot, stopped long enough to curse the deserters. Captain Henry Dearborn noted in his journal:

Our men made a general prayer, that Colonel Enos and all his men might die on the way, or meet with some disaster equal to the cowardly, dastardly and unfriendly spirit they discovered in returning back without orders, in such a manner as they had done, and then we proceeded forwards.

As soon as Enos and his division arrived back at Cambridge, Washington had Enos arrested for "quitting his commanding officer without leave." But, as some of the officers sitting on his court martial were his friends, and there was no one from Greene's division on hand to testify against him, he was acquitted. The court ruled that "the return of the division was prudent and reasonable." Had he gone on with Arnold, his whole division would "have perished in the woods for want of sustenance." After enduring eight days of cold silence after the trial, Enos resigned his commission and never served in the war again.

Between Arnold, near the Height of Land, and Enos, at the Great

Carrying Place, young John Joseph Henry was with those who were progressing up the flooded Dead River valley. The trials these men suffered at the hands of the swift current are vividly related by Henry:

Oct. 23d. The river flowed with terrifying rapidity. None but the most strong and active boatmen entered the boats. The army marched on the south side of the river, making large circuits to avoid the overflowings. This was one of the most fatiguing marches we had as yet performed, though the distance was not great in a direct line. But having no path and being necessitated to climb the steepest hills, and that without food, for we took none with us, thinking the boats would be near us all day. In the evening we arrived at the fall of four feet. Alas! all the boats of the army were on the opposite side of the river. The pitch of the fall made a dreadful noise, and the current ran with immense velocity. We sat down on the bank sorely pinched with hunger, looking wistfully towards our friends beyond the torrent, who were in possession of the provisions, tents and camp equipage, convinced that the most adventurous boatman would not dare the passage, for the sake of accomodating any of us. We were mistaken.

The force of the central current naturally formed considerable eddies at each side of the river, close under the pitch. Simpson now disclosed his amazing skill. The stream forced his boat down the river, but he recovered and brought it up. He called in his loud voice to Robert Dixon, James Old and myself to enter the boat. We entered immediately. He pushed off; attempting the start by favor of the hither eddy, which was the main thing - we failed. Returning to the shore, we were assailed by a numerous band of soldiers, hungry, and anxious to be with their companions. Simpson told them he could not carry more with safety, and would return for them. Henry M'Annaly ... jumped into the boat. He was followed by three or four other inconsiderate men. The countenance of Simpson changed. "O God," said he, "men we shall all die." They would not recede. Again we approached the pitch; it was horrible. The bateau swam deep, almost ungovernable by the paddle. Attempting again to essay the departure - we failed.

The third trial was made: it succeeded. As lightning we darted athwart the river. Simpson called to the men in the bow, to lay hold of the birch bushes - the boat struck the shore forcibly; they caught hold, but like children their holds slipped, at the only spot where we could have been saved. Letting go their holds, the bow came round to the stream, and the stern struck the shore. Simpson, Dixon, and myself now caught the bushes, but being by this time thrown into the current, the strength of the water made them as so many straws in our hands. The stern again swung round: the bow came again ashore. Mr. Old, Tidd, and M'Annaly, and the rest, sprung to the land to save their lives. Doing this, at our cost, their heels forced the boat across the current.

Though we attempted to steady it, the boat, being broad side to the current, turned; borne under, in spite of all our force, by the fury of the stream. The boat upsetting, an expression, going into the water, fell from me, "Simpson we are going to heaven." My fall was head-foremost. Simpson came after me - his heels, at the depth of fifteen feet or more, were upon my head and neck; and those grinding on the gravel. We rose nearly together. Swimming was tried, but it was a topsyturvy business. The force of water threw me often heels overhead.

In the course of this voyage, after a few hundred

yards, Simpson was at my side, but the force of the stream prevented the exertion of swimming; the impetuosity of the current kept us up. Floating along with my head just above water - prayers in sincere penitence having been uttered - my eyes became closed. Driving with the current some hundred yards more, the most palpable feeling recollected was the striking of my breast against a root or hard substance. My head came above water. Breathing ensued; at the same moment Simpson raised his head out of the water. Neither of us could have crept out. We should have there died but for the assistance of Edward Cavanaugh, an Irish man, an excellent soldier, who was designated in the company by the appellation "Honest Ned." He cried out "Lord, Johnny! is this you?" and instantly dragged me out of the water. Simpson immediately appearing, he did him the same good office.

Lying on the earth perhaps twenty minutes, the water pouring from me, a messenger from the camp came to rouse us. Roused we went to it. But all eyes looked out for Dixon, all hearts were wailing for his loss. It was known he could not swim ... In some time we had the inexpressible pleasure of Dixon in our company. He had stuck to the drift wood some miles below; and in this way he was saved. Arriving at the camp our friends had a large fire prepared. Immediately the breeches were off and stuck upon a pole to dry. Simpson was so much exhilarated by our escape that, seated on a stump, he sung "Plato" in great glee. It became a favorite with us.

Benedict Arnold, with a few men and a wooden dugout canoe, went ahead of the army, and crossed the Height of Land. He sent back letters to the three division commanders, informing them that he was going ahead to purchase provisions from the first Chaudiere River settlement, that the carry was too difficult to bring along the boats, and that after crossing the Height of Land the army should keep to the high ground and skirt around the swamp that lay before Lake Megantic.

Arnold's instructions to not try to carry the bateaux over the Height of Land was welcome news to the men. "With inexpressible joy," the Pennsylvanian, George Morison, wrote, "we dropped these grievous burdens." Arnold had entrusted the bulk of the gunpowder, as well as the money chest, to Captain Daniel Morgan, of the Virginia riflemen. Morgan's company had seven bateaux remaining, and he was not about to risk these indispensable supplies not reaching Quebec. John Henry recalled:

> Morgan determined to carry over all his boats. It would have made your heart ache to view the intolerable labors his fine fellows underwent. Some of them, it was said, had the flesh worn from their shoulders, even to the bone. By this time an antipathy against Morgan as too strict a disciplinarian had arisen.

George Morison, many years later, recalled the trek over the Height of Land, or what he called the "Terrible Carrying Place."

> Every one of us shivering from head to foot. Men whose weakness was reduced to the lowest degree, struggling among rocks and in swamps and falling down upon one another in the act of mutually assisting each other. We had all along aided our weaker brethren. These friendly offices could no longer be performed. Many of the men began to fall behind. It was impossible to bring them along; and if we tarried with them we must have all perished. It was therefore given out by our officers for every man to shift for himself and save his own life if possible. When will the remembrance of

that mournful period cease to disturb my mind?

When we moved off from them, calling out to us as well as their feeble voices would allow: "Will you leave us to perish in the wilderness?" Never will that heart piercing interrogatory forsake my memory. It was an exclamation that overwhelmed our souls with indescribable horror - some of those who were advanced turned back, and declared that they would prefer death to leaving them; others stopped their ears and moved off with all the expedition in their power.

With heavy laden hearts we marched on. Passed musketmen eating dog. They devoured this strange repast with extream voracity, not excepting the skin, the feet or entrails. We encamped, our strength so reduced that but a few of us were able to raise a fire. Our spirits were so depressed by the occurrences of this day that death would have been a welcome messenger to have ended our woes.

John Henry also noted the unavoidable death wish and eating "this strange repast:"

We came to a fire. I sat down on the end of a long log, against which the fire was built, absolutely fainting with hunger and fatigue, my gun standing between my knees. Seating myself, that very act [upset] the kettle, which was placed partly against the log, in such a way as to spill two thirds of its contents. At that moment a large man sprung to his gun, and pointing it towards me, he threatened to shoot. It created no fear. Death would have been a welcome visitor. Simpson soon made us friends. Coming to their fire, they gave me a cup of their broth. A tablespoonful was all that was tasted. It had a greenish hue, and was said to be that of a bear.

This was instantly known to be untrue, from the taste and smell. It was that of a dog. He was a large black Newfoundland dog, belonging to Thayer's and very fat.

We left these merry fellows, and marching quickly, toward evening encamped. We had a good fire, but no food. To me the world had lost its charms. My privations in every way were such as to produce a willingness to die. The idea occurred, and the means were in my hands, of ending existence. The God of all goodness inspired other thoughts. One principal cause of change (under the fostering hand of Providence) in my sentiments was the jovial hilarity of my friend Simpson. At night, warming our bodies at an immense fire, to animate the company he would sing "Plato." The music added strength and vigour to our nerves. This evening it was, that some of our companions washed their mockasins in the river, scraping away the dirt and sand, with great care. These were brought to the kettle and boiled. The poor fellows chewed the leather, but it was leather still: not to be macerated. My teeth, though young and good, succeeded no better. Disconsolate and weary, we passed the night.

Though a few dozen died from hunger and fatigue, most of the nearly 700 men remaining on October 27th did overcome the Height of Land. They hoped it would be the last obstacle in their path to Quebec. At the top they found a "beautiful meadow," from which they could look down and see long, narrow Chaudiere Pond, or Lake Megantic. Dr. Senter described the meadow as "not a little delightsome, considering its situation in the midst of an amazing wilderness." At the far end of the lake would be the Chaudiere River, which would lead them past French villages (hopefully friendly) and directly to Quebec. They also knew, from Arnold's letters, that he was somewhere on that river, proceeding "as fast as possible with 4 bateaux and 15 men to the inhabitants ... [to] send back provisions as soon as possible."

What the men could not see from the beautiful meadow was the seven miles between them and the lake. In this seven mile stretch were a large swamp and a deceptive second lake, neither of which were on Montresor's map. By the next morning, October 28th, all ten companies were lost in the swamp. A Connecticut private later described this new difficulty:

> The top of the ground was covered with a soft moss, filled with water and ice. After walking for a few hours in the swamp we seemed to have lost all sense of feeling in our feet and ankles. As we were constantly slipping, we walked in great fear of breaking our bones or dislocating our joints. To be disabled from walking in this situation was sure death.

Arnold had sent back clear directions and a guide, so the army would not walk into the swamp. The letter was addressed "To the Field officers and captains. To be sent on, that the whole army may see it."

> The bearer, Isaac Hull, I have sent back in order to direct the people in coming from the Carrying-place to Chaudiere Pond. From the west side, before they come to the Meadows, strike off to the right hand and keep about a north by east course, which will escape the low swampy land and save a very great distance; and about six miles will bring you to the pond. By no means keep the brook, which will carry you into a swamp, out of which it will be impossible for you to get.

With the guide and directions and a copy of Montresor's map, the men were confident that they would "find the way into the country without difficulty." But Isaac Hull could not find the way, and soon the freezing, starving army "kept to the brook," and became lost in the ice-covered swamps. By the third day of hopelessly wandering in the swamps, Dr. Senter noted, "Hunger and fatigue had so much the ascendency, that some of them were left, nor heard of afterwards."

No longer a column, the army was now composed of groups of panicky men passing each other, going in different directions, each group sure the others were going in the wrong direction. Each evening they found islands in the swamp just big enough for a man to lie down on, and hope the night did not bring more rain. John Henry recalled these desperate days:

> This morning, the first of November, breakfasting on our bleary [water and flour], we took up the line of march through a flat and boggy ground. About ten o'clock we arrived [on] a narrow neck [of land] covered by a coat of ice, half an inch thick. Here Simpson concluded to halt a short time for the stragglers or maimed of Hendrick's and Smith's companies to come up. There were two women attached to those companies. One was the wife of Serjeant Grier, a large, virtuous and respectable woman. The other was the wife of a private of our company, a man who lagged upon every occasion.
>
> These women being arrived, it was presumed that all our party were up. We were on the point of entering the marsh, when some one cried out "Warner is not here." Another said he had "sat down sick under a tree, a few miles back." His wife begging us to wait a short time, with tears of affection in her eyes, ran back to her husband. We tarried an hour. They came not. Entering the pond, breaking the ice here and there with the buts of our guns and feet, as occasion required, we were soon waist deep in the mud and water.

Abner Stocking's journal tells what happened to Jemima Warner after she found her man:

> His affectionate wife tarryed by him until he died,
> while the rest of the company proceeded on their way.
> Having no implements with which she could bury him
> she covered him with leaves, and then took his gun and
> other implements and left him with a heavy heart. After
> travelling 20 miles she came up with us.

Daniel Morgan's company was the first to fall upon the right route
out of the swamp. Morgan then went back, with the seven bateaux he
had forced his men to carry over the mountain, to hail the nine other
lost companies and ferry them across the swamps and streams. Sight-
ing Morgan and his rescue boats, the men shouted "three huzzas."
Morgan soon left the ferrying to others and rejoined his own company,
to lead the army down the River "Chaudiere," a French word meaning
caldron or boiler. It was aptly named, because "for 60 or 70 miles it is
a continued rapid," as it descends to the St. Lawrence. John Henry
continues his account, now marching along the riverbank.

> Marching hastily, we came within view of a tremen-
> dous catarack [the Falls of Sault] in the river, from 12 to
> 20 feet high. The horror this sight gave us, fearing for
> the safety of our friends in the boats. Turning the point
> of a steep cragg, we met those very friends; having <u>lost</u>
> <u>all</u> [including the bateaux, smashed on the rocks] but
> their lives, sitting around a fire on the shore. Oh God!
> what were our sensations! Poor M'Cleland ... was lying
> at the fire; he beckoned to us. His voice was not audi-
> ble; placing my ear close to his lips, the word he uttered
> scarcely articulate was "Farewell." Simpson, who loved
> him, gave him half of the pittance of food which he still
> possessed; all I could give was a tear.
> We passed on, fearful for our own lives. Coming to a

75

long sandy beach of the Chaudiere, some men of our company were observed to dart from the file and with their nails tear out of the sand roots which they esteemed eatable and ate them raw, even without washing. The knowing one sprung, and half a dozen followed. Strokes often occurred.

Soon Dr. Senter thought his eyes were deceiving him, as he saw

a vision of horned cattle. Upon a nigher approach our vision proved real! Exclamations of joy, echoes of gladness resounded from front to rear. A heifer was slain and divided accordingly. Each man was restricted to one pound of beef. Soon arrived two more Canadians in b[irch] canoes, ladened with a coarse kind of meal, mutton, tobacco, etc. Each man likewise drew a pint of this provender. The mutton was destined for the sick. They proceeded up the river.

"Provisions in sight! Provisions in sight!" resounded from hill to hill. Throwing down their guns, those who still had them, they sprang forward like a pack of famished wolves and struck at one of the cattle with their tomahawks. They were eating its flesh "before the creature was dead."

After further marching, the men arrived at a settlement - Sartigan, populated by French Canadians and Abenaki Indians. While at Sartigan, Natanis, the Indian whom John Henry's advance scouting party had been ordered to kill on sight, walked up to Henry and his companions, much to their surprise, "and shook hands in the way of an old acquaintance." Natanis had traveled within sight of the army during the last few weeks. When asked, "Why did you not speak to your friends," he replied, "You would have killed me." Two nephews of Natanis were hired to paddle their birch canoes from Sartigan up the Chaudiere, each canoe bounding "like an egg-shell over the surface of

76

the waves of every opposing ripple." They hurried to the Falls of Sault and brought back Lieutenant McCleland. "The following day he died, and his corpse received a due respect from the inhabitants."

After marching down the bank of the Chaudiere, wading through numerous ice-cold tributaries, Abner Stocking reached Sartigan. Like the other diarists, he recorded his surprise and gratitude at how the French Canadians received them:

> November 3d. This day we proceeded down the river about 20 miles, waiding several small rivers, some of which were up to our middles. The water was terrible cold as the ground was at this time covered with snow and ice. At evening we came in sight of a house which was the first we had seen for the space of 31 days.
>
> The kindness and hospitality of the inhabitants was to us very pleasing. After having been our late enemies, at war with us, we did not expect to experience from them so much friendship.
>
> Our cloathes were torn in pieces by the bushes and hung in strings, few of us had any shoes ... beards long and visages thin and meagre. I thought we much resembled the animals which inhabit New Spain, called the Ourang-Outang. The French appeared a little surprised at the first sight of us; and had not Colonel Arnold gone forward to apprise them of our approach, they might have fled from their habitations.

Approximately eighty men had died of starvation, hypothermia, pneumonia and exhaustion between the headwaters of the Dead and Chaudiere Rivers. The habitants of the Chaudiere Valley admired and respected "les bons Bostonnais" who had defied the wilderness at such a late season. "Surely," said one, "God is with this people, or they could never have done what they have done."

Exposure to these devout Roman Catholics was quite an experience for a Protestant Yankee like John Pierce:

> November 1 1775 We were very friendly received by the inhabitance and treated very kindly this night. I slept between two Frenchmen in a French house. It was very odd to hear them at their devotion ... very precise in saying their prayers, counting their beads and crossing themselves.
>
> Novem. 13 The French had a fine ball last evening with which we were entertained and had each of us a dram [of rum] and a piece of bread gratis. We had musik of diverse sorts such as bag pipes fiddle fife German flute and some vocal musike &c. Playing cards and some other gaming on Sunday. They do not labour on said day but all recreation is lawfull such as hunting gaming and all sorts of sports and plays.

The army stayed near Sartigan (present St. Georges) four days, to gather itself together and to recuperate somewhat. The new danger was overeating, which can be fatal after weeks of starvation. "Reasoning had no influence" for two men that John Henry observed. They "seemed to defy death for the mere enjoyment of present gratification, and died two days after their imprudence."

At Arnold's headquarters, five miles below Sartigan, the Abenakis met with Arnold and, through an interpreter, demanded to know why he had brought an army into their homeland, pretending that they did not know. After the chiefs' dignified speeches, Arnold gave one of his own, trying to convince them that the colonists' quarrel with the English King should also be their own. It was convincing enough, especially the ending, when he offered payment. Natanis and at least 40 other Indians were hired, more for the transportation their canoes would provide across the St. Lawrence than for any help they might provide in fighting Carleton's forces. The Abenakis quickly found a name for the swarthy, sharp-eyed Arnold: Dark Eagle. Before departing, Natanis addressed Arnold:

> Dark Eagle comes to claim the wilderness. The wilderness will yield to the Dark Eagle, but the Rock [the clifftop Quebec fortress] will defy him. The Dark Eagle will soar aloft to the sun. Nations will behold him and sound his praises. Yet when he soars highest his fall is most certain. When his wings brush the sky then the arrow will pierce his heart.

CHAPTER FOUR
ATTACK ON QUEBEC
NOVEMBER - DECEMBER 1775

"My Dear Father: If you receive this, it will be the last this hand shall ever write you. Orders are given for a general storm on Quebec this night; and heaven only knows what may be my fate; but whatever it may be, I cannot resist the inclination to assure you that I experience no reluctance in this cause, to venture a life which I consider only lent, to be used when my country demands it."

- John Macpherson,
December 31, 1775.

On November 10th, the army began arriving at the St. Lawrence. The place was Pointe Levis, only a few miles from Quebec, visible on the far side of the river, which was one mile wide here. Due to the traitorous Eneas and Sabatis, who had been entrusted by Arnold with his letter to Schuyler, the army's arrival was by now expected. The lieutenant-governor, after reading the intercepted letter, had ordered anything on the south shore that could float be removed or destroyed.

Near Pointe Levis, through the assistance of a sympathizer at a grist mill, the army was able to confiscate a large supply of wheat and flour. Although the mill owner, Colonel Henry Caldwell of the Canadian militia, was loyal to the governor, the manager of the mill had been secretly stealing and stockpiling supplies ever since he learned Americans were on the Chaudiere. The musketmen had shown their imprudence by overeating at Sartigan. Now the riflemen were about to show theirs at the grist mill, when Caldwell sent a boat to salvage what remained of the mill's supplies. John Henry describes the encounter:

> A hurried and boisterous report came from headquarters, that the British were landing on our left at a mill about a mile off. Each one grasped his arms. The running was severe. We perceived a boat landing, which came from a frigate. The boat came ashore. A youth sprang from it. Morgan, apprehensive of a discovery of our presence, fired at the boat's crew. They pulled off shore, beyond the range of our guns. The hapless youth plunged into the river, hoping to regain his boat. His friends flying from him - he waded, he swam, yet could not reach the boat. At the distance, perhaps of one hundred and fifty yards, nothing but his head above water, a shooting match took place; the balls within a few inches of his head. It gives me pain to recollect that my gun was discharged at him.
>
> [The boy] seeing that his boat's crew had deserted him, showed a desire to surrender, by approaching the shore. The firing ceased. Sabatis, the Indian, sprung forward, scalping knife in hand. The humanity of Morgan or Humphreys was excited. One or the other of them, it is not now recollected which, by his agility and amazing powers of body, was enabled to precede the Indian by several yards. This [race] was observed with great interest. Morgan brought the boy to land.

Arnold kept the men at Pointe Levis busy building ladders for scaling Quebec's walls, while he waited for the rest of his army to arrive. He sent a detachment "to purchase birch canoes twenty miles distant." The crossing was further delayed by high winds, producing very choppy waters on the St. Lawrence. This was the same storm that, further up the river, was preventing Governor Carleton's ships from sailing a gauntlet past Montgomery's artillery battery at the narrows of

Sorel.

By November 13th, Arnold was able to write to Washington, "I intend crossing this evening with about 40 canoes. To prevent which, the *Hunter* sloop and *Lizard* frigate lie opposite - however, expect to be able to evade them." Conditions were perfect for a crossing that night: calm water, cloudy sky, moon not due to rise until long after midnight. Even the tide - going out - would help the canoes in their crossing. The landing site would be near Wolfe's Cove, where in 1759 General Wolfe had landed his army prior to the climactic battle atop the cliffs, on the Plains of Abraham.

So, about 9 p.m., Colonel Arnold, Dr. Senter, Captains Thayer and Topham, and a few others pushed off and led the first wave. The canoes would have to return several times to bring over the entire 600. The crossing was not without adventure. One of the canoes, in mid-stream, burst open, spilling its men into the frigid water. They all managed to clamber aboard other canoes, except Lieutenant Steele, who swam to a full canoe. He was instructed "to throw his arms over the stern." For the remaining distance, one of the men was "seating himself upon them," lest the numbing effect of the cold water cause Steele to loosen his grip. To the first crossers' surprise and relief, there was no enemy party to oppose their landing. The men were soon warmed, and the wet ones dried out, by a fire quickly made in an abandoned house near the shore.

However, "The fire was spied by one of the patrolling barges who came towards the shore" to investigate. Arnold hailed the boat. When its crew did not answer their challenge, Arnold ordered his riflemen to fire. Shrieks of pain followed, and the watchboat quickly headed away to alert the *Lizard*. With this shooting incident, the element of surprise was now gone. And, with the moon soon to rise, it was judged too risky to send the canoes back for the rest of the men and the ladders. They would have to cross some other night.

Arnold led his troops along Wolfe's path up the cliff, considerably widened since 1759. On top, a council was held to set a plan of action. Captain Morgan and a few others were for immediately storming the city before daylight broke. The scouts Arnold had sent out had just returned to report there were no signs of alarm yet from the walled city. But, by a majority of one, the officers felt an immediate assault would be unwise, since the army was not entirely crossed over and most of the scaling ladders were still on the other side of the river. In addition, the watchboat that Arnold fired upon would be warning the defenders any minute now. The consensus was to wait. A few days later, refugees from the city informed the Americans that one of the gates was open that night, and those who had crossed over could have "entered unknown and even unseen," had Arnold ordered an immediate attack after landing.

For several days, Arnold's men resided in a nunnery and a school, coming out to shoot at the sentries atop the high fortress walls. The British Captain Thomas Ainslie commented on the practice in his diary:

> Dec. 8th. There fell six inches of snow last night, the wind in SW today freezing clear weather. Skulking riflemen watching to fire on those who appear on the ramparts. We saw a man drop; we pop at all those who come within musket shot, knowing their intention is to kill any person walking on the ramparts. This is the American way of making war. The indignation of our militia is raised against these fellows who call themselves soldiers. They are worse than savages, they will ever be held in contempt with men of courage. Lie in wait to shoot a sentry! A deed worthy of Yanky men of war.

A British cannon ball hit one American. It was Robert Dixon, who had barely escaped drowning with John Henry on the Dead River.

> Dixon was carried on a litter to the house of an English gentleman. An amputation took place. A tetanus followed. The lady of the house, though not one who

approved of our principles of action, was very attentive to our wounded companion. She [on Dr. Senter's advice] presented him with a bowl of tea. "No madam," said he. "It is the ruin of my country." Uttering this noble sentiment, this invaluable citizen died.

From refugees coming out of the city, Arnold learned that Colonel Maclean, with 200 men and seven field pieces, was planning to venture out for a surprise attack against his unsuspecting and poorly armed force. Lacking a sufficient supply of gunpowder to defend against such a threat, Arnold retreated with his army twenty miles upriver to Pointe aux Trembles (Aspen Point). A few lucky soldiers had now "furnished ourselves with seal-skin moccasins, which are large, and accordingly to the usage of the country, stuffed with hay or leaves to keep the feet dry and warm." However, "most of the soldiers were in constant misery, as they were bare footed and the ground frozen and very uneven. We might have been tracked all the way by the blood from our shattered hoofs."

As they marched along the riverbank, they observed a boat heading downriver for Quebec, and soon heard the booming of cannon, celebrating the return of its passenger, Governor Guy Carleton. Quebec's defense would surely improve now, under the direction of the very capable General Carleton.

Tradition has it, that while Arnold's army camped at Pointe aux Trembles, Aaron Burr was hunting in the woods with his Abenaki princess, Jacataqua, who had traversed the wilderness with him from their first meeting at Fort Western. They stopped at a brook for water. Having no cup, Burr was proceeding to use his hat, when a British officer, alone in the woods on a scouting mission, chanced to come upon the same brook from its other side. He politely offered Burr his own drinking cup. The two men struck up a friendship and, upon departing, pledged to remain friends despite the war. They met again, secretly, several times over the next few months, and the British officer arranged for Jacataqua, who was pregnant by Burr, to be taken in and cared for at one of Quebec's nunneries.

Arnold waited at Pointe aux Trembles twelve days until General Montgomery arrived with 300 men, mostly New Yorkers. Montgomery had had to leave garrisons at St. Jean and Montreal, and almost all his New Englanders had gone home soon after Montreal was taken. Livingston, the Old Subject from Chambly, brought up a regiment of Canadians a few days later. Montgomery clothed Arnold's men as he had his own - in new British uniforms, part of a shipment that had just arrived, destined for the Regulars formerly at St. Jean.

Arnold and his men liked Montgomery from the start, describing him as one "born to command" and possessing "a captivating address." The general was likewise impressed with Arnold's men. He wrote to General Schuyler, "there is a style of discipline among them much superior to what I have been used to see this campaign."

Montgomery and Arnold lost no time in returning to resume the siege. Arnold's men took up residence in a monastery and a hospital run by nuns in St. Roche, north of the city. Montgomery's men moved into houses in the villages near the Plains of Abraham, northwest of Quebec. Inside the city, Carleton heard rumors that Montgomery had brought "many cannon and 4500 men" to join Arnold. Lacking confidence in his defensive force, "men unused to war" whose loyalty was suspect, Governor Carleton wrote to Lord Dartmouth, "I think our fate extremely doubtful."

Carleton had been with Wolfe back in 1759, when Montcalm came out from his fortress to do battle on the Plains of Abraham. Montcalm lost that battle, and with it Canada. Now, faced with a similar situation, Governor Carleton remembered that lesson and would not venture from behind his secure walls, knowing his strength lay in holding tight until the spring thaw would see British reinforcements sailing upriver. While Arnold had been away at Pointe aux Trembles, Carleton had laid in as much food as he could purchase from the countryside and settled in, well-stocked for a long siege.

Wary of the enemy within, on November 22 Carleton issued a proclamation ordering all inhabitants unwilling to fight against the

Americans to flee the city. Many of the militia secretly favoring the Americans took this opportunity to join them, to the relief of Captain Ainslie:

> Thus was our militia purged from all those miscreants who had already taken arms with a design no doubt of turning them against us when a fair opportunity shou'd offer. Many people fear'd more the internal enemy than the avowed rebels without the walls. Their banishment made the minds of the people easy.

The refugees were accepted by the Americans, and placed under their fellow Canadians, Livingston and Duggan, who had joined Montgomery's army at Chambly.

Montgomery tried using his artillery, brought up from St. Jean, to breach the walls of the fortress, but soon had to admit that their "fewness and lightness" had "very little effect" on the 20-foot thick walls. And it was a dangerous experiment, as John Henry explains:

> The earth was too difficult for the intrenching tools to pierce. The only method left was to raise a battery composed of ice and snow. The snow was made into ice by the addition of water. The work was done in the night time. Five or six nine-pounders and a howitzer were placed in it. It was scarcely completed, and our guns had opened on the city, before it was pierced through and through by the weightier metal of the enemy. Several lives were lost on the first and second day. Yet the experiment was persisted in till a single ball, piercing the battery, killed and wounded three persons.

The balls, weighing 32 pounds apiece on average, that the British were hurling at them brought devastating results - both physical and psychological - when they hit their mark. Arnold's engineer, John

Pierce, was at the ice-covered breastwork when the ball Henry referred to smashed through it. One of the artillerymen it hit "was shot through his belly and had one of his armes shot off and all his inwards lay on the platform which was very awfull to behold." Further attempts to bombard the city were abandoned.

The Americans were also being bombarded in suburban St. Roche. Captains Thayer and Topham were sharing a bed when a cannon ball passed through the roof and landed between them, waking them but, amazingly, sparing their lives. General Montgomery, himself, called at Menut's tavern, leaving his horse and carriage outside the door. Minutes later, a cannon ball took off the horse's head, demolishing the carriage.

Eagerly anticipating their enlistment expiration on New Year's Day, many of the troops were "determined to get to New England as soon as may be." The frostbitten men were weary of the extreme cold, and they missed their families. To add to their troubles, "a number of women loaded with the infection" had come into the American camps and, thus, "the smallpox had already begun its ravages." Besides smallpox, the army had "lice itch, jaundice, crabs, bed bugs and fleas." Feelings were strong against being pressured to stay on. John Pierce, of Massachusetts, on Christmas Day recorded in his journal, "There is a certain number of officers who propagate a plan too much favouring tyranny with regard to keeping their men longer than they inlisted for." Only the three rifle companies assured Montgomery they would stay.

By now, Montgomery was weary of the Canadian campaign and the insubordination, and decided to resign his commission as soon as a replacement could be sent north. He secretly wrote to General Schuyler, "I am much obliged to you for communicating to Congress my desire of retiring. I wish, like a New Englander, for the moment of my release."

Governor Carleton refused to let Montgomery's letters, addressed to him and "the principal merchants" and demanding capitulation, be brought into the city. A messenger bearing a white flag was sent back three times by cannon shot before a woman finally smuggled the letter in. But Carleton burned the unopened envelope in front of her, threw her in jail, and the next day had her drummed out of town. So copies were attached to arrows and shot over the city walls. But words alone would not conquer the mighty fortress city.

Since Carleton would not give up, and siege tactics were out of the question, Montgomery was now for "storming the place," despite the likely "melancholy consequences" of heavy casualties that such a dangerous plan would bring. On December 20th, the British Captain Thomas Ainslie wrote in his journal:

> Montgomery is reported to have said that "he wou'd dine in Quebec or in Hell on Christmas." We are determined he shall not dine in town & be his own master. The weather is very severe indeed. No man, after having been exposed to the air but ten minutes, cou'd handle his arms to do execution. Ones senses are benumb'd. If they ever attack us it will be in mild weather.

Montgomery planned his attack for the evening of the 23rd. But on the 22nd a Canadian prisoner escaped from the American camp and brought word of the plan to Governor Carleton.

The informer also told him that Montgomery was having trouble persuading his men "to undertake a step so desperate." To induce them, he had promised each man $800 worth of plunder. Captain Ainslie remarked, "Can these men pretend that there is a possibility of approaching our walls loaden with ladders, sinking to the middle every step in snow! It will be a fatal attempt for them, they will never scale the walls."

Carleton was not as skeptical as Captain Ainslie. The next night he posted 1000 men along the Upper Town's extensive walls, staring out across the snow until sunrise. They suffered from the frigid weather. It was so cold that it was impossible to handle metal of any sort. One sentry had the lids of his "eyes frozen together, and was carried blind into the guard house."

But Montgomery cancelled the scheduled attack, after being notified of the prisoner's escape. Now that Carleton's sentries would be on the alert, Montgomery concluded he would have to sneak up on them. Therefore, he waited for the poor visibility a snowstorm would bring.

The awaited snowstorm arrived on December 27. But, to his dismay, Montgomery found that many of the New Englanders "appeared unwilling to attempt so daring an enterprise." It became necessary "to have the approbation of all the officers and soldiers." Three captains - Hanchet, Hubbard and Goodrich - who earlier had "incurred Colonel Arnold's displeasure by some misconduct" proposed forming a separate corps under Major John Brown, of Montgomery's division. Brown had disliked Arnold ever since the attack on Ticonderoga the previous May. Montgomery refused their proposal, whereupon the three companies then appeared to be "very averse" from the proposed assault. Isaac Senter offered to head one of the companies. Arnold refused the doctor's offer, telling him, "you will be wanted in the way of your profession."

General Montgomery met with the recalcitrant officers, "to compose some matters, which were happily settled," then spoke to Arnold's entire force, when paraded, addressing them "in a very sensible spirited manner, which greatly animated" them. One of Hanchet's men wrote of Montgomery's speech, "The fire of patriotism kindled in our breasts, and we resolved to follow wherever he should lead."

Just when the men were poised for the attack, the snow stopped falling, the clouds drifted off, and the moon came out. The frustrated Montgomery called off the attack, to wait for a more "favorable opportunity." The next day, Captain Topham's Rhode Islanders took four men who had feigned sickness the night before, and drove them from place to place amongst the camps with halters around their necks, prodding them and kicking them as the watching troops hooted. Topham wrote in his diary, "a man that inlists in this service should not be afraid of dying."

The same day, a New York sergeant deserted. When he reached the fortress walls, he held his musket upside down in the manner that signified surrender. Rather than opening the gates, sentries hauled him up on ropes. He informed Carleton, in detail, of the plan of attack. So now Montgomery had to formulate a new plan. Dr. Isaac Senter outlined the new plan in his journal:

> The arrangements of the army was as follows, viz., General Montgomery on the right wing, with the majority of the troops from Montreal. Colonel Arnold on the left, with his division of "Famine proof Veterans." Colonel Livingston's Canadian Regiment, to assault the [west] walls at St. John's gate, with combustibles for firing the gate, and thereby to draw the attention of the enemy that way, and at the same time attempt the walls a little distance with scaling ladders, &c.
>
> The place where the General was to assault was on the bank of the St. Lawrence, at the [southern] termination of the city walls, and where large piquets [wooden fences] were substituted. For this purpose instruments were carried to make the breach.
>
> Arnold was to attack at the other [northern] extremity of the town, where he first expected to be opposed by some small batteries before he arrived in the lower town, where the two extremes were to form a junction. To discriminate our troops from the enemy in action, they were ordered each officer and soldier to make fast a piece of white paper across their caps.

On December 31st, it began to snow. As the night wore on, the "outrageous" storm turned into a blizzard with a "cold wind extremely biting" that would not allow the men to look forward as they walked into it. Hail now mixed with the "thick small snow" that kept falling during the night. It was New Year's Eve. Officers passed from billet to billet, knocking on doors and alerting the men to "be ready at twelve" midnight.

Montgomery's division set out at 3:30 a.m. and marched southward across the Plains of Abraham. They descended the cliff known as Cape Diamond to the narrow beach at its base, which led to the southern end of the Lower Town. The beach was so narrow that the 300 men were forced to march single file. While Arnold's column, advancing from the north, was encountering snowdrifts five feet high, Montgomery's column was faced with a different obstacle. They discovered that, because the base of the 300-foot cliff was "washed by the river ... enormous and rugged masses of ice had been piled on each other, so as to render the way almost impassable." These conditions made for a much slower march than expected.

Three hundred feet above Montgomery's column, 100 Americans under Captain Jacob Brown, backed by cannon fire, rushed the Upper Town's walls. When "the flashes from their muskets made their heads visible," the defenders, led by Captain Ainslie, "briskly returned their fire." Still, the rebels came on, until they were almost at the gates. Then, suddenly, they broke and ran. The other diversionary attack, Livingston's Canadians, achieved similar results. Both parties had diverted, at least for a while, the attention of the defenders away from the main attack points. Now it was time for Montgomery and Arnold to take advantage of these diversions, and converge on the Lower Town.

At 5 a.m., when Brown and Livingston began their diversionary attacks, they sent flares skyward to signal Montgomery and Arnold. But the rough going in the ice and snow delayed them so much that, by the time the diversionary attacks were completed, the two columns were not yet near the blockhouses leading to each end of the Lower Town. And now the flares had alarmed the city. "The bells were all set on ringing, and drums beating." The defenders, who had been sleeping fully clothed and lying on their weapons for the past several nights, quickly ran to their positions.

It did not take long for the governor to realize that the attacks by Brown and Livingston were feints, and that the real attack would be directed against the Lower Town, the city's relatively weak point. Quickly, he organized a detachment of men and field pieces, under Colonel Maclean, to locate the main attack.

Arnold's force, about 600 strong, including Captain Lamb's New York City artillerists, had embarked at 3:30 a.m. They approached the Lower Town from St. Roche. Here, the suburbs merged with the city in tall warehouses, the backs of which overlooked the St. Charles River, as it emptied into the St. Lawrence. At the foot of these buildings, above the rocky shore, was a path that led down around the northern edge of the Lower Town. Arnold, with a local guide and an advance company of thirty men, marched about 100 yards ahead of "the artillery company, with a field piece mounted on a sled; then [came] the main body, of which Capt. Morgan's company was first." In order, behind them, marched Arnold's other rifle and musket companies, as well as a few Canadians and the 40 Indians recruited at Sartigan. John Henry remembers:

> The snow was deeper than in the fields, because of the nature of the ground. The path made by Arnold, Lamb, and Morgan was almost imperceptible because of the falling snow. Covering the locks of our guns with the lappets of our coats, and holding down our heads, we ran along the foot of the hill in single file.

By the dim light of the bursting shells, the guards noticed Arnold's long column of men pasing along the rocky path to the harbor. Since the column was directly below them, the angle was too sharp for cannon to be directed against the invaders. So the militia opened up with their muskets from atop the walls, and likewise the sailors from the windows of the Hotel Dieu. Lanterns on long poles were held out from the walls and windows, to cast circles of light on the ground below.

Arnold's men, some carrying the long, heavy ladders, made painfully slow progress on the snowy, rocky path. For about a third of a mile, they were "exposed to a dreadful fire of small arms which pour'd down on them." They suffered casualties, but kept marching, "powerless to return the salutes we received, as the enemy was covered by his impregnable defences. They were even sightless to us - we could see nothing but the blaze from the muzzles of their muskets."

Finally, they were out of range of the enemy muskets above them. Soon they reached their first barrier to the Lower Town - a "battery, which was raised upon a wharf." Major Return Meigs explains how the plan for taking this battery went awry:

> When our field piece had given them a shot or two, the advanced party were to rush forward, with the ladders, and force the battery above mentioned, while Capt. Morgan's company was to march round the wharf, if possible, on the ice [to attack from the rear]. But the snow being deep, the piece of artillery was brought on very slow, and we were finally obliged to leave it behind. The field piece not coming up, the advanced party, with Captain Morgan's company, attacked the battery, some firing into the port holes or kind of embrasures, while others scaled the battery with ladders, and immediately took possession of it, with the guard, consisting of 30 men.
>
> This attack was executed with so much despatch, that the enemy only discharged one of their cannon. In this attack we lost but one or two men, the enemy lost about the same number. In the attack of this battery, Col. Arnold received a wound in one of his legs with a musket ball, and was carried to the General Hospital.

According to Simon Fobes, "Arnold directed two soldiers to help him back to the encampment, while at the same time he ordered the troops to push on. 'Rush on, brave boys,' said he." John Henry had been marching near the lead with his rifle company, but fell down a declivity. He struggled back up, and fell in with a musket company.

Arnold called to the troops in a cheering voice as we passed, urging us forward; yet it was observable among the soldiery, with whom it was my misfortune to be now placed, that the Colonel's retiring damped their spirits. A cant phrase, "We are sold," was repeatedly heard in many parts throughout the line.

But they didn't break and run. They had suffered too much to quit now. They proceeded on, "enfiladed by an animated fire" from the ramparts high above them.

After Arnold had been hit in the leg, Daniel Morgan had wasted no time seizing the moment. Abner Stocking explains:

Morgan rushed forward to the battery at the head of his company, and received from one of the pieces, almost at its mouth, a discharge of grape shot which killed only one man. A few rifles were immediately fired into the embrazures, by which a British soldier was wounded in the head.

Now it was time for the ladders. Daniel Morgan's own account tells us that he quickly ordered the ladders placed against the walls.

This order was immediately obeyed and, for fear the business might not be executed with spirit, I mounted myself and was the first man who leaped into town among McLeod's guard, who were panic struck and after a feint resistance ran into a house that joined the battery and platform.

I lighted on the end of a heavy piece of artillery which hurt me exceedingly and perhaps saved my life, as I fell from the gun upon the platform where the bayonets were not directed.

Corporal Charles Porterfield, who was then a cadet in my company, was the first man who followed me. The rest lost not a moment, but sprang in as fast as they could find room. All this was in a few seconds. I ordered the men to fire into the house and follow up their fire with their pikes. This was done and the guard was driven into the street.

I went through a sally port at the end of the platform, met them in the street, and ordered them to lay down their arms, if they expected quarter. They took me at my word and every man threw down his gun. We then made a charge upon the battery and took it and everything that opposed us, until we arrived at the barrier gate [at the intersection of Sault-au-Matelot and Mountain Street] where I was ordered [earlier] to wait for General Montgomery.

The sally port through the barrier was standing open. The guard left it, and the people came running and gave themselves up in order to get out of the way of the confusion. I went up to the edge of the Upper Town with an interpreter to observe what was going on, as the firing had ceased. I found no person in arms at all. I returned and called a council of war of what officers I had, for the greater part had missed their way and had not got into the town.

Here I was overruled by hard reasoning: it was stated that if I went on I would break an order, in the first place. In the next, I had more prisoners than I had men. If I left them, they might break out, retake the battery, and cut off our retreat. General Montgomery was certainly coming, so we were sure of conquest if we acted with caution.

What was keeping Montgomery? He had been marching at the head of his struggling column of 300 men, heads down, fighting the biting wind and its snow and hail. The general came to a picket log fence put up as an initial barrier from the cliff's base to the shore. Here he stopped and helped the three carpenters, brought along for just this purpose, to saw and pull down an opening in the fence.

As he waited for the long, strung out column to come up, in the dim light he could see ahead of him the dark mass that was the blockhouse he would have to capture - the only barrier to his rendezvous with Arnold's division in the Lower Town. "We will be in the fort in two minutes," he said to Aaron Burr, who stood beside him. Montgomery then turned to the troops, and, drawing his sword, shouted, "Come on, men of New York, your general bids you come on!" He then "advanced boldly and rapidly at their head, to force the barrier."

There are two versions of what then ensued. The first is from the diary of the British Captain Ainslie:

> Capt. Barnsfair, master of a Merchantman, had charge of the battery that morning; he had his men by the guns with lighted matches. A strict look out was kept; men were seen approaching. A band advances within fifty yards of our guns - there they stood as if in consultation. In a little while they sprang forward. Capt. Barnsfair called <u>Fire</u>. Shrieks & groans followed the discharge. Our musketry & guns continued to sweep the avenue leading to the battery for some minutes. When the smoke clear'd away there was not a soul to be seen. Much has been said in commendation of Mr. Coffin's cool behaviour; his example had a noble effect on his fellow soldiers, they behav'd with the greatest spirit.

The above account is corroborated by a letter the following July from Colonel Maclean to Coffin, the volunteer who fired the cannon. Maclean commended him for "the great coolness with which you allowed the rebels to approach, and the very critical instant in which you directed Capt. Barnsfair's fire."

The other version of what happened is retold by Abner Stocking and John Henry, in their accounts of the battle. This is what they were told, while prisoners, by their British guards:

> The guard placed at the blockhouse, being chiefly Canadians, having given a random and harmless fire, threw away their arms and fled in confusion. A drunken sailor returned to his gun, swearing he would not forsake it while undischarged. Applying the match, this single discharge deprived us of our excellent commander.

Besides Montgomery, two captains, a sergeant and a private were also slain by the grapeshot "when the American front was within forty paces" of the blockhouse. One of the two captains, Jacob Cheeseman, a few hours earlier had shaved himself with great care and dressed meticulously in his best linen and uniform. He put in his waistcoat five Portuguese gold coins known as "half-joes," saying to his companion, "That should be sufficient to bury me decently." The other captain, the general's young aide-de-camp, John Macpherson, had written a letter to his father, a veteran of many sea battles during the French Wars. "I am tired of leading a life of so much ease, while other officers are exposed to hardships almost double what I experience. Headquarters are extremely agreeable, but I wish for the roughs as well as the smooths of a soldier's life." The evening before his death, Macpherson wrote another letter, this one to be mailed only in the event of his death:

> My Dear Father:
> If you receive this, it will be the last this hand shall ever write you. Orders are given for a general storm on Quebec this night; and heaven only knows what may be my fate; but whatever it may be, I cannot resist the incli-

nation to assure you that I experience no reluctance in this cause, to venture a life which I consider as only lent, to be used when my country demands it.

Alas, if only Montgomery's second-in-command, Colonel Campbell, had felt the same way. Campbell had recently deserted the British Army and fled his native Scotland to New York, to avoid imprisonment for huge gambling debts he could not pay off. He had been Montgomery's quartermaster, concerned with the ordering of supplies, not the commanding of men in the face of enemy cannon and musketry fire. According to Campbell's letters, upon Montgomery's death he immediately ordered six soldiers to aim their muskets at the blockhouse and "Drive those rascals from that window." Six triggers were squeezed, but none fired - the powder having been dampened by the falling snow. John Henry commented on Colonel Campbell:

> If rushing on as military duty required, and a brave man would have done, the block house might have been occupied by a small number. From the block house to the centre of the lower town, where we were, there was no obstacle to impede a force so powerful as that under Colonel Campbell. Campbell retreated, leaving the bodies to be devoured by the dogs. The disgust caused amongst us, as to Campbell, was so great as to create the unchristian wish that he might be hanged. Though he was tried, he was acquitted; that was also the case of Colonel Enos, who deserted us on the Kennebec.

The three hundred New York troops slowly marched back up the rocky path and returned to camp, "and left the garrison at leisure to direct their undivided force against" Morgan's men, ignorantly waiting for Montgomery's division.

While Daniel Morgan anxiously waited for Montgomery, a group of schoolboys rushed into the Place d'Armes and shouted to the governor, "The enemy's in possession of the Sault aux Matelot." The Sault aux Matelot, which means Sailors' Lock, was the long street in which Morgan's men were waiting. Carleton sent Colonel Maclean out to verify the information. When Maclean returned, confirming the story, Carleton dispatched Captain Laws with 200 Highland Emigrants and sailors, and a few field pieces, to go out the Upper Town's Palace Gate, and circle down to the Lower Town, using the very same path that Arnold had taken, in hopes of coming up behind them. The governor then sent another party through the streets, to oppose the Americans at the second barrier, from the front.

Also searching for Arnold's main column were some Americans: Captain Henry Dearborn and his company. They had been camped on the opposite side of the St. Charles River and received a late message to come across for the attack. By the time they arrived on the waterfront, the battle had already commenced, and they were destined to meet up with the larger enemy force under Captain Laws that was trying to circle around behind Morgan. Here is Dearborn's account:

> I met several men who said they knew where our people were, yet none of them would pilot us untill I met one who said he would show me the way. He miss'd it and carry'd us quite wrong, but when he found his mistake he declared he did not know where we were, and he immediately left us. We were all this time harass'd with a brisk fire [from above]. It now began to grow a little light, the garrison had discover'd us and sent out two hundred men, who took possession of some houses which we had to pass. We pushed on as fast as possible, but the enemy took some of my rear, and kept a brisk fire upon us from the houses, which we had pass'd.
>
> I came to a place where I could cover my men a little, while I could discover where our main body was. I heard a shout in Town, which made me think that our people had got possession of the same. The men were

so thick within the picketts, I was at a stand to know whether they were our men or the enemy, as they were dress'd like us. I was just about to hail them, when one of them hail'd me. He asked who I was. I answer'd a friend, he asked me who I was a friend to. I answer'd to liberty. He then reply'd Goddamn you, and then rais'd himself partly above the pickets. I clapt up my piece which was charged with a ball and ten buck shott certainly to give him his due. But to my great mortification my gun did not go off. I new prim'd her, and flushed and try'd her again, but neither I, nor one in ten of my men could get off our guns they being so exceeding wet.

They fired very briskly upon us from the picketts. Here we found a great number of wounded men, and some dead, which did belong to our main body. I order'd my men to go into a lower room of a house, and new prime their guns, and prick dry powder into the touch-holes. We now found ourselves surrounded by six to one. I now finding no possibility of getting away, my Company were divided, and our arms being in such bad order, I thought it best to surrender after being promis'd good quarters and tender usage. I told my men to make their escape, as many as possible could, and in the confusion a considerable number did, some of them after they had given up their arms.

In the Sault aux Matelot, Daniel Morgan's wait for Montgomery would eventually be violently interrupted by a large party led from the Upper Town by Colonel Caldwell. Caldwell's suburban house had been occupied for a time by Arnold, until Governor Carleton had ordered it burned down to keep it out of rebel hands. Now Caldwell wanted revenge on Arnold.

Earlier, in response to the feint attack on the Upper Town's St. Louis Gate, Carleton had dispatched Caldwell to that scene. It had not taken Caldwell long to realize that the rebel attack at St. Louis Gate was a feint. After some searching for the real attack, Caldwell had concluded it must be down by the harbor, near the Sault aux Matelot. As he made his way to the Lower Town, he ordered every group of defenders he met to join him. By the time he reached the second barrier, below which Morgan had halted to wait for General Montgomery, his force had grown to 160 men - militia, sailors, and a few Regulars.

After a run of two miles, Caldwell's motley force reached the second barrier, where the "sally port" was still open. Just ahead of Caldwell, running faster, were a naval officer named Anderson and some of his soldiers. They saw Daniel Morgan approaching this second barrier, which led to the Upper Town. Morgan, by now, had given up waiting for Montgomery. One of Morgan's men, Abner Stocking, saw Anderson run through the barrier's open sally port and, seeing Morgan, foolishly yell to the Virginian to surrender. According to Stocking, "Captain Morgan answered the British captain by a ball through his head. His soldiers drew him within the barricade and closed the gate."

Caldwell quickly ordered his men to take up positions. Caldwell provides his own account of the action:

> The enemy had got in at the Sault au Matelot, but, neglecting to push on, as they should have done, were stopped at the second barrier which our people got shut just as I arrived. As I was coming up, I found our people, the Canadians especially, shy of advancing towards the barrier, and was obliged to exert myself a good deal. I posted people in the different houses [behind the barrier] that commanded the street of Saint au Matelot. The Fusileers I posted in the street with fixed bayonets, ready to receive the enemy in case they got on our side of the barrier.

The Americans in the narrow street, led by Morgan, Hendricks,

Steele and the former dissident Hubbard, tried to climb the log barrier with their ladders. John Henry was among them and describes the attempt:

> The army gathered into the narrow pass, attempting to surmount the barrier, which was about twelve or more feet high, and so strongly constructed that nothing but artillery could effectuate its destruction. There was a construction fifteen or twenty yards within the barrier, upon a rising ground, the cannon of which much overtopped the height of the barrier; hence we were assailed with grape shot in abundance. This erection was called the platform. Again, within the barrier, and close in to it, were two ranges of musketeers, armed with musket and bayonet, ready to receive those who might venture the dangerous leap. Add to all this that the enemy occupied the upper chambers of the houses in the interior of the barrier, on both sides of the street, from the windows of which we became fair marks.
>
> Humphreys, upon a mound which was speedily erected, attended by many brave men, attempted to scale the barrier, but was compelled to retreat by the formidable phalanx of bayonets within, and the weight of fire from the platform and the buildings. Morgan, brave to temerity, stormed and raged. Hendricks, Steele, Nichols, Humphreys, equally brave, were sedate, though under a tremedous fire. The platform, which was within our view, was evacuated by the accuracy of our fire, and few persons dared venture there again.
>
> Now it was that the necessity of the occupancy of the houses on our side of the barrier became apparent. Orders were given by Morgan to that effect - we entered. This was near daylight. The houses were a shelter from which we could fire with much accuracy. Yet even here

some valuable lives were lost.

Hendricks, when aiming his rifle at some prominent person, died by a ball through his heart. He staggered a few feet backwards and fell upon a bed, where he instantly expired. He was an ornament to our little society. The amiable Humphreys died by a like kind of wound, but it was in the street before we entered the buildings. Many other brave men fell at this place, perhaps fifty or sixty non-commissioned officers and privates. The wounded were numerous, and many dangerously wounded. Captain Lamb, of the York artillerists, had nearly one half of his face carried away by a grape or canister shot. My friend Steele [atop a ladder] lost three fingers as he was presenting his gun to fire; Capt. Hubbard and Lieutenant Fisdle were also among the wounded.

Private Simon Fobes, of Captain Hubbard's Worcester, Mass., company, was also in the narrow street, and later wrote this account:

It continued to snow furiously. Many of the gunlocks had become so wet that the guns could not be fired. The battle became more and more desperate, the enemy firing from the walls of the city, from the windows of the houses, and from every lurking-place they could find. Our troops were mowed down in heaps. I well remember that Captain Hendricks was shot down dead. I saw my Captain Hubbard leaning on the side of a building. I spoke and said, "Are you wounded, Captain?" He replied that he was, but said, "March on; march on."

The orderly Sergeant was shot down by my side. He fell on his back. He said to me: "I am a dead man. I wish you would turn me over." I complied with his wish. Having strict orders, before we marched, not to stop for the wounded or the dying, I left him to be trampled on in his blood.

At one point the Americans swung a ladder over the top, to climb down to the other side while covered by the sharpshooters in the second floor windows. But a burly habitant named Charland foiled their plan. He ran up to the barrier, exposing himself to point blank fire through the loopholes in the stockade, and wrenched the ladder away.

The riflemen in the second floor had already forced the artillerists from their platform, and were making things hot for the other defenders. So one of Maclean's Highlanders quickly took Charland's ladder and placed it up against one of the windows. He scrambled up it, followed by a few others, to engage the riflemen inside with close range firing and hand-to-hand combat. Colonel Caldwell's account tells us that the Highlanders "soon dislodged them into the street." This allowed the artillerists to return to their guns on the platform behind the barrier.

Once again, grapeshot rained down on the Americans, and now solid shot was aimed at those in the houses. They were forced to fall back and regroup. Major Meigs tells us that, after falling back, Daniel Morgan held a quick consultation of the remaining officers, where "it was the unanimous opinion that it was impracticable to retreat." They decided to wait again for Montgomery's appearance.

A few minutes before Morgan decided to fall back, Caldwell had left the defense of the second barrier in the capable hands of Colonel Maclean, and then snuck down to the other end of the street to see whether the detachment Carleton had ordered there had yet arrived to trap the rebels.

> I had a narrow escape, for going at day break to reconnoitre on the wharf under them, just as they took post there, they asked, "Who is there?" At first I thought they might have been some of Nairne's people, who I knew were next door to them, and answered, "A

friend - who are you?" They answered, "Captain Morgan's company." I told them to have good heart for they would soon be in the town, and immediately got behind a pile of boards beside me, not above ten or twelve yards from them, and escaped. Their fire, however, a good deal slackened towards nine o'clock, after I brought a nine-pounder on Lymeburner's wharf to bear upon them, the first shot of which killed one of their men and wounded another.

The party under Captain Laws, that Carleton had sent forth to come up behind the Americans, was "delayed in taking some straggling prisoners" (Dearborn's company). But now Laws was anxious to move on. Shouting to his men to follow, he raced toward the first barrier. Captain Laws should have looked over his shoulder - he was outdistancing his entire command. Brandishing his sword, he burst in upon the wounded, the exhausted, and the faint-hearted that Morgan had left at the first barrier when he had pushed on to the second barrier. A British officer's account of the embarassing scene:

> Captain Laws rushes into the midst of the rebels crying out, with the greatest sang froid, "You are all my prisoners." You may well conceive the surprise of [the Americans] at being addressed in such language.
>
> "How," said they, "are we your prisoners? You are ours." "No, no my dear creatures," replied he, "I vow to God you are all mine, don't mistake yourselves." "But where are your men?" "O, ho," says he, "make yourselves easy about that matter, they are all about here, and will be with you in a twinkling."
>
> A proposal was made to kill him, which was overruled; in the interim his party arrived [and] made themselves masters of the post.

106

Although the rebels quickly took up defensive positions, the 200 men that Captain Laws had alluded to soon came around the bend, and proved to be too numerous for the American party. They came and, in John Henry's words, they

> fully and handsomely cooped us up. Many of the men, aware of the consequences, and all our Indians [except Natanis and another] and Canadians escaped across the ice which covered the bay of St. Charles, before the arrival of Captain Laws. This was a dangerous and desperate adventure, but worth the undertaking, in avoidance of our subsequent sufferings. Its desperateness consisted in running two miles across shoal ice, thrown up by the high tides of this latitude - and its danger in the meeting with air holes, deceptively covered by the bed of snow.

By ten o'clock, it was obvious that Montgomery would not be coming. Escape was sealed off by the cannon and substantial force of musketmen commanded by Captain Laws. The officers and men trapped along the Sault aux Matelot, almost out of ammunition, and concerned that their wounded needed medical attention, listened to the enemy shouting "Good quarters!" A few at a time, the Americans began throwing down their guns and stepping out of the houses with their hands held high above their heads.

Daniel Morgan was the only one left now who had not surrendered. Ever since 1759, when he was given those 499 lashes for striking a British officer, he had hated the British with a passion. It was Morgan who had brutally forced his starving, exhausted company to carry seven bateaux over the Height of Land so that they could bring enough gunpowder and lead down the Chaudiere to attack Quebec. Now, backed up against a wall, he held his sword in defensive posture against a swarm of bayonets surrounding him. They were shouting at him to lay down his sword, and he was cursing them all, telling them they would have to kill him to take his sword. Finally, he spotted a man standing to the side, wearing a black cape. Morgan yelled to the man, "Are you a priest?" He answered, "I am." "Then I give this sword to you. No scoundrel of these cowards shall take it out of my hand."

So ended the ill-fated attack on Quebec. Sixty attackers lay dead in the snow, another 426 were captured. Of the defenders, only five were killed and thirty wounded. Whether the Americans could have succeeded if Colonel Campbell had pushed on after his commander was shot down, as Morgan did, will never be known. Or what result would have come had Morgan disregarded orders and his fellow officers' advice, and immediately pushed on through the open sally port of the second barrier, instead of halting to wait for Montgomery. His adversary, Colonel Caldwell, reflected on it: "Had they acted with more spirit, they might have pushed in at first and possessed themselves of the Lower Town, and let their friends in at the other side, before our people had time to have recovered from a certain degree of panic, which seized them on the first news of the post being surprized." But, even if the Americans had taken possession of the Lower Town, the objective - the Upper Town with its fortress - would have remained to be taken. It is unlikely that their possession of the Lower Town would have forced Carleton's hand, despite the Americans' feelings that the "inhabitants, to secure their property, would compel the governor to capitulate."

In the suburb of St. Roche, the few dozen of Arnold's division that had avoided being killed or captured now huddled in several houses, wondering what the fate of their comrades was. Dr. Senter was manning a temporary hospital set up for the wounded, when Colonel Benedict Arnold was carried in, a bullet lodged in his leg.

> I easily discovered and extracted it. Before the Colonel was done with, Major Ogden came in wounded through the left shoulder, which proved only a flesh wound. The Major gave it as his opinion that we should

not be successful. The fire and re-fire continued incessant. No news from the General and his party yet, which gave us doubtful apprehensions of their success. Not long had we remained in an anxious suspense ere an express came down from the plain informing of the fatal news of his death, and that the remainder of his division had retreated, and that the enemy were advancing towards the Hospital! ...

We entreated Colonel Arnold for his own safety to be carried back into the country where they would not readily find him. He would neither be removed, nor suffer a man from the Hospital to retreat. He ordered his pistols loaded, with a sword on his bed, &c., adding that he was determined to kill as many as possible if they came into the room. We were now all soldiers. Even to the wounded in their beds were ordered a gun by their side. That if they did attack the Hospital to make the most vigorous defence possible.

But, despite Caldwell's urging, Carleton did not venture out of the city to destroy the depleted American army. Carleton contented himself for the next few months with solidifying his defenses, lest a sizable contingent of Americans arrive from upriver. Spring would bring British reinforcements and the pursuit of the American "rabble in arms," if they should persist until then in their preposterous siege.

Brigadier-General Montgomery died before ever learning that Congress, three weeks before his death, had voted to promote him to major-general. As soon as Governor Carleton heard Montgomery had been killed and was still lying on the battlefield, he ordered "a genteel coffin" and a burial with full military honors for the former British officer. Montgomery had helped capture Quebec from the French back in 1759, but he had not been so fortunate this time. A British officer noted in his journal on January 1, 1776, "Those who knew him formerly in this place sincerely lament his infatuation" with the rebel cause.

Carleton looked upon the prisoners as "our brethren." His subordinates, however, as was more customary for British officers, had nothing but contempt for the Americans. Typical was this excerpt from a letter home to England:

> You can have no conception what kind of men composed their officers. Of those we took, one major was a blacksmith, another a hatter. Of their captains, there was a butcher, a tanner, a shoemaker, a tavern-keeper, etc. Yet they pretended to be gentlemen.

But Carleton did not disdain these Americans, who he believed had been deceived by republican propagandists. He was confident that, with humane treatment, they could be dissuaded from continuing to support the rebellion. The prisoners were "allowed good house rooms, straw bed and two blankets a piece per man, and good victuals and drink." The nuns provided medical attention to the wounded prisoners, bringing to a realization the wish of that rifleman who, in early September, had predicted a winter "among the sweet nuns" of Quebec.

CHAPTER FIVE
RETREAT FROM CANADA
JANUARY - JUNE 1776

"No mortal will ever believe what these suffered unless they were eye witnesses."

- Dr. Lewis Beebe, June 25, 1776, on Isle aux Noix, in the Richelieu River.

In the early months of 1776, Colonel Benedict Arnold doggedly kept up his futile blockade of Quebec. If he succeeded in taking the city, and could also repel the expected British reinforcements in the spring, Canada would become "the fourteenth colony" and the other thirteen would be safe from attack from the north.

Arnold was directing operations from his bed, while his shattered leg slowly healed in the cold Canadian winter. He was determined not to leave "this proud town until I first enter it in triumph." His requests for reinforcements were largely ignored by General Wooster, now in charge of the northern army. The sixty-year-old Connecticut general spent the remainder of the winter drinking enormous quantities of hot flip at his headquarters in Montreal. A Congregationalist, Wooster was convinced that the Catholic populace all around him would butcher his little army if he depleted it by sending any men forward to assist Arnold. Like Carleton, Wooster was also waiting for spring's reinforcements. During the winter, a few hundred Americans managed to travel over frozen, windswept Lake Champlain, though many froze to death in the attempt and were left upon the snow.

Congress sent north four commissioners, headed by Benjamin Franklin, to win the affections of the habitants by promising them freedom of religion. But the Canadians were opposed to a union with the other colonies. And they flatly refused to honor the Congress's paper currency. One commissioner wrote back to Congress that the Canadians will not support the army "till they see our credit recovered and a sufficient army arrived to secure the possesion of the country."

The winter was a severe one, with temperatures at times dropping to 24 below zero. Both sides suffered much while on duty. The following diary entry of January 29, 1776, was written by a British artillerist:

> This morning about 5 o'clock when the field officer of the day was going his rounds he hailed a sentry who had not challenged him & was very angry for the sentrys negligence. "God bless Your Honor," replyed the sentry, "I am glad you are come, for I am blind." On the officers examining him he found the mans eyes had watered with the severity of the cold & that his eye lids were froze together - his face was tender he durst not rubb them. The officer was obliged to carry him to the guard to be thawed.

Inside the city, Captain Daniel Morgan and 400 other Americans were prisoners of war. Governor Carleton offered Morgan a commission as a colonel in the British Army, a rare compliment to a colonial. Morgan refused it with contempt, telling Carleton only a "scoundrel" would choose to betray his country. Congress rewarded Benedict Arnold with a brigadier-generalship in January, but Daniel Morgan would go unrecognized until exchanged a year later.

Governor Carleton allowed 94 of the prisoners, those born in the British Isles, to enlist in a loyalist regiment. This did not set too well with the British Regulars in the garrison, and "wagers were laid that the greatest part of them will take the first opportunity to desert." This proved to be the case, and the remainder who had not deserted were returned behind bars.

Meanwhile, many of the American-born prisoners, held in another location, were planning a mass escape and uprising timed to coincide with an attack by Arnold. During the long winter nights, while two prisoners stood "constantly on the watch," iron hoops found within the prison were fashioned into crude swords, and a few smuggled knives were attached to thin planks from the beds to serve as spears. One prisoner escaped a few days early to make his way to Arnold's head-quarters and tell him the signal for the escape. The prisoners hoped that, upon this signal, Arnold would assault the city. A British officer who later learned of the plan described it as follows:

> When they got out, their first attack was to have been directed against St. John's Gate, where they meant to cut and destroy every one they met with. This done, they intend to turn the guns in that quarter on the town, and set fire to three different houses. The rebels [outside] were expected to advance with all speed to that gate.

In late March, the plan ran into a snag. The cellar door, which was to be the escape point, was obstructed by a thick layer of ice on the outside. The escapees began patiently, and relatively quietly, sawing the ice through a crack around the door hinges, using a knife which had been notched to resemble a saw's teeth. But not everyone was willing to wait so long. John Henry, one of the prisoners, explains how even "the best imagined schemes may be defeated by a thought-less boy, the interference of an idiot, or a treacherous knave:"

> Two lads from Connecticut, without consultation or authority from their superiors, descended into the cellar, and with hatchets picked at the ice at the doorsill. The operation was heard. The guard was instantly alarmed. You cannot form an idea of the pangs we endured. My heart was nearly broken by the excess of surprise and burning anger, to be thus deprived of the gladdening

113

hope of a speedy return to our friends and country. ...
[It was resolved] to kill the person who should disclose
the general plot.

About sunrise the formidable inquisition took place
[by] Major Murray. The officers and the guard were departing, fully persuaded that it was no more than the
attempt of one or two persons to escape. Major Murray
was the last to recede. ... [The informer] had posted
himself close to the right jamb of the door, which was
more than half opened for the passage of the major.
Those of us who were determined to execute our last
night's resolution, armed with our long knives, had
formed a half-circle around the door, without observing
the intrusion and presence of the deserter. Major Murray was standing on the threshold, speaking in a kindly
manner to us, when the villain sprung past the major,
even jostling him. Touching Major Murray's shoulder,
"Sir," says he, "I have something to disclose." The
guards hurried him away to the Governor's palace.

The leaders were soon put in irons and the rest guarded more
closely. A British officer relates Governor Carleton's next step:

The Governor, pleased with this unexpected discovery, and being possessed of the signal expected by the
enemy, immediately resolved to decoy them within range
of the ramparts. Two small brass field-pieces were
brought down to St. John's Gate, and three different
fires were kindled in various directions, as if so many
houses were burning; when immediately the two guns
fired away, and continued repeated discharges of blank
cartridge for about ten minutes. The garrison being now
supposed to be alarmed, all the church bells were set
ringing, and the drums beating; at the same time, small

arms were fired in various directions, while a party kept hallooing, "Liberty, Liberty for ever!" Not a single man of the enemy appeared in the face of our works. Had our plan succeeded, and they boldly advanced, they would have met with such a reception as would have completely put an end to the blockade.

It was good for the prisoners that the plot was discovered, for after a few more scurvy-plagued months Carleton released them and sent them back home. Their comrades outside Quebec's walls, though, would suffer quite a different fate.

* * * * *

With Quebec isolated from help by the frozen St. Lawrence, the governor patiently waited, hoping relief ships bringing food and troops would arrive before his supplies ran out and Congress reinforced Arnold. Relief was indeed on the way, part of a three-pronged British plan of attack aimed at winning the war in the summer campaign of 1776.

One prong would be the 25,000 men being sent to join Howe and attack Washington's army at New York. Another was a much smaller force on its way to the Carolinas, to establish a base around which Southern loyalists could rally. And finally, nearly 10,000 British and German troops were being sent to serve under General Carleton. His task would be to first kick the American northen army out of Canada, and then sweep down the Lake Champlain-Hudson River waterway and cut off Washington's New England supply line. With the less rebellious colonies isolated from New England, eventually the rebels' will to resist would crumble, and Congress would sue for peace.

The initial plans for raising and equipping such a massive force - larger than England had ever sent at one time to North America during any of the French wars - had been going slowly. Then, two days before Christmas, 1775, the appalling news reached London that St. Jean and Montreal had fallen, and two rebel armies were converging on Quebec.

Hearing this terrible news, the Secretary of War, Lord George Germain, had immediately driven over to the admiralty offices and collared the only admiral who had not yet gone home for the holiday recess. Germain hurried him off to 10 Downing Street, where they found Prime Minister Lord North just entering his carriage to ride off to his country seat. Germain insisted that the three of them go inside, sit down, and plan how to meet the emergency. After all, Germain argued, unless the machinery was immediately put in motion, relief would not reach Carleton until June, perhaps too late.

As a result of this meeting, preparations were handled more expeditiously. Transports carrying provisions and 200 Regulars set out on March 11, 1776, accompanied by three war-ships. The main fleet was to follow three weeks later.

On April 12th, the lead ship, the 50-gun *Isis*, found itself in the Northwest Atlantic, blocked by an ice field 10 to 12 feet thick. The captain could alter his course, delaying his arrival in Quebec, or he could risk his ship and career by trying to break his way through. Captain Douglas determined to put forth "an effort due the gallant defenders of Quebec." A gale coming up, he ordered as much canvas as possible and sailed into the ice field at five knots. The bow of his ship struck the ice. The whole ship shuddered and came to a stop. After a long pause, the ice loudly cracked and split apart. "Encouraged by this experiment," the *Isis* sailed forward, plowing a channel for itself and the other relief ships. However, progress was so slow that the troops at times were lowered to the ice, where they practiced their battle maneuvers beside the vessels.

After overcoming the further obstacles of fog and adverse winds, the ships on May 5 came in sight of that besieged city on a rock - Quebec. Atop a flagpole could be seen a blue pennant flying above the Union Jack - the agreed signal that Quebec was still in British hands. Five cannon roared a welcome from the fort, and seven from the lead ship answered - a counter signal, informing the governor they were indeed relief ships.

As soon as the three ships arrived, Carleton ordered the 200 Regulars and the marines to join his own forces from the city and immediately march against the Americans outside, "to see what those mighty boasters are about." Dr. Isaac Senter describes the arrival of the first British reinforcements on May 6:

> A report from down the river brought us by some of the honest peasants [claimed] that a fleet was coming up. To this there was not sufficient credit given, imagining it impossible for any arrival so early in the spring.
>
> Immediately upon landing their marines, soldiers, &c., they rushed out. The army was in such a scattered condition as rendered it impossible to collect them either for a regular retreat or to bring them into action. In this dilemna, orders were given to retreat. In the most irregular, helter skelter manner we raised the siege, leaving every thing: all the camp equipment, ammunition, and even our clothing, except what little we happened to have on us.

Private Lemuel Roberts, recently arrived from Massachusetts:

> A groupe of exceeding pale faces appeared around me. One cried, "I cannot carry my pack!" another "I must leave my clothes!" The pale symptoms were rather more evident in the officers than among the men.
>
> My pack was too valuable for me to abandon. And while I was preparing to swing it, our ensign offered me two good shirts if I would carry a third for him, and I packed them up. Our captain, too, wanted me to take a pair of his shoes, and a pair of his son's, and I obliged him - and kept receiving from one and another till my pack weighed about seventy pounds.

I swung my pack and started with them on our march for the bank of the river. We perceived two British vessels had passed us and lay at anchor some distance from the shore, on the line of our projected march. On our coming opposite to them, a great part of our men crept along up the bank among the bushes and [only] a few kept on the flats, in sight of the enemy.

Setting down in this place with one of my comrades, on a pile of rails which lay in the road, and looking at these vessels, I humorously observed to him that as long as I had been a soldier I never yet had an opportunity to fire at the enemy, and was thinking to improve it now. On this, levelling my piece about topmast high and discharging it in fun - at that very instant the vessels gave us one or two broadsides each. And it became laughable to see the skulkers scamper out of the bushes into the road as the balls made tearing work among the brush, while they entirely overshot the flats.

The Americans had broken camp on such short notice that the pursuing enemy found "that they had left cannon loaded and their match lighted, without firing a gun." Two tons of gunpowder, camp utensils, blankets, and food were also left behind, as well as 500 muskets just arrived from Ticonderoga. Upon entering General Thomas's headquarters, the enemy helped themselves to his midday meal, cooked but untouched, on the dining room table.

Those fleeing in bateaux "threw out many of their sick men upon the beach" to lighten the boats. The British frigates overtook several boats before "the turning of the tide" forced the frigates "to come to an anchor, and the bateaus rowed close to shore and got off." Altogether, the British found 200 men either left behind or too weak to get far in the woods. Carleton ordered a "diligent search for all such distressed persons." He sent them "to the general hospital, where proper care shall be taken care of them."

Three months later, the governor would give these new captives, and all those captured earlier in the unsuccessful assault on the city, "free liberty to return to their respective provinces," on parole. (Several of the officers refused to sign the parole, which would have required them "not to take up arms against His Majesty" ever again. They signed a different parole, in which they promised not to fight again until exchanged for captive British officers of the same rank.) Before boarding the ships bound for the colonies, they were given clothes, a little money, wine and mutton by Governor Carleton. He said, "Since we have tried in vain to make them acknowledge us as brothers, let us send them away disposed to regard us as first cousins." Some of the prisoners, such as Captain Thayer, soon broke parole and "took up arms again in defence of my country." Most of Carleton's officers disapproved of such magnanimity to "murderers and deluded fools."

Colonel Caldwell, of the Canadian militia, was frustrated that most of the fleeing Americans escaped Carleton's initial pursuit on May sixth. Caldwell hoped to "follow the Rebells close at their heels and not give them time to recover from the panick." However, with thousands of British and German Regulars soon to arrive, Carleton called off the chase until their arrival. The Americans slipped away and regrouped upriver at Sorel.

* * * * *

A few days later, action was taking place 35 miles west of Montreal at an American post called The Cedars. A British captain from Fort Detroit, George Forster, was leading a mixed force of 60 Regulars, 40 Canadians and 500 Indians, but no cannon, against some American arthworks held by 390 men and two cannon, under New Hampshire's Colonel Timothy Bedel. The Americans were well supplied with ammunition and had enough food to hold out for 30 days. Only 35 miles away was a larger American force in Montreal under General Benedict Arnold.

Upon learning that an enemy force was approaching the area, Bedel set out alone for Montreal - to seek reinforcements, according to one report; to attend an Indian council, according to Bedel's later court-martial testimony. He left Major Isaac Butterfield in command at The Cedars.

After some initial skirmishing, the Indians informed the British captain they would have nothing to do with a frontal assault on a fortified position, and they began to leave. Captain Forster was about to give up the attack due to this depletion of his strength, when a rider came up bringing news of the rout at Quebec. Forster then sent a messenger to his American adversary, threatening an assault followed by "the inevitable consequences of savage custom" (torture and death to all captives) if Butterfield did not "surrender at discretion within thirty minutes." Over the objections of his subordinate officers, who reported no casualties as yet and wanted to sally forth to meet the enemy, Butterfield surrendered the entire post of 390 men.

When Arnold learned the next day that The Cedars was under attack, he immediately sent 100 men under Major Sherburne to their assistance, while he himself prepared to follow with a larger force. The Indians were waiting in ambush for Sherburne:

> [They] rose up and poured upon them a tremendous fire, making at the same time a most hideous noise called the war-whoop, which sounds thus: "Woo-woo-woo-whoop!" ... [The] last syllable is raised to a monstrous scream or yell, and this is kept up so incessantly that it is impossible to hear the word or command from your officers.

After a battle of two hours, Sherburne, finding himself surrounded, "was obliged to give up." This would bring to nearly 500 the total number of prisoners in the vicinity of The Cedars. However, according to our diarist:

No sooner were his men prisoners than the Indians, exasperated from the loss of some of their best chiefs and warriors, fell to work stripping and leaving stark naked those who had clothes fit for anything, despatching the wounded by knocking them on the head with their axes and tomahawks and scalping the dead, that is, tearing the skin and hair from the top of their heads. Previous to being slain, the wounded had to suffer the torments inflicted by the children of the savages. The dead were also divested of their clothing and laid by the road-side, where our remaining troops were driven past them like cattle to witness the spectacle, the Indians brandishing their knives and tomahawks over their heads, and howling and screaming like madmen or devils. Thus they were taken to the Cedars.

Encouraged by his success so far, Captain Forster started downstream in a fleet of bateaux and birch bark canoes to "relieve Montreal from the oppressive tyranny of the rebels." By now, Arnold was on the march with 500 men, all that he could spare, since "two thirds of our troops were down with smallpox." Private John Greenwood was sent forward with a guide ("a former British soldier who had deserted") to reconnoiter the enemy. We pick up Greenwood's account as he, armed with a sword, and his guide with only a tomahawk, have stopped at a habitant's house in the woods:

We had not been in the place more than ten or fifteen minutes before the war-whoop of the Indians was heard; we had got ahead of them, and they were now flying before General Arnold. The building was a one-story stone structure with two rooms on the ground floor. In one of these was a bed under which this fellow Jack and myself quickly ensconced ourselves. In a minute or two the house and the entire road were filled with Indians,

121

making a most hideous noise and retreating as fast as they could. In about an hour, they had all passed by without discovering us; had they found us we would have been burned alive.

Jack now borrowed from the Canadian his spare clothes and, putting them on, left his own behind, saying "We will follow them and see what they are about." So after them we went, not by the road but across the fields, and at length came to the settlement where the enemy had stopped.

Private Greenwood waited by a log picket fence.

My companion, being disguised, went into the town to observe their movements. I was to remain until he returned. Had he been taken prisoner, I should have been obliged to stay there until daylight and be taken prisoner myself, for I never could have found my own way back to our detachment. I began to think what a situation I was in, standing in a nook between two posts of the fence, within hearing of the savage Indians. Every minute appeared an hour; sometimes I heard them walking by me in the road, then again I would fancy they were looking after me; in short I had but a very unpleasant time of it.

A signal had been agreed upon between the guide and myself: he was to come along the fence with one hand touching it until he touched me, then I might be sure it was he. In about an hour he returned and touched me; it made my heart beat again. "Come along," he said, "the Indians are crossing the river, and will be all over before our troops can come up with them. We must go and inform the general." In haste we took our route back over the fields. It was quite dark and I, being slipshod, had the misfortune in getting over a high picket fence to drop one of my shoes, and jumping down on a sharp stone, cut a large gash in my right heel. This hurt me considerably before the end of the two remaining miles. However, we reached this point near daylight and informed the general as to the situation of the enemy.

The troops were soon mustered for pursuit, but as I could not walk without much pain, I was obliged now to get into one of the boats. General Arnold was in a birch canoe paddled by two Indians who belonged to a party of 200 that had joined us. As we passed a small island, our boat being near it, a naked man up to his middle in the water was seen coming off to us. We rowed toward him and took him in, when he proved to be one of our men who had escaped the Indians, anxious for his revenge against them, eager to conduct us where they were, and apparently no more concerned about his appearance than if he were dressed like a prince.

We pushed on until within musket-shot of the shore. The landing place was covered with woods, and behind every tree were three or four Indians who poured or showered their bullets upon us as thick as hailstones. As it was now sundown, General Arnold thought proper to give the signal of retreat to the other side of the river, so back we went.

The English had drawn down their two field-pieces to the shore and now began to play amongst us with them, which made our Indians fly with their birch canoes like so many devils; they do not like to see large balls skipping over the water, for a single one would knock their paper boats to pieces.

On landing, as we were in sight of the enemy, a great number of fires were ordered to be kindled to make them suppose we were many in numbers, so about midnight a flag of truce came over.

As soon as the Indian scouting party that had shot at Arnold brought back word that the famed Dark Eagle (Arnold) was leading a large force, most of Forster's remaining Indians quietly slipped away and went home. But Forster knew he held an ace in his hand - the 500 American captives. He sent forth their Major Sherburne to deliver a message to Arnold. The Indian chiefs, with Forster in agreement, had told Sherburne "that every man of the prisoners should be put to instant death" if Arnold chose to attack. Majors Sherburne and Butterfield had signed an agreement, or "cartel," that Forster drew up, promising that if the 500 captives were freed on parole, then an equal number of Regulars captured the previous fall at St. Jean would also be released.

Arnold was furious when he read the document, and "extremely averse from entering into any agreement." But, at length, he was "induced to [sign] it by no other motive than that of saving the prisoners from cruel and inhuman death." Forster quickly departed after releasing all the captives, except ten who would be "adopted" into the tribes.

However, Congress refused to honor the cartel. The captive British Regulars remained prisoners in Connecticut. Of the ten Americans not released, the British eventually ransomed seven; the other three chose to stay with their adopted tribes.

* * * * *

The "scandalous surrender at The Cedars" occurred during the second week of May. The next three weeks saw the long expected arrival of reinforcements for both armies. General "Gentleman Johnny" Burgoyne and General Baron Friedrich von Reidesel brought the nearly 10,000 British and German troops up the St. Lawrence. The highest ranking general, Carleton, took charge of the entire army. On the American side, Congress ordered north several thousand newly recruited troops, bringing the total in Canada to nearly 7000.

The American northern army was now centered at the village of Sorel. The Sorel area - chiefly a sandy, mosquito-infested marsh near where the Richelieu empties into the St. Lawrence - did nothing to help the rapidly worsening smallpox epidemic. The head of the Northern Department of the Continental Army was General Schuyler but, due to ill health, he stayed in Albany and Ticonderoga. While Schuyler concentrated on directing the supply line, he left the combat duties to his top field officer in Canada, General Thomas.

General Thomas was violently opposed to the natural method of vaccination - cutting under a fingernail and inserting pus from a pock, or pustule, of an infected person. From Dr. Lewis Beebe's diary:

On Thursday [May 16] general orders were given by Gen'l Arnold for inoculation. On fryday Gen'l Thomas arrived at head quarters from Quebeck and gave counter orders, that it should be death for any person to innoculate.

Tuesday 21t May. Early this morning I was called upon to visit General Thomas, who upon first sight evidently had the small pox.

Sunday 26 [Dr. Beebe and General Thomas are in Chambly] I have been much unwell, troubled with the quick step [dysentery] attended with severe grippings. If ever I had a compassionate feeling for my fellow creatures, who were objects in distress, I think it was this day, to see large barns filled with men in the very height of the small pox and not the least thing to make them comfortable.

Saturday June 1t. 1776. After breakfast 18 drums & as many fifes paraded about 1200 men, who went thro part of the manual exercise, and many manoevres, with surprising dexterity and alertness. Had we a W-n or a Lee, to take command from a sett of haughty, ambitious miscreants who only pride in promotion & honour, we might have hopes of regaining Quebec.

Sunday 2d June. This morning Gen'l Thomas expired.

> Thomas is dead that pious man,
> Where all our hopes were laid.
> Had it been one, now in command,
> My heart should not be griev'd.

[June 7] In the hospital is to be seen at the same time some dead, some dying, others at the point of death, some whistleing, some singing & many cursing & swearing. A strange composition wonderfully calculated for a campaign. ...

[June 10] Orders from the great Mr. Brigadier Gen'l Arnold to proceed to Sorrell immediately. Is not this a politick plan, especially since there is not ten men in the reg't but what has either now got the small pox or taken the infection [through inoculation]. Some men love to command, however ridiculous their orders may appear.

It is enough to confuse & distract a rational man to be surg'n to a reg't. Nothing to be heard from morning to night but "Doct'r, Doct'r, Doct'r" from every side 'till one is deaf, dumb & blind, and almost dead. Add to all this, we have nothing to eat; thus poor soldiers live, sometimes better but never worse.

When Major General Thomas died of the smallpox on June second, the command in Canada fell to Major-General John Sullivan, of New Hampshire, who arrived at Chambly the day Thomas died. Sullivan was confident that he could bring "the army to order, and put a new face upon our affairs here." To Washington, he wrote, "I am determined to hold the most important posts." So determined was Sullivan that he did not even stick around Chambly for Thomas's burial later that same day. He was sure that under his leadership the British could be pushed back to Quebec, and even that reinforced fortress could be taken by the Americans. Like Thomas before him, Sullivan assumed the Regulars that had chased the army away from Quebec were a few hundred men sent north by General Howe. Sullivan, as yet, knew nothing of the 10,000 Regulars fresh from Europe.

So, upon arriving at Sorel on June sixth, Sullivan immediately sent off nearly 2000 Americans to make a surprise attack on the British outpost at Trois Rivieres. Sullivan's intelligence reports estimated British strength there between 500 and 700, but by the time Sullivan attacked two days later it would grow to several thousand. And the British at Trois Rivieres had artillery (the Americans didn't), and strong intrenchments. Also, the sloop *Martin* had just arrived and was cruising slightly upriver from where the Americans would cross.

Brigadier-General William Thompson, originally a rifleman from Pennsylvania, was chosen to lead the attack, assisted by Colonels St. Clair, Irvine and Wayne, all of Pennsylvania. Captain John Lacey described the plan of attack: "The armey was to cross over in bateaus, land [three miles] above the Three Rivers and attack the enemy at daylight."

Once across, General Thompson left a small party to safeguard the fifty bateaux. The rest he led on a march to Trois Rivieres, guided by a local habitant named Gautier. In the darkness of the night woods, the guide seemed to lose the path, and led the army into an impenetrable swamp, up to their knees in muck. Then Gautier disappeared. Thompson, suspecting treachery and faced with rapidly approaching daylight, which would give the attack away, ordered the troops back to the riverbank road. When he regained it, an enemy gunboat, detached from the *Martin*, sighted his long column and quickly came over, raking them with artillery fire.

The column took cover in the woods, and proceeded on toward Trois Rivieres. After nearly three hours marching through waist-high water in "the most horrid swamp that ever man set foot in," they finally set foot on dry ground. They were immediately met by a party of British, sent out when the artillery fire had alarmed their camp. One member of that welcoming committee was Sergeant Roger Lamb, of the Royal Welsh Fusiliers. From his diary:

> June 8th. At three o'clock this morning our drums beat to arms, and we soon marched out of the village to meet our foe. This being the first skirmish I ever was engaged in, it really appeared to me to be a very serious matter, especially when the bullets came whistling by our ears. In order to encourage the young soldiers amongst us, some of the veterans who had been well used to this kind of work said "there is no danger if you hear the sound of the bullet which is fired against you, you are safe, and after the first charge all your fears will be done away."

The Americans, though outnumbered, were pushing the British party back toward the village. Lieutenant-Colonel Simon Fraser, in command at Trois Rivieres, sent word to the transports in the river to quickly bring ashore their troops and "for God's sake" any field artillery. One of Fraser's men was Lieutenant William Digby:

> The troops on shore were ordered to line every avenue from the village to the wood, and take post in the best manner possible; those on board ordered to land with the greatest dispatch. A strong reinforcement of our troops with some field pieces arrived, which soon swept the woods and broke their columns, the remains of which were pursued by us.

Had the Americans arrived an hour sooner and "not lost their route," wrote one British officer, they would have succeeded in taking Trois Rivieres. Led by Colonel Anthony Wayne, the vanguard of the American force had pushed the British detachment back to their lines. But, after giving battle there for some time, General Thompson's attack force found it could not maintain its position under fire from both the Regulars and the guns on the British ships, which had arrived in time to join the fight. So they headed back to their bateaux, three miles to the rear. Captain Lacey explains that yet another surprise was in store for them when they reached the place where their boats had been beached:

> Major Woods, who was in command of the batteaus and baggage, found himself cut off from the American armey, discovering two of the enemies frigates nearly abreast of the batteaus. He ordered those in the batteaus to proceed directly with them to the mouth of the Sorrel, about 45 miles, with all possible dispatch, thus abandoning the armey to make the best of their way through horrid swamps up the north side of the river.

One of the retreating Americans was Private Lemuel Roberts:

> On the day this retreat commenced I was taken exceeding severely with the dissentery, and being on the rear guard I was obliged to drop behind, and was most severely put to it to regain my place.
>
> Endeavoring to do it, I came up to an imperious young officer stationed in the rear. This man, feeling the importance of his commission, used me with very rough language for straggling behind with intention, as he suggested, to be taken by the enemy.
>
> I resented this insult with spirit; and he, furnishing himself with a heavy club, threatened me with loud sounding words, and told me how he would serve me if I did not run. I told him I was unable to run, and he came at me with apparent fury. But having a tomahawk in my hand, I stood my ground; and he was careful not to come within my reach. We soon parted company.

About 1100 of the 2000 men finally made it back to Sorel, travelling through woods and swamps, instead of on the riverbank road, to avoid the British gunboats. Of the nine hundred that didn't reach Sorel, two hundred were captured, and most of the others bypassed it and headed straight for home.

General Thompson and Colonel Irvine were with one group that was lost. After 24 hours of wandering, they were exhausted and "concluded it would be better to deliver ourselves up to British officers than to run the risk of being murdered in the woods by the Canadians." They surrendered to a British colonel, who showed his contempt for the high-ranking rebel officers by making them march, at double-time, the six miles back to Trois Rivieres. Once there, though, Generals Carleton and Burgoyne treated them very politely. Burgoyne even served the refreshments. General Thompson and Colonel Irvine remained prisoners for two years until they were finally exchanged.

Carleton's arrival assured the escape of most of Thompson's men. The governor ordered the recall of British parties that were out scouring the countryside. He could not afford to feed any more prisoners; provisioning the army was hard enough. He hoped these "misguided cousins" would go home and persuade their neighbors to quit their futile rebellion.

Soon after the defeat at Trois Rivieres, General Sullivan received reports confirming the size of the enemy force slowly bearing down on him - to his surprise it was "exceedingly superior to ours." But he felt he still must make a stand, if only to seek "a glorious death or a victory obtained against superior numbers." John Hancock, writing to him for the Congress, was still "fully convinced of the absoute necessity of keeping possession of Canada." George Washington, who was preparing New York's defenses, also sent encouraging words: "I hope vigorous exertions will be attended with success, notwithstanding the present unpromising appearances." Unpromising appearances indeed! There was no money to buy food, no medicine for the sick. Reinforcements were coming north all the time, worsening the food shortage, and catching the smallpox almost as soon as they arrived.

The scattered army now listed at 6241, but only 3591 were "effectives" - that is, healthy enough for duty.

Part of the advancing enemy (Germans marching to Montreal) was sighted on June 13th on the north shore of the St. Lawrence, across from Sorel. Sullivan quickly called his top officers together for a council of war, where "it was decided it was advisable for the whole American armey to evacuate Canada ... and make a stand at Ticonderoga." Sullivan had been outvoted by his officers! Disappointed, he wrote to his superior, General Schuyler, then at Albany:

> I found myself at the head of a dispirited army, filled with horror at the thought of seeing their enemy. Smallpox, famine and disorder had rendered them almost lifeless. I found great panick among both officers and soldiers. No less than 40 officers begged leave to resign.

That same day, Arnold wrote to Schuyler from Montreal, advising him to quickly send north all vessels, especially the sloop and schooner captured at St. Jean the previous year. They would be needed to prevent Carleton from pursuing the fleeing army onto the lake. On an inspection of St. Jean, Arnold spotted another schooner, one-third complete, at the shipyard there. He ordered it dismantled and each piece marked for reassembly later on American soil. Unlike Sullivan, Arnold had finally seen the light, as he explained in his letter to Schuyler, "I make no doubt the enemy will pass Sorel and Montreal, march immediately for St. Johns and endeavour to cut off our retreat." Arnold, who had burned with an intense desire to be Canada's conqueror ever since he helped Ethan Allen take Fort Ticonderoga more than a year earlier, was now resigned to the hopelessness of the situation. He wrote to Sullivan the day Sullivan's council voted to retreat:

> The junction of the Canadians with the Colonies, an object which brought us into this country, is now at an

end. Let us quit them and secure our own country before it is too late. There will be more honour in making a safe retreat than hazarding a battle against such superiority.

These arguments are not urged by fear for my personal safety. I am content to be the last man who quits this country, and fall so that my country rise - but let us not fall all together.

Besides the Germans marching toward Montreal, two British divisions were pursuing Sullivan. Less than one hour after Sullivan broke camp and headed overland for St. Jean, Burgoyne's division landed at Sorel. The British fleet sailed "past a very great number of small islands" at the narrows near Sorel. Lieutenant Enys called the sight "one of the most agreable prospects I ever saw, the islands and shipping being so interspersed one with another." To another British officer, the eighty ships appeared like a moving forest."

Arnold was right in his prediction: three divisions, led by Burgoyne, Carleton and Riedesel, were trying to converge on St. Jean before the rebel army could pass it and reach Lake Champlain. Riedesel would go overland from Montreal, as Burgoyne would from Sorel. A British soldier named Thomas Hughes explains:

> The rest of the fleet [under Carleton] continued their way up the St. Lawrence with an intention, if the wind had continued favourable, to have got up as high as Longeuil [across from Montreal], landed, and cross'd to Chambly or St. Johns, and cut off the rebels' retreat; but the wind and our plan fail'd together, and the rebels made good their escape.

Unlike the precipitous retreat from Quebec, this retreat was orderly. Sullivan would later report to Congress, "with all our disadvantages we saved the whole of the public stores & left not one of our sick behind us" - only a slight exaggeration. The stores and the sick were placed in the bateaux, which were rowed, pulled and pushed up the Chambly rapids by those who were still healthy. Even many of the heavy cannon were brought along. Sullivan led by example, helping on the tow ropes at the rapids, encouraging the exhausted, starving men struggling in the humidity and heat of mid-June. The lead roofing was stripped from one of the houses and brought along, all two and one half tons of it, to be later melted down to make ammunition.

The retreating army stopped for a few hours at St. Jean on June 18th, where Sullivan called a council of war. His officers advised him to burn the fort, as they had at Chambly, and continue south. Sullivan reluctantly took their advice. The last of Sullivan's army to leave St. Jean were Benedict Arnold and his aide-de-camp, young James Wilkinson, who provides the details:

> After the last boat but Arnold's had put off, at his instance we mounted our horses and proceeded two miles down the direct road to Chambly, where we met the advance of the British division under Lieutenant-General Burgoyne. We reconnoitered it a few minutes then galloped back to St. Johns. Stripping our horses, Arnold shot his own and ordered me to follow his example, which I did with reluctance.
>
> The sun was now down, and the enemy's front in view, and we took an affectionate leave of Colonel Lewis, the faithful chief of the Caughnawaga tribe. He cast a sorrowful look at our boat and retired precipitately into the adjacent forest. General Arnold then ordered all hands on board, and resisting my proffers of service, pushed off the boat with his own hands, and thus indulged the vanity of being the last man who embarked from the shores of the enemy. We followed the army twelve miles to the Isle aux Noix, where we arrived after dark.

Although Burgoyne had pushed his light infantry forward "on a trot" the last few miles, they arrived an hour too late to catch the Americans. One Regular that night recorded in his diary, "Thus was Canada saved with much less trouble than was expected on our embarking from Great Britain." Any British advance in large numbers was effectively stopped by the Chambly rapids. Other than harassment by Burgoyne's Indians, the pursuit would be put off for "want of boats." There was no road from St. Jean to the Lake Champlain settlements. Carleton now began the tedious process of carting the smaller boats around the fast water, and dismantling the larger ones. Like some brought from England in pieces, they would be reassembled at St. Jean.

Sullivan halted his army at Isle aux Noix and began sending the sick troops southward. Private Charles Cushing, of Massachusetts:

> Here what boats could be spared were sent to Crown
> Point with sick and stores, as a great part of the army
> were sick. Here we were obliged to wait for boats eight
> days, where we could get nothing but pork and flour.
> The island being small, not more than one mile in length
> and a quarter of a mile in width, the land low, the days
> hot, and at night great dews; and such a number of men
> on so small a spot, and many of them sick - the place
> stunk enough to breed an infection.

The victims of smallpox were dying in droves. Swarms of black flies and mosquitoes added to the miseries of the men, especially the sick ones unable to fend them off. Malaria and dysentery were also in epidemic proportions. The overwhelmed doctors were helpless without medicines. Dr. Lewis Beebe, though, found that he could "effect greater cures by words than by medicine." Another doctor, Samuel Meyrick, also remembered these trying days on Isle aux Noix: "Great numbers calling on us for help and we had nothing to give them. It broke my heart, and I wept till I had no more power to weep."

It is easy to imagine Dr. Meyrick weeping at the sight of these poor creatures, tortured by the constant burning and itching caused by smallpox, their faces unrecognizable due to the sores and swellings, and the air around them permeated with the overpowering stench emanating from the sores. Many of them, like General Thomas had, went blind during the advanced stages of their smallpox. Their hoarse croaks for coolness and water went unanswered. They felt that God had forsaken them, and their torture was compounded by intense homesickness. The worst time of day was sunrise, when the ravages made in the night became apparent. A man could easily see what was soon in store for him by observing those lying near whose cases were slightly more advanced.

Sullivan reported to Schuyler, "Heaven seems at present to frown upon us in this quarter & take off those by pestilence who have escaped the sword." Captain John Lacey, walking about the island, came upon a big, fly-buzzing pit into which men were tossing dead soldiers. He was told that each night another thin layer of earth was thrown over that day's bodies, and the whole procedure repeated the next day. We return now to the diary of Dr. Beebe, as he arrives at Isle aux Noix:

> [June 17] Was struck with amazement upon my arrival, to see the vast crowds of poor distressed creatures. Language cannot describe nor imagination paint the scenes of misery and distress the soldiery endure. Scarcely a tent upon this isle but what contains one or more in distress and continually groaning & calling for relief, but in vain! Requests of this nature are as little regarded as the singing of crickets in a summers evening. The most shocking of all spectacles was to see a large barn crowded full of men with this disorder, many of which could not see, speak, or walk - two had large maggots, an inch long, crawl out of their ears, were on almost

every part of the body. No mortal will ever believe what these suffered unless they were eye witnesses. ...

[June 26] Death is now become a daily visitant in the camps. But as little regarded as the singing of birds. We have here pointed out our own mortality, in the most lively colours. Strange that the frequent instances of so solemn a scene as this should have such an effect, that it should harden, and render us stupid, and make us wholly insensible of the great importance of so serious a matter. Somewhat remarkable, that a reg't so distressed with sickness as ours is should be so engaged in fatigue and doing duty, that they can by no means find time to attend prayers night & morning or even preaching upon the Sabbath.

[June 29] Alas! what will become of our distressed army. Death reigns triumphant. - God seems to be greatly angry with us, he appears to be incensed against us for our indominable wickedness. We remain insensible of our danger, and grow harder and harder in wickedness, and are ripening fast for utter destruction.

By early July, what remained of the Northern Department of the Continental Army, now down to less than 4000 men because of small-pox and desertion, reached Crown Point and Ticonderoga. We return to teenager John Greenwood for an account of the trip south, up Lake Champlain:

On the route the rations, served out to us each day, consisted of a pint of flour and a quarter-pound of pork for every man, and to cook this we were allowed to land at noon. We were without camp kettles or any utensils whatever to make bread. [The flour was] mixed up with water from the lake, by fellows as lousy, itchy, and nasty as hogs. I have seen it, when made and baked upon a

136

piece of bark, so black with dirt and smoke I do not think a dog could eat it. But with us it went down, lice, itch, and all, without any grumbling, while the pork was broiled on a wooden fork and the drippings caught by the beautiful flour cakes. Such was the life of our Continental soldiers who went to Canada.

At least one man found that life was now too depressing to continue. Brigadier-General Baron de Woedtke, who had come over from Germany to help the cause and was given a commission by Congress, took to the bottle even more than usual and drank himself to death. Just before he died, he begged the chaplains, both Congregationalists, to give him the last rites of the Catholic Church, but neither felt authorized to do so. One of the chaplains "endeavoured to show him that God did not require it." Too weak to press the point, he died. The campaign had been a far cry from his glorious campaigns under Frederick the Great.

* * * * *

Meanwhile, Carleton was stalled at St. Jean. Aware that the Americans' three small ships fitted for war controlled the lake, and thus prevented his advance, he set about building a superior fleet. Watching the calendar, he found "the tediousness" of the preparations

far from pleasing. We had everything to build, battows [680 of them] to convey the troops over, and armed schooners and sloops to oppose theirs. It was thought that everything would be ready in 7 or 8 weeks, but the undertaking was a great one.

Indeed, it would take fully three months. During that time, reinforcements of various kinds arrived: 3000 more Germans; and 200 loyalists from New York's Mohawk Valley. They were led by Sir John

Johnson, son of the late Sir William Johnson, the "Great White Father of the Iroquois," of French and Indian War fame.

While in Canada, the British Lieutenant James Hadden had been struck by the ways of both the habitants and the Indians. The amazed Hadden heard that the soil near the St. Lawrence and Richelieu Rivers was so fertile that "the people throw all their dung on the ice in order that it may float away when the Winter breaks up." Much more amazing, though, were the customs of the "savages," as he relates:

> I was present at a Congress of Savages held here. The men are in general tall, active & well made, qualifications absolutely necessary for a race of hunters. A small tuft of hair is left on the back part of their heads, to which they fasten & wear a feather for every scalp taken in war, the rest being pluckt out as soon as they are of an age to go to war. During this operation the young hero sings a war song.
>
> Their ears are slit and they wear a number of small rings round their seperated gristle. They also wear mock jewels &c. by way of ear rings, and the gristle of the nose being bored serves to support a small kind of silver bob & ring. When prepared for war they paint themselves with vermilion & other colours.
>
> Their dress is a blanket and arse clout, or covering for the privities; at great war dances they are sometimes totaly naked. At the end of the penis the head & neck of some handsome bird is fasten'd. The nation of Fox Indians were thus equiped on the present occasion, and some others had their bodies painted in stripes of different colours. ... The sprouts on a certain part are carefully pulled out with what is called an Indian razor. This resembles a cork screw except in having many more turns; and being made of wire, when compressed together lays hold of the hairs, and being suddenly pulled

off from the part, carries them with it. The men git rid of their beards & all other superfluous hair in this way.

Their complexions are swarthy, and their hair very coarse & black. They (particularly the women) cover themselves with greese as a defence against ye mousqueeto's & other flies. This makes them far from tempting and we are therefore not surprised to see their women employed in all laborious occupations, except hunting. The barter with them is blankets, cloth, rum and trinkets. These go up in canoes which return loaded with furs of various kinds. Savages are immoderately fond of spirits, of this the traders make their advantage, tho' sometimes in a state of intoxication the whole is seized and the unhappy traders scalped.

The Indians are cunning and treacherous, more re-markable for rapid marches and sudden attacks than courage. Presents to them are usually silver bracelets, gold laced hats, & coats, feathers, paints, arms of vari-ous sorts &c., in all of which both government and the Indians are much cheated by the traders who on these occasions are interpreters. The time of amusing them with tinsel & such baubles is over; they want useful or valuable [goods] ...

Their arms are a wooden ball fixed to a handle, a tommy hawk or hand hatchet, and a scalping knife. Those employed in our service had a kind of light musquet which they use very skilfully. I shall conclude remarking that the most mischievous and treacherous nations are those who are nearest & mix most with the Europeans; they acquire only our vices & retain their fe-rocity.

"A wretched, motley crew of landlubbers."

> *- Benedict Arnold, describing his men*
> *before the battle on Lake Champlain.*

While the British feverishly worked the summer away preparing a fleet to control the lake and take them to Ticonderoga, the Americans were trying to organize themselves amidst chaos. Colonel Joseph Wait reported that the army had "generals without men, and a small artillery without supplies, and commissaries without provisions, pay masters without money, and quartermasters without stores, and physicians without medicines." Under such circumstances, coupled with the discouragement caused by the flight from Canada, it is not surprising that many of the men went home. One frustrated engineer, Lt.-Colonel Jeduthan Baldwin, wrote in his journal that he had had enough of "this retreating, ragged, starved, lousey, thievish, pockey army in this unhealthy country." He stayed on, though, and supervised the construction of a strong battery atop a hill on the "Hampshire Grants" (Vermont) side, opposite Ti. Late in July, after a copy of the Declaration of Independence reached the fort, the hill was christened Mount Independence.

In June, Congress appointed a Virginian and former British officer, Major-General Horatio Gates, to command the army in Canada. John Adams wrote to Gates, "We have ordered you to the post of honour, and made you dictator in Canada for six months, or at least until the first of October. We don't choose to trust you generals with too much power for too long time." By the time Gates arrived at Ticonderoga, he found that Sullivan had already brought "the army in Canada" back to Ti.

Sullivan was hurt and angered that Congress did not select him for the command. He rode off to Philadelphia to tender his resignation, just as Wooster had done when superceded by Thomas.

For a while, Gates and Schuyler became rivals for overall command of the Continental Army's Northern Department. But Congress settled the matter: due to his poor health, Schuyler would remain in Albany, while Gates would lead the army in the field - the same arrangement Schuyler previously had with Montgomery, Wooster, Thomas, and after Thomas's death, Sullivan.

Gates soon displayed his administrative abilities and brought some order to the chaos. To prepare them mentally for the enemy's appearance, all troops were now required to practice drilling each day. Gates sent all the sick to a post on Lake George. And, because he found "the officers as well as men of one colony insulting and quarreling with those of another," he segregated them. New Englanders were assigned to the Mount Independence redoubts in progress on the Hampshire Grants side. On the New York side, Gates set the Pennslyvanians to work rebuilding Ti's crumbling walls.

Colonel Anthony Wayne found digging outside Ticonderoga to be an eery experience, with grisly reminders of General Abercrombie's 1758 unsuccessful assault on this old French fort. He wrote home to a friend in Pennsylvania:

> [Ticonderoga] appears to be the last part of the world that God made & I have some ground to believe it was finished in the dark. I believe it to be the ancient Golgotha or place of skulls - they are so plenty here that our people, for want of other vessels, drink out of them, whilst the soldiers make tent pins of the shin and thigh bones of Abercrombies men.

At a council attended only by the generals, it was decided unanimously to abandon the old fort at Crown Point, which seemed beyond repair. However, in a petition to Congress, more than twenty officers objected that this would leave western New England open to attack if the enemy established a base there. George Washington agreed, and sent a reprimand to Schuyler. Schuyler stood his ground, though, and sent Washington details of the fort's condition, pointing out that the fort was on a peninsula. This meant its garrison could easily be cut off from communication with Ti, and starved into submission. And, as for the abandonment of Crown Point leaving northwestern New England unprotected, Schuyler predicted that British and German troops would have an unpleasant welcome if they ventured into the home of the Green Mountain Boys and the hardy pioneers of New Hampshire and western Massachusetts.

An American fleet was being constructed at nearby Skenesborough (present day Whitehall, New York), where a Tory named Skene had previously built a forge and two sawmills. Directing the works was a bumbling New York colonel, Jacobus Wynkoop. An incident on the lake that summer illustrated his incompetence. While cruising near Crown Point, he thought he sighted white sails approaching from the north. Quickly he ordered his ships to retreat. A few moments later, the "white sails" arrived as a flock of sea gulls passed by, flying low over the lake.

To build the fleet, hundreds of carpenters, blacksmiths, riggers, sailmakers and oarmakers were lured away from their seaports, from Maine to Philadelphia, by promises of daily rum rations and thirty-four and two-thirds dollars per month - "prodigeous wages." To Schuyler's surprise, when they arrived they refused to work for paper continentals and insisted on hard currency. Progress on the fleet was slow. Many of these artificers contracted malaria, but others often "sham-sick." Gates was disturbed by "the laziness of the artificers" and "the neglect of those whose duty it is to see them diligent in their work." So he named Brigadier-General Benedict Arnold to replace Jacobus Wynkoop as commander of the fleet, and director of construction.

A former sea captain himself, Arnold drove the men 12 to 14 hours a day, and by September had ready what one soldier dubbed "the Mosquito Fleet." Thirteen small vessels joined the two schooners and one sloop captured from St. Jean and Skenesborough the previous year. Somehow, Philip Schuyler, back in Albany, managed to meet Arnold's demands for materials. Schuyler often called on Connecticut's Governor Jonathan Trumbull. The term "Brother Jonathan," the predecessor of "Uncle Sam," can be traced to Jonathan Trumbull's work for the Continental Army. Often General George Washington, frustrated with the inability of Congress to supply his army, would say to his aides, "we will have to ask Brother Jonathan again."

Arnold sent recruiting officers to New England seaports for crews to man his new fleet, but they came back empty-handed. Every available seaman was already serving elsewhere, either with the infant U.S. Navy - eight ships roaming the Atlantic - or on a privateer that paid in shares of booty from captured British supply ships. So, reluctantly, General Arnold manned his fleet with "a wretched, motley crew of land lubbers, few of them ever wet with salt water." And Arnold's "marines" - musketmen capable of boarding enemy vessels for hand to hand combat - were "the refuse of every regiment." Arnold's fearless and energetic leadership would have to make up for what his "sailors" lacked.

Schuyler, rejecting the protest of ousted Colonel Jacobus Wynkoop, declared that Arnold was the only one "equal to the command of such a fleet as we now have." But Benedict Arnold always seemed to be in the center of a controversy. Outspoken, he was intolerant of, and abusive to, officers he considered cowardly or incompetent. Men either greatly admired Arnold or hated him. One who hated was Dr. Lewis Beebe, our descriptive, bitter diarist. Beebe was a friend of Moses Hazen, a former classmate of John Brown, and brother-in-law of Ethan Allen, all men who had had confrontations with Arnold. On July 9th, Beebe was again writing about Benedict Arnold in his diary:

Col Beadle [Bedel] & Maj'r Butterfield remain under an arrest [for the scandal at The Cedars]; pray that they may soon be try'd & hanged. Gen'l Arnold is very busy in making experiments [interrogations] upon the field officers and others; within 2 days he has arrested Col Hazen & Col Dehose, together with 5 or 6 captains; but for what offense I know not. I heartily wish some person would try an experiment upon him, to make the sun shine thro his head with an ounce ball; and then see whether the rays come in a direct or oblique direction.

Arnold had to take a week off from supervising construction of the fleet in order to defend himself at a court-martial. He was accused of stealing goods at Montreal during the retreat. He had purchased food and other supplies on credit and sent them, under a Major Scott's care, forward to the army, then at Chambly. Ignoring Arnold's orders to safeguard the receipts and the goods, Colonel Moses Hazen, a Canadian who had joined "the cause," had allowed his men to plunder the goods. The names and labels of the merchants were also destroyed, making it impossible for Arnold to settle his accounts, and eventually resulting in reports to Congress that Arnold had stolen the goods.

The court-marital board was packed with officers friendly to Hazen and hostile to Arnold. Major Scott, Arnold's star witness, who had seen Hazen's actions firsthand, was not allowed to give testimony. Enraged, Arnold denounced the trial as "unprecedented and unjust." Shocked, the board's president, Colonel Enoch Poor (a friend of Colonel Enos, another enemy of Arnold), asked for an apology. Arnold refused, but offered to give the "satisfaction" each board member's "injured honour may require" - a separate duel with each one! The board then demanded Arnold's arrest, charging that "the general's conduct during the course of the trial was marked with contempt and disrespect" and that "by his extraordinary answer he has added insult to injury."

Rather than arrest him, Gates sent a transcript of the court proceedings to Congress for a ruling, which he well knew would take two or three months to arrive. In the meantime, Arnold was free to contest the lake with Carleton. In his letter to John Hancock, Gates made it clear that "The United States must not be deprived of that excellent officer's services at this important moment." Unfortunately for Arnold's later career, his heroic actions on the field of battle would never quite overshadow this and other disparaging reports that from time to time would reach Congress. It should have been remembered by officers like Arnold, aspiring to ever higher command, that the war was being run from Philadelphia by fifty privileged, jealous and often petty civilians with little or no military experience.

By August 24, reinforcements (mostly militia, not Continental Army regulars) had built Gates's army up to more than 9000 men, almost 5000 of them fit for duty. Schuyler's ability to alleviate some of the supply shortages, coupled with the competence and contagious spirit of men like Gates, Arnold and Wayne, had had an effect on morale. The engineer, Jeduthan Baldwin, who had been disillusioned in July, by September was able to boast that his "men work with life & spirits this day, which shows a determined resolution to defend this place to the last extremity."

That spirit may have been dampened for some after a few routine artillery tests on the lake. The first of two incidents involved a large mortar, or howitzer. Although Arnold was decades ahead of his time in attempting to use mortars on boats rather than on unwieldy rafts, Baldwin's jounal indicates the first tests were not encouraging:

> August 1. At sunset one howet was fired on board a large gundalow by way of experiment. The shell brok in the air. One 13 inch bomb was also thrown from the same gundelow on bord of which were about 20 men. When the bomb went of, the morter split & the upper part went above 20 feet high in the air over the mens heads into the water & hurt no man. The piece that blowd of weighed near a ton. I was nigh & saw the men

146

fall when the morter burst, & it was a great wonder no man was kild.

August 2. This morning I went early to Independent Point where we charged the other 13 inch morter, by way of tryal. When she was fired she burst just in the same mannar, so that we have no large morter here now. These 2 morters were carried from this place [the previous winter] to Cambridge & brought back & went down to Canada & then back to this place, at an immence cost, altho they were worth nothing.

Three days later another incident occurred, this one a tragedy all too common in those days of muzzle-loading cannon. It involved the "scaling" of a 12-pounder in the newly launched gondola, *Providence*. Scaling is the discharging of powder in a cannon to rid its bore of rust and other impurities that accumulate from lack of use. Bayze Wells, of Farmington, Conn., provides the account. First the men in the *Providence* fired a charge, then they sponged the bore to rid it of sparks prior to a second firing.

They spunged the bow gun and put in [the second] cartritch. One Solomon Dyer who served spung went to ram down the cartritch. There being fire in the gun [an unextinguished spark], it went off while he was standing before the mouth of the cannon, which blew both his hands & one nee almost of, and likewise the spung rod, part or all of it, went through the left part of his body at the root of his arm, blew him overboard. We could not find him until 7th [of August, when] he rose and floted. We took him up and buried him decently.

At the end of August, Arnold set off with what boats were ready by then. In front of Windmill Point, at the northern end of the lake, he lined them up in battle formation and fired thirteen charges of powder:

to celebrate the Declaration of Independence under British noses, but also to challenge Carleton to come out and fight.

Carleton's sea captains had earlier asked for permission to venture onto the lake, and now they pleaded with him to let them blow the upstart rebel commander out of the water. They already outnumbered the Americans in war vessels and in "weight of metal" - firing capacity. However, Carleton, perhaps impressed by the enemy's modest fleet, decided to wait for completion of his last ship - the *Inflexible*. A 180-ton, three-masted sloop, *Inflexible* would carry eighteen 12-pounders, almost by herself equalling the entire firepower of the rebels. As had earlier been done with the schooner *Maria*, the *Inflexible* had been built at a lower St. Lawrence shipyard. After sailing upriver, it was dismantled into thirty sections to be carted twelve miles around Chambly rapids to the St. Jean shipyard.

The reassembly took until the end of September. This additional wait meant that, once on the lake, Carleton would have to quickly seize control of it by destroying the rebel fleet, then capture Crown Point, Ticonderoga, and the Lake George forts. Finally, he would have to push overland to the Hudson through enemy territory to unite with Howe. All this before winter set in!

Returning from his show of strength off Windmill Point, Arnold stopped for three days to send work crews ashore to cut fascines (bundles of sticks) "to fix the bows and sides of the gondolas, to prevent the enemy from boarding them and to keep off small shot." The first two days, covering parties were sent ashore with the work crews. Unmolested both days, on the third day "they neglected that precaution." British Lieutenant William Digby recorded the consequences in his journal:

> [Sept.] 6th. Lieutenant Scott went up towards the enemy who were still cruising off the island Amott, about 30 miles from us. He had a cannoe full of Indians, and was if possible not to return without a prisoner. When night came on, he paddled his birch cannoe through their

fleet. This the reader will think rather improbable; but the Indians have a method of putting the paddle in the water and taking it up again without the smallest noise, and the night being very dark favoured him. He thus got through their fleet undiscovered, and at day break covered himself and party in some bushes on shore side, where he did not long remain until a battow of theirs came on purpose to cut wood for fuel.

They, not dreaming of danger, left their arms in the boat on going ashore. The first who landed, an Indian starting from his ambush caught him by his pouch-belt, but the fellow by a sudden exertion, and being greatly frighted, disengaged himself, the belt breaking, and ran with all his speed to alarm his comrades in the battow; who before they could make use of their arms, received a heavy fire from the Indians, which did great execution among them, and left but a very few to row back.

Lieutenant Digby, besides relating the incident above, also tells us that the British soldiers smoked tobacco as "a preservative of the health against dews." And, like the Americans camped further south at Crown Point, Digby mentions the "great flocks of wild pidgeons" "which flew over us thick enough to darken the air. They roosted at night" in the pine trees above the troops. The tremendous weight soon brought the branches crashing to the ground, where the soldiers clubbed them. The passenger pigeons "helped out His Majesties allowance of beef and pork very well." Digby was also impressed with the forests at the northern end of the lake.

The wood was so thick round us, that some of our men were near losing themselves on straggling a small distance from camp, against which there were particular orders. It is surprising, with what a degree of certainty an Indian will make his way from one country to another through the thickest woods, allowing the sun to be constantly hid from his sight, where a person not used to such a country would soon be lost, and the more attempts made to extricate himself serve to entangle him the deeper.

Thirsty for intelligence about Carleton's naval strength, Arnold almost constantly had scouts going to Canada and back. One of them, a Connecticut man named Whitcomb, wanted to bring back a British prisoner. In the woods near St. Jean, he observed one of Burgoyne's subordinate generals riding alone. Whitcomb aimed his rifle for the shoulder - a live general would be worth much more than a dead one. Unfortunately, the impact was not strong enough to throw the general; he clung to his horse and got away. Eight days later he died from an infection that had set in at the shoulder wound. Whitcomb's identity was discovered, and the outraged Governor Carleton offered 100 pounds to anyone who could bring the bushwhacker in, dead or alive.

But Whitcomb eluded capture, and later returned to the same vicinity and captured two officers. When questioned, they told Benedict Arnold about the big ships under construction at St. Jean. This intelligence was confirmed by "two prisoners [released from Quebec] who had liberty to return to there homes on the lake. By them we larn that the Regulars are in a readiness to pay us a visit."

Now that he knew his adversary's fleet was stronger, Arnold searched the lake for a defensive position. He found one at Valcour Island, about halfway between Crown Point and the northern end of the lake. Valcour Bay, a channel three-fourths of a mile wide between the island and the lake's western shore, was protected from the north by rocky shoals. So the only approach to the channel was at its southern end. On October 5th, Arnold located his little Mosquito Fleet just inside the bay's southern entrance and waited for the enemy to approach. Valcour Island's steep sides and tall pines would hide them from sight until the British, sailing between Valcour and Grand Isle, went past the tip of the island. Then, after spotting Arnold's boats, the five big British vessels, without oars, would have a hard time beating against the wind to come back and give battle. And they would have to swing past his line one at a time, fully exposed to a broadside from all 16 of Arnold's boats.

On the morning of October eleventh, the British made a grand spectacle, as they proceeded up the lake, sailing southward between Grand Isle and Valcour Island. Sailors with spyglasses high up in each ship's rigging searched Grand Isle's jagged coastline for Arnold.

In the lead were the big ships: the *Inflexible*; followed by the *Carleton* and *Maria*, each mounting fourteen guns apiece; then the *Loyal Convert*, an American gondola captured at Quebec and mounting six guns; and finally the *Thunderer*, a huge "radeau" or floating battery, manned by 300 sailors and mounting six 24-pounders, six 12-pounders and two howitzers. Next came 24 little gunboats, each with a 12-pounder in its bow. If well-orchestrated, these could combine to deliver surprising firepower. Following the war-ships were dozens of "northern" canoes from as far away as Lake Superior, some of them carrying as many as thirty warriors.

Spread out in the wake of all this were over 600 bateaux bringing along part of the army, their scarlet greatcoats contrasting sharply with the lake water. Half the bateaux were filled with troops, the other half with provisions and supplies. It was a massive effort to provision this army - by now up to 13,000 men, plus a few hundred women and children. For example, 25,000 gallons of rum were brought along when the army came over from England.

Escorting the grand procession were numerous scouting boats, each carrying a 3-pounder, although these scouts apparently could not find Arnold in time to warn the *Maria*, whose Captain Pringle had been appointed by Carleton as commander of the fleet.

In narrow Valcour Bay, Arnold waited, his sixteen boats positioned in a crescent to allow a wide firing arc. This would make best use of their meager firepower - less than half that of the enemy. There were eight gondolas, each with a 12-pounder in its bow and a pair of 6-pounders amidship. There were also four row galleys, three schooners, and one sloop. These boats, all slightly larger than the sixty-foot gondolas, carried between six and twelve guns apiece, mostly 6- and 4-pounders. Total "weight of metal" would decidedly be in favor of the British. But the Americans would have better maneuverability, due to the prevailing northerly winds (although they might also become trapped in the narrow bay). The American boats were equipped with long oars, and had shallow draft suitable for a lake battle requiring maneuvering close to shore.

The poorly-clad, largely barefoot and blanketless Americans waited for six days on their boats in Valcour Bay. Then, dawn on October 11 brought an icy wind from the north, and with it came the big British ships, their sails taut in the bitter wind. Bayze Wells recorded their approach in his journal:

> Friday 11 Octr. This day the wind at North and clear. Thare was snoe to be seen on the mountains on the west shore. About eight a.m. the guard boat came in and fired an alarm and brought news of the near aproach of our enemy. About ten a.m. a twenty-two gun ship hove in sight and two sixteen gun schooners and two sloops and one floteing batery which mounted twenty-four pounders and a large number of boats.

The British war-ships sailed past the southern tip of the island without noticing the American fleet. Arnold waited until the *Inflexible*, *Thunderer*, and *Loyal Convert* were well past before he took advantage of the north wind and ordered the schooner *Royal Savage* and three row galleys out to attack the smaller ships, *Carleton* and *Maria*, then come back to the line. A British Army captain, Joseph Pell, observed that the British gunboats "immediately rush'd in amongst them and engag'd them without waiting for orders."

From the deck of the *Congress* galley, Arnold counted the British gunboats at twenty-four, more than twice as many as he had expected! He quickly signaled his four boats to immediately return to the line.

The crews of the row galleys, using their oars, had no trouble getting back, but the schooner, not having oars, lagged behind and came under heavy fire from the gunboats. Three times, solid shot struck the *Royal Savage*, sending sprays of splinters amongst the "landlubber" crew. They panicked, and the American schooner ran aground on an underwater ledge near the southern tip of the island.

The captain of the *Carleton*, Lieutenant Dacres, without waiting for the other four big British ships to come up, headed for the bay and joined the gunboats in slowly bearing down on the helpless *Royal Savage*. A longboat with anchor aboard pushed off from the stricken schooner, hoping to drag the ship afloat by hauling in the anchor cable. But Lieutenant Dacres guessed the rebel's plan and concentrated his fire on the longboat; it soon capsized. The *Carleton* neared its objective and altered course to present its guns and give the immobile *Royal Savage* a devastating broadside. Benedict Arnold's line of boats stood helplessly by, not firing for fear of hitting the *Royal Savage*, the largest ship in the American fleet.

But their turn was coming. After a second broadside, the *Carleton* was now crossing in front of the rebel line as it moved toward the west shore of the lake on its intended U-shaped route in and out of the narrow bay. Most of the British gunboats had come up closer, and those not directly behind the *Carleton* were busy defending it. "A tremendous cannonade was opened on both sides," observed Baron von Riedesel. But, suddenly, owing to the island's trees blocking the wind, her foresail went slack and she swung around out of control "nearly into the middle of the rebel half moon." Fully exposed, her bow pointed now toward the middle of the American line. In such a position, the *Carleton* was unable to use her guns. The rebels used this opportunity to rake the defenseless schooner. Solid shot burst great holes in her hull, while grape-shot wrecked havoc on her deck. Exposed to grapeshot flying all around them, Dacres's men performed heroic maneuvers with the rigging and managed to swing the *Carleton* around so she could continue on her route out of the bay.

As she slowly moved to the west, the *Carleton* was now able to give the rebel line a few broadsides, but she still had to suffer their concentrated fire. The other four big British ships were still trying to make their way up to the bay and could not help her yet. Among the casualties was Lieutenant Dacres, who was knocked unconscious. Nineteen-year-old Midshipman Edward Pellow assumed command. He climbed along the bowsprit (the long beam that extends beyond the bow) and flung himself against a sail in an effort to scoop some wind. Exposed to the hail of metal, he miraculously was not hit, but the sail still would not draw wind. Eventually, two gunboats approached from the rear, and Pellew threw them lines. Slowly, still under fire, they towed the ailing vessel out of the bay. The *Carleton*, assisted only by the little gunboats, had withstood the concentrated fire of Arnold's sixteen boats for a full hour, but had not struck her flag.

During this action, one of the gunboats received a direct hit to her powder magazine. The German Captain Pausch, chief of the Hanau artillery, observed the explosion from one of the other gunboats. Later he had a chance to record the action:

> Close to one o'clock in the afternoon, this naval battle began to get very serious. Lieut Dufais came very near perishing with all his men; for a cannon-ball from the enemy's guns going through his powder magazine, it blew up. The sergeant who served the cannon on my batteau [gunboat] was the first one who saw the explosion, and called my attention to it as I was taking aim with my cannon. At first I could not tell what men were on board. But directly, a chest went up into the air and, after the smoke had cleared away, I recognized the men by the cords around their hats. I hurried toward it. All who could, jumped on board my batteau, which being thus overloaded, came near sinking.

Finally, by late afternoon, the *Inflexible* and *Maria* had at last made it into the bay and were now passing the same route in front of the rebel boats. Captain Pausch described the action at this point as

> very fierce and very animated. The *Maria*, having His
> Excellency von Carleton aboard, advanced and opened a
> lively cannonade. As she in turn retreated, the *Inflexible*
> took her place, only to retreat as the others had done.
> One of the enemy's frigates began to career over on one
> side, but in spite of this continued her fire. The cannon
> of the Rebels were well served.

The numerous, heavier British guns repeatedly struck the smaller American vessels. One galley had twelve holes in her hull, another a shattered mainmast. A gondola sank and two more were so badly damaged they would sink the next morning. The *Royal Savage*, still stuck, had been set on fire. Up in flames went all of Arnold's official correspondence, accounts, etc., and his personal baggage.

In his report of the battle, Arnold noted that "at five o'clock" the enemy "thought proper to retire to about six or seven hundred yards' distance and continued the fire til dark." They hoped to seal off the bay and finish off the badly damaged rebel fleet the next morning. Captain Pausch described the cordon of boats that night: "a chain [of gunboats] was formed, and every one had to be wide awake and on the alert." In the morning, wrote Lieutenant Digby, only "a few hours would determine who should be masters of the lake."

As darkness arrived, General Arnold met with his subordinates, General Waterbury and Colonel Wigglesworth. They took account of the injuries and the fleet's prospects for resumption of the battle at dawn. Several vessels had been destroyed or were beyond repair and would sink within hours. Killed and wounded amounted to about sixty. Only three of the small British gunboats had been sunk, and all the big ships might be able to fight in the morning. Even the *Carleton* was not beyond repair. Although the "incessant fire" from the Indians onshore had been ineffective so far, by morning they would be supplemented. And, Arnold noticed, in the distance the "enemy had, to appearance, upwards of one thousand men in batteaux prepared for boarding." The Americans' ammunition was three-fourths gone, and the competence of the crews had not been encouraging. Arnold reported that the fleet "suffered much for want of seamen and gunners. I was obliged myself to point most of the guns on board the *Congress*."

It appeared that dawn must bring a capitulation by the Americans. But Benedict Arnold was not one to give up so easily. He proposed an attempt to escape through the blockade, under cover of darkness and the fog now settling on the lake.

To reduce noise to a minimum, oar locks and other contact points were greased and stuffed with rags, and each oar was wrapped in a shirt. The boats still afloat proceeded "Indian file" through the fog. At each boat's stern was placed a lantern covered with a canvas sack, to guide the one behind. There was just enough deep water between the New York shore and the western end of the blockade to slip past, one at a time. They gauged their distance from the shore (between ten and twenty yards) by the sound of the waves on the rocks. In each bow stood six stout men with oars, ready to use them as poles, in case the boat touched bottom.

As they neared the enemy line of boats, hoping not to hit any rock and alarm the enemy, they stopped rowing and slowly drifted by with the slight north breeze. Before long it turned southerly, and they had to man the oars. The daring escape was later noted by British Lieutenant James Hadden in his journal:

> The enemy, finding their force diminished and the rest so severely handled, determined to withdraw to Crown Point, and passing through our fleet at night effected it undiscovered; this the former position of the gun boats would probably have prevented. All the enemies vessels used oars and on this occasion they were muffled. This retreat did great honor to Gen. Arnold. Their retreat was discovered at day break.

"The astonishment next morning was great," wrote Riedesel, "as was Carleton's rage." With the wind now from the south, the runaways could not reach Crown Point that day. The day after, October 13th, a new northwest wind filled the British sails, allowing them to catch up with the runaways near Split Rock, a few miles north of Crown Point. The American fleet was now down to eleven vessels. Arnold, in the row galley *Congress*, ordered Waterbury, in the *Washington*, to assist him in a rear-guard action to allow the other, slower vessels to continue on to Crown Point.

The *Inflexible* and *Maria*, the partially repaired *Carleton*, and several gunboats surrounded the *Washington*. General Waterbury struck her colors without firing a shot. He and over 100 men were taken prisoner. But Arnold's *Congress*, boasting a meager eight guns, half of them 4-pounders, kept up a running fight with the seven British ships. "They kept up an incessant fire on us," Arnold wrote, "for about five hours with round and grapeshot, which we returned as briskly, the sails, rigging and hull shattered and in pieces." Arnold was assisted by four gondolas that had been leaking too badly to escape with the others to Crown Point.

After 27 of his crew of 83 men on the *Congress* were dead, Arnold finally ordered the rest, though weak from exhaustion and hunger, to man the oars again and head for the east shore (the British had positioned themselves to prevent Arnold from reaching the west shore and Crown Point). Fortunately, the wind had shifted to southerly again, so the rebels were able to put distance between themselves and Carleton's oarless ships.

After an hour of frantic rowing, the exhausted men beached their boats on the shore of Buttonmould Bay, "ten miles from Crown Point, on the east side." The muskets and ammunition were brought ashore, then the five vessels were set ablaze. The British ships kept up their bombardment, but from too far away to be effective. Arnold's party of survivors, nearly 200 in all, stood in formation watching the boats burn until the flags were consumed, then he led them into the forest. Still lacking a favorable breeze, Carleton gave up the chase.

Arnold's 200 survivors were safely brought across that evening, when their march brought them to Chimney Point, across from Crown Point. They had "very luckily escaped the savages," who were one hour too late to catch the last members of the heroic Mosquito Fleet. Arnold reached Ticonderoga at four o'clock the next morning "exceedingly fatigued and unwell, having been without sleep or refreshment for near three days." Roger Lamb, the British officer, observed Arnold burning his beached boats:

> In this perilous enterprize [blowing up the boats] he paid attention to a point of honor. He did not quit his own galley till she was in flames, lest our sailors should board her, and strike her flag. The result of this sea fight [October 11 and 13], though unfortunate to the Americans, raised the reputation of Arnold higher than ever; in addition to the fame of a brave soldier, he acquired that of an able naval officer.

Ironically, although the British fleet's lack of seamanship off Valcour Island gave little indication, four of the men aboard the British vessels would eventually become admirals in the British Navy. A few months after the battle, Lieutenant John Schank (who commanded the *Inflexible* and later invented the centerboard) wrote a scathing report of the battle, criticizing Captain Pringle, who commanded the fleet from the *Maria*.

Schank cited three points of error which prevented the total victory that should have been attained by such a superior force: 1) Letting Arnold get the advantage of the weather, by not discovering him until the British ships were down-wind. In fact, Schank claimed in the report that Pringle knew Arnold's location the night before the battle, but did not put the information to use. 2) Failure to get the *Maria* and *Inflexible* in range until after the *Carleton*, assisted only by the gunboats, was nearly sunk. Since the *Carleton* had been able to make it fairly quickly, Schank asserted that the others could have, too. He hinted that cowardice on Pringle's part might have had something to do with his late arrival. 3) The retiring of the line of gunboats to 700 yards from Arnold's line at day's end. This took the British out of the narrow bay, and allowed Arnold enough room to sneak past in the night. Schank's report was ignored, and both he and Pringle later rose through the ranks to become admirals.

The British landed at Crown Point the day after Arnold made his escape. The few Americans still at Crown Point retreated without contesting the place, burning the barracks before an advance force of Indians and Tories reached it. According to Jeduthan Baldwin, the inhabitants near Crown Point ran for several miles

> in the woods with women & children in the greatest distress, leaving all there housel stough. But we may expect a more melancholly seen to morrow or soon. God prepair us for it & grant us a compleat victory over our enemy.

The next day the Americans at Ticonderoga received not an attack, but "Genl Waterbury & 106 prisoners" captured in the naval battle. Governor Carleton was again showing his magnanimity toward his prisoners of war. He dined with Waterbury, then released him and his men after they signed a parole promising not to take up arms again until formally exchanged. Lieutenant Digby's journal tells us that the American General Gates

> sent the general a letter of thanks, but would not permit the prisoners to enter the fort, but sent them directly away ... as their informing their country men how well they had been used might induce some of them to turn on our side.

* * * * *

Governor Carleton had accomplished the first step in his expedition to Albany - control of the lake. But he still needed to take Ticonderoga and keep moving through enemy territory all the way to Albany. He was concerned about the oncoming winter's "frequent squalls on the lake," and freezing temperatures which would threaten his supply line from Canada. He was opposed to a bloody assault on the fort. That strategy had failed for General Abercrombie in 1758 against the French, and it would fail again, unless Gates was too ill-prepared or cowardly to put up much of a fight. Because Gates was a former British officer, Carleton ruled out cowardice. And the time-consuming process of "regular approaches" (digging trenches) was, at this late season, out of the question.

Perhaps the fort was not adequately supplied to withstand an assault. On October 28th, according to Digby, "Gen. Carleton and General Phillips, who command[ed] the artillery, went up towards their lines to reconnoitre their strength." They concluded that the American batteries were "of great extent & force," and by deserters had "heard they were then receiving fresh supplies of cannon and other stores." Reports of the American strength ranged from 12,000 to 20,000 men. In contrast to his Indians, who were advising Carleton to wait until spring, his generals urged him to attack at once. They secretly ridiculed him for listening "to the whim of a drunken Indian."

The Americans were prepared and expecting an assault. Their weapons included "poles, about twelve feet long, armed with sharp iron points, which each soldier is to employ against the assailants when mounting the breast works." Spirits were high, and the men were eager to prove themselves. A few days earlier, about a hundred "poor, emaciated, worthy fellows" demanded their discharge from the hospital at Lake George. Reporting their arrival at Ticonderoga, Anthony Wayne wrote that "they were determined to return to this place and conquer or die with their countrymen and brother soldiers."

Gates expected the attack to be "rash and sudden," and counseled each officer "to be deliberate and cool in suffering his men to fire." Rather than let them "throw away their shot in a random, unsoldierly manner," they should execute "one close, well directed fire." Captain John Lacey was impressed with the various reactions of the officers and men at the approach of battle:

> On the morning of the 28th of October, word was brought by our scouts and look-out boats on the lake that the enemy were approaching both by land and water. A general alarm was fired, and every one hurryed to his post. All was bustle ... Collem after collem presented their fronts along the lines, with fixed byonet, whose glissening fire arms reflecting the bright raise of the sun presented a luster more radiant than the sun itself. The sounds of the drums to arms, the reports of the alarm cannon, and the crye of the sargents to the men in hurrying them from their tents of "Turn out! Turn out!" would make even a coward brave.
>
> I will throw a vail over some names, who but the evening before bosted over a glass of grog what feats they intended to do on the approach of the enemy, now srunk with sickning apathy within the cover of their tents and markees, never appeared to head their men, leaving that task to their subalterns to perform. On finding at last the enemy had made a halt, and that this movement was only to cover a reconnoitering from them, they came out as boald soldiers as ever, complaining only of a little sick headake.

Carleton judged that Gates was indeed well prepared and determined. The "want of time" to take the fort before the onset of the "severe season," he wrote, must "force us back to Canada." Therefore, within a week, he returned with the army and the fleet to Canada.

Gates and many of the American troops at Ti went south to join Washington's army as it retreated across New Jersey, and eventually

161

would surprise Howe by counterattacking at Trenton. But most of the Americans in the northern army returned to their farms and villages. Colonel Anthony Wayne, soon to be a brigadier-general, was left in charge at Ti for the winter. Almost 4000 Pennsylvanians and New Englanders stayed with him. Several hundred of them, before winter's end, would perish of disease, starvation and exposure.

"Here ended the Northern Campaign for the year 1776." So wrote Captain John Lacey. Congress had taken a bold step, back in 1775, by invading Canada. Bad weather, smallpox, and unrealistic expectations of support from the Canadians all contributed to a disastrous waste of men and material that might better have been used in defending New York.

If the Americans had succeeded in taking Quebec, could they have held it against the British Army that arrived in the spring? Probably not.

And could Carleton have taken Ticonderoga and gone on, all the way to Albany? Perhaps. General Baron von Riedesel thought so. "If only," he lamented, "we could have begun our expedition four weeks earlier." They had spent four weeks waiting for construction of the *Inflexible* to be finished. The malaria-ridden artificers at Skenesborough had slaved the summer away, allowing Arnold to put enough boats together by late August to give the appearance of a formidable foe, and thus convince the cautious Carleton to wait. Those four weeks gained Carleton assurance of a naval victory, but they gave America another full year to continue its revolution.

CHAPTER SEVEN
"GENTLEMAN JOHNNY"
BEGINS HIS EXPEDITION
JUNE - JULY 1777

"This army must not retreat."

> *- General John Burgoyne, at
> Crown Point, June 30, 1777.*

Two years after Lexington and Concord, the rebellion was still going strong. The illegal Continental Congress had had the audacity to declare the colonies an independent nation the previous July.

After being provided with a seemingly invincible army, General Sir William Howe had not yet been able to destroy the pitiful rebel army led by George Washington. Clearly, force alone was not enough to break the will of the rebel army and Congress. Instead, force should be coupled with strangulation: the colonies must be divided and their army cut off from its main supply line.

Massachusetts provided more men, and Connecticut more supplies, than any of the other colonies. Virtually all of these reached the army via the few roads that led out of southern New England to the Hudson River. There the men and supplies had to be transported across the river on boats. This often involved unloading and reloading wagons. All this took time and could not easily be accomplished if British boats patrolled the river. The key, therefore, to cutting off the rebel army's sustenance was to control the Hudson River.

Once New England was isolated, the other colonies to the south (where rebellious fervor was not as universal) would likely sue for peace, and the rebellion would collapse.

This was the plan that Governor Carleton had intended to follow in 1776. But, by the time he reached Fort Ticonderoga, he had found it well defended, with winter fast approaching. Time consuming siege tactics were out of the question. Reluctantly, Carleton had ordered a return to Canada, to await a resumption of the campaign in the early spring.

However, while Carleton remained in Canada, his ambitious second in command, General John Burgoyne, returned to London. There he spent the winter lobbying for an independent command. He suggested to the Colonial Secretary, Lord George Germain, that an invasion from Canada be attempted again, but this time led by "a more enterprising commander."

Burgoyne knew Germain would be receptive to his idea of a change in command. Germain had held a bitter hatred for Carleton ever since the last war, when Carleton had testified at Germain's court-martial. Germain had been found guilty of disobediance on the field of battle, and was declared forever ineligible for any kind of military service whatsoever. Ironically, by virtue of his political connections, Germain rose to the position of Colonial Secretary and now was responsible for Britain's entire military effort in America. Knowing that the King was furious over Carleton's failure to reach the Hudson, or at least take Ticonderoga, Germain saw his chance to even the score with Carleton. He urged Burgoyne to put down his ideas in a formal proposal, which he promised to present favorably to the King. Burgoyne gladly wrote a lengthy treatise, *Thoughts on Conducting the War from the side of Canada.*

During the previous war, when King George III was just a boy, Burgoyne had gained fame as a dashing cavalry captain, and became one of young George's heroes. Now, in the winter of 1777, the two of them frequently were seen riding their horses together in London's Hyde Park. It came as no surprise, then, that Burgoyne's proposal was accepted, and the author, newly promoted from major-general to lieutenant-general, was given command of the expedition.

Burgoyne arrived in Quebec on May 7, 1777, and presented a letter from Colonial Secretary Germain to Governor-General Guy Carleton. In a very insulting manner, Germain explained to Carleton that he had been superceded and that Carleton's future role would be expressly limited to staying in Canada and providing "all possible assistance" to Burgoyne. A lesser man might have reacted with a spiteful lack of cooperation. The governor, however, swallowed his pride. According to Burgoyne's own subsequent testimony, Carleton "could not have shown more indefatigable zeal than he did to comply with and expedite my requisitions and desires."

The plan to cut the colonies in two, along the Hudson River, was logical and looked good on paper in London. However, events sometimes interfere with even the best made plans. The plan stated that "the sole purpose of the Canada army [was] to effect a junction with General Howe." But General Howe was certainly not expected to stay at New York all summer, and do nothing but wait for the right moment to sail up the Hudson to meet Burgoyne. Howe was given a free rein to go ahead with his own plans "to the southward," namely his proposed attack upon Philadelphia. Germain trusted that Howe would complete his operations to the southward in time to return and form the junction on the Hudson River by the close of the campaign.

Burgoyne, for his part, was expected "to force his way to Albany," through whatever resistance the rebels could muster. No one expected much resistance to be offered, once Ticonderoga was captured. Burgoyne would quickly push on to the Hudson, "get possession of Albany, and open communication to New York." As events would turn out, however, Burgoyne would find it not as easy as he and everyone else imagined to "force his way to Albany," and Howe would be too busy fighting Washington's army outside Philadelphia to return to the Hudson for the "junction" with Burgoyne.

* * * * *

The British and German soldiers, for the most part, were the same ones Carleton and Burgoyne had led south the previous campaign.

They had spent the winter quartered with the habitants, "2 or 3 in each house," in the villages along the St. Lawrence and Richelieu Rivers. The winter had been unusually mild, and for many years afterward was remembered by the habitants as "the winter of the Germans."

The Europeans adapted readily to Canadian ways. When the soldiers had originally arrived from Europe, after several months on transports, many of them were suffering from scurvy. But they found that "by drinking plentifully of spruce beer" they soon were "all in perfect health." Another pleasant surprise for them was a Canadian custom for celebrating New Year's Day:

> The Canadians have a very singular custom among them: at the commencement of the year, the men go round the city and salute the ladies upon the cheek; when he has saluted one, the lady presents the other. The lady is under the necessity of receiving the salute of every one.

The soldiers found that the severity of the Canadian winter did not deter the habitants from their favorite pastime - socializing. Thomas Hughes recorded his observations in his diary, which he entitled, *A Journal of Thos. Hughes, For his Amusement & Designed only for his Perusal by the time he attains the Age of 50 if he lives so long.*

> During the winter, we amused ourselves with carrioling. The carriole is form'd in the body like a one horse chair, with a seat in front for the driver; but instead of wheels it is supported by two pieces of timber shod with iron. It is only us'd on the ice or snow, is drawn by one or two horses, goes very expeditious, and is the easiest mode of travelling I ever experienc'd. The travellers, as they are entirely expos'd to the weather, are always so wrapt in furs that you often pass intimate friends without knowing each other.

Thomas Anburey, serving as a "gentleman volunteer" in a British grenadier regiment, was also impressed that these carrioles would "go with ease fifteen miles an hour upon the ice."

> The inhabitants think nothing of a journey of forty or fifty miles to see a friend, and returning the same day. The river is entirely frozen over, yet there are certain warm springs that never will congeal. To caution travellers, every parish, as soon as the river is frozen over, is obliged to fix large pine trees in the ice, distant from each other about ten feet, which receiving moisture from the ice and being an evergreen continue so the whole winter, so that when travelling it appears as if you were going between an avenue of firs.

The end of March brought a thaw and "the breaking up of the ice." Two British captains were out carrioling that day and "unfortunately lost their lives" when their carriole fell through. Winter's end also was "the time the wolves and bears come from the woods to pick up food." Someone from Lieutenant William Digby's company "killed a fine bear and his flesh proved not bad; at least it was a variety. It had a young cub which we tamed."

Life was not so pleasant for all the soldiers in this strange land. For the Germans the language barrier was a problem, and they missed their schnapps and sauerkraut. They also suffered from dysentery and many of them grew desperately melancholy. In the hospital, "They talked day and night of fathers, sisters, cousins and aunts. For this disease there is but one remedy in the world, namely peace and a speedy return." Unfortunately, many of them died. Captain Georg Pausch attributed their deaths to homesickness. Thomas Anburey remembered seeing many of these victims, stored in "a long room" in the hospital "where they remain froze till the warm weather allows them burial."

The superintendent of this room, an apothecary, being a man of whimsical ideas, had placed the dead bodies of the poor Germans in various postures, some kneeling with books in their hands, others sitting with pipes in their mouths, many standing erect against the wall. As they have their clothes on, you can scarcely at first imagine they are dead; but, upon nearer approach, what with their long mustaches and their ghastly countenances, you cannot picture to yourself anything so horrible, yet at the same time so truly laughable and ridiculous.

* * * * *

After five weeks of preparations, the army set out on June 16th from St. Jean on the Richelieu River. The main fighting force consisted of 8000 Regulars, half of them British and half Germans. There were also 100 American Tories, 150 Canadian militia, and a sizable complement of officers' servants, musicians, sutlers, and "batmen" - Canadian laborers who would help haul the supplies, care for the horses, etc. And, despite Burgoyne's attempts to limit the number of camp followers, a total of 297 women and an unknown number of children accompanied the army.

Burgoyne also brought along the extraordinary total of 138 pieces of artillery, for he intended to use formal siege tactics to reduce the fabled Fort Ticonderoga. In Europe it was sometimes called "the Gibraltar of North America," due to Abercrombie's unsuccessful assault in 1758 against the then French-occupied fort, when more than 2000 British and American lives were lost. Carleton's decision the previous October to return to Canada, rather than attack the fort, added to Ti's reputation.

The heavier field pieces would be left behind once the fort was taken, but 42 of the lighter pieces would be brought south on the trek through the wilderness to the Hudson. After observing Bunker Hill,

Burgoyne was convinced that artillery was indispensable to dislodge Americans from the redoubts and breastworks they were "so adept in constructing and behind which they fought with tenacity."

The expedition, of course, was followed closely back home, and Burgoyne would be criticized often in the London papers for bringing so many cannon through the almost roadless wilderness south of Ticonderoga. The lack of transport would become a critical factor, once the army left the lake and began traveling overland. Governor Carleton, despite a diligent search, was only able to provide half the 1400 horses Burgoyne requested. Besides the artillery, an enormous amount of equipment and provisions must be transported. Five hundred two-wheel carts were constructed before the army set out from Canada. Just the champagne and clothes for Burgoyne and his mistress required more than thirty carts.

Observing all this, a veteran German officer named DuRoi expressed his disgust in his journal, "It is impossible to get an idea of the excessive amount of baggage carried along with the army. An army which is of any use in these parts must be almost without baggage, and with no more tents than can be taken by boats." The horses were not the only ones with a difficult task ahead of them. Sergeant Lamb describes the typical British foot soldier's burden:

> In marching through a difficult country, he carried a knapsack, blanket, a haversack containing four days provisions, a canteen for water, and a proportion of his tent furniture, which, superadded to his accoutrement, arms and sixty rounds of ammunition, made a great load and large luggage, weighing about sixty pounds.

While the artillery and heavier baggage was floated down the lake, most of the army marched along the west shore. They averaged eighteen miles per day, stopping long before dark to take elaborate precautions, even to the point of building breastworks, for protection against surprise attacks by the rebels. It was not the kind of march the

German soldiers expected, according to DuRoi:

> The banks of the lake are covered with the thickest woods, and every time a camp had to be pitched trees had to be cut down and the place cleared. In spite of the hard work, no other provisions were furnished than salt meat and flour. As each soldier had to bake his own bread, and no ovens for baking the same were there, he had to either bake it in hot ashes or on hot stones. This bread was, of course, very hard and heavy, and required good teeth. ... We were not accustomed to this and did not know how to do it. Every other army furnishes bread to the soldiers; even the Russian army, whose soldiers are known as hardened, takes baking ovens along during the wars.
>
> Furthermore, there was neither whisky nor tobacco, which the German soldiers were accustomed to have. I consider these last indispensible for soldiers.
>
> We had already made the acquaintance of mosquitoes in Canada, but never before had we suffered from them as much as today, for these insects attacked us in such quantities that it was impossible to protect ourselves from them, neither smoking of tobacco, nor the smoke of smallfires all around the camp being of any avail. We nearly suffocated from the smoke and could not keep our eyes open. It was impossible to wrap ourselves up in blankets on account of the heat, and the bloodthirsty mosquito would sting even through three-fold linen. It is impossible to describe the torture; indeed, I think myself justified in stating that nobody could endure it continuously for more than a few days and nights without becoming insane. If anybody could have watched us from a distance without being molested himself, or knowing what was going on, he would have

thought the whole camp full of raving maniacs.

The army halted for a week at a point on the western shore across from what is now Burlington, Vermont. Here, where the Bouquet River empties into Lake Champlain, Burgoyne held a conference with the chiefs of approximately 1000 braves who had arrived from New York and Canada. They listened to Burgoyne speak the words of "the great father beyond the great lake." He praised their past loyalty and performance, and their more recent restraint in waiting so patiently for "the King your father's call to arms." Then Burgoyne said the words they wanted to hear: "Warriors, you are free - go forth in might and valor. Strike at the common enemies, disturbers of public order, peace, and happiness." Then, in a firm tone, he laid down the rules by which they must "regulate" their "passions":

> I positively forbid bloodshed when you are not op-
> posed in arms. Aged men, women, children, and
> prisoners must be held sacred from the knife or hatchet,
> even in the time of actual conflict. You shall receive
> compensation for the prisoners you take but you shall be
> called to account for scalps.
> In conformity and indulgence of your customs which
> have affixed an idea of honour to such badges of victory,
> you shall be allowed to take the scalps of the dead, when
> killed by your fire and in fair opposition.

An old Iroquois chief then spoke on behalf of the others, promising "a constant obedience to all you have ordered and all you shall order." After the meeting broke up, the naive Burgoyne told one of his aides that he was "highly pleased to find the Indians so tractable." The next few months would reveal to him that the Indians had no intention of having their passions regulated. To their way of thinking, letting an enemy captive live to fight another day was foolish, granting him the chance to kill you later.

An account of Burgoyne's speech to the Indians reached London and was read aloud in Parliament, bringing tears of laughter to Lord North's eyes. An outraged Edmund Burke, knowing the Indians would do as they pleased, declared the speech would have the same effect as turning loose captive bears, wolves and hyenas, telling them to "go forth, but take care not to hurt man, woman or child."

Thomas Anburey was with a part of the army camped at Button Mold Bay, on the eastern shore. He crossed the lake with some other officers to hear Burgoyne, the famous London playwright, address the savages. On the way there, he passed the Indians' encampment.

> We observed a young Indian who was preparing for the war-dance, seated under a wigwam, with a small looking-glass placed before him, and surrounded with several papers, filled with different paints. At our stopping to observe him, he was at first a little disconcerted, and appeared displeased, but soon after proceeded to adorn himself. He first smeared his face with a little bear's grease, then rubbed in some vermilion, then a little black, blue, and green paints. And having viewed himself for some time in the glass, in a rage he wiped it all off and began again, but with no better success, still appearing dissatisfied.
>
> We went on to the council, which lasted near two hours, and on our return found the Indian in the same position, and at the same employment, having nearly consumed all his stock of colours! What a pity it is the ladies in England, adept in this art, have not such a variety of tints to exercise their genius with!

Within three days of the chiefs' promise to refrain from scalping non-combatants, ten scalps were brought into camp. However, like many of the officers, Thomas Anburey considered the use of Indians to be "essential ... [they] being extremely skillful in the art of surprising,

172

and watching the motions of an enemy." Indeed, they proved to be a good shield, preventing American scouts from Ticonderoga from getting close enough to gauge the strength of the advancing army.

At this time, Burgoyne also wrote a *Proclamation* intended for "the eyes and ears of the temperate part of the public" and those loyal subjects who he claimed were suffering under "the completest system of tyranny" in human history. In this bombastic document he explained that "the intention of this address [was] to hold forth security, not depredation to the country." He offered "encouragement and employment" and pledged to "find means to assist" any persons who would partake of the "glorious task of redeeming their countrymen." Those who did not come forth to join his army would be left unharmed, "provided they remain quietly at their homes [and] do not suffer their cattle to be removed, nor their corn or forage to be secreted or destroyed. Every species of provision brought to my camp will be paid for at an equitable rate, and in solid coin."

Solid coin, so precious in those days of inflated paper Continentals, was tempting bait, yet very few of the inhabitants responded positively to it. Instead, they were more impressed by the ominous warning with which he concluded his proclamation:

> And let not people be led to disregard it [his advice], by considering their distance from the immediate situation of my camp. I have but to give stretch to the Indian forces under my direction, and they amount to thousands, to overtake the hardened enemies of Great Britain and America, wherever they may lurk.
>
> If the phrensy of hostility should remain, I trust I shall stand acquitted in the eyes of God and men in denouncing and executing the vengeance of the state against the wilful outcasts. The messengers of justice and of wrath await them in the field; and devastation, famine, and every concomitant horror that a reluctant but indispensable prosecution of military duty must occasion will bar

the way to their return.

This was enough to scare away the inhabitants, even some of the most ardent loyalists. Decades of frontier living had taught them that when Indians on the warpath suddenly appear on your homestead they do not stop to ask which side you are on. The people reading this proclamation somehow doubted that their "security" was Burgoyne's primary concern when he hired mercenaries and savages as his "messengers of justice."

Burgoyne's other hired mercenaries were, of course, the Germans. King George III had contracted with several landgraves, who each ruled their own principality, to supply him with soldiers to fight his war in America. The Germans in this army were nearly all from Brunswick - unlike those of Howe's army further south, who were mainly from Hesse-Cassel and Hesse-Hanau (and thus commonly re-ferred to as "Hessians").

Burgoyne's Germans were led by 39-year-old General Baron Friedrich Adolph von Riedesel (pronounced Ree-day-zel, but most Americans and British said "Red Hazel"). Short, stocky, balding and personable, he was a strict disciplinarian, thoroughly competent, and more experienced than Burgoyne. Riedesel admired Carleton's mili-tary judgement, and offered his opinions in a letter to the Duke of Brunswick. Riedesel thought it was "a great mistake ... a great risk to remove a man who was so peculiarly fitted for so important a posi-tion." Carleton "went to work more carefully and safely and made no plan until he was convinced it could be carried out." Burgoyne, on the other hand, "judges somewhat hastily." However, despite his personal reservations, Riedesel would admirably serve under his new com-mander.

Burgoyne made it a point in his general orders to remind the troops in all the brigades to continue to rely on the bayonet when attacking the enemy. Riedesel, however, was more open minded. He had spent many hours during the past year training his troops in new methods of warfare better suited to North America than the traditional European mass volley and bayonet charge. "I perceived," he wrote, "that the American riflemen always shot further than our forces - consequently I made my men practice at long range and behind trees, that they might at least be enough for them." This was necessary, Riedesel was convinced, because the terrain would not be conducive to European style fighting. "Aside from a few cultivated regions on the rivers, all the hills are covered with woods. In the whole of America there is no spot where six battalions could be placed in a good position."

On June 29th, Burgoyne's army reached Crown Point. The Americans posted there had abandoned it. This old French and Indian War fort, now in disrepair, would serve as headquarters and a supply depot until Ticonderoga could be taken. The last day of June brought the following general orders from Burgoyne, to be read to the army:

> G.O. The army embarks tomorrow, to approach the enemy. We are to contend for the King, and the constitution of Great Britain, to vindicate law, and to relieve the oppressed - a cause in which his Majesty's troops and those of the princes his allies will feel equal excitement. The services required of this particular expedition are critical and conspicuous. During our progress occasions may occur in which no difficulty, nor labour, nor life are to be regarded. This army must not retreat.

Burgoyne's soldiers, "in high spirits and perfect health," dismissed the thought of retreating to Canada again as being extremely unlikely. This time their leader meant business. Instead of the cautious Carleton, they were now led by "Gentleman Johnny." Lieutenant William Digby explained the soldiers' feelings in his journal:

> [Carleton] was far from being the favorite of the army. Genl Burgoyne alone engrossed their warmest attachment. He possesses a winning manner in his appearance and address. Idolized by the army, his

orders more like recommending subordination than enforcing it. On every occasion he was the soldiers friend.

In contrast to "the severity of Carleton" and almost every other British general, Burgoyne treated his troops like human beings (an uncommon practice in an age when it was thought that only harsh and frequent discipline could hold an army together). Burgoyne absolutely forbade his subordinate officers from striking or even swearing at their men. It was his aim to substitute "the point of honour in place of severity." He even recommended his officers use "an occasional joke in talking to the men as an encouragement." When the army set out from St. Jean, "Gentleman Johnny" placed himself at the river's edge so every soldier passing on foot or in the boats could see their commander. During the march to Crown Point, Burgoyne made it a point each evening to wander through the camps, casually talking to the men sitting around the campfires. This was the kind of commander for whom British soldiers would willingly suffer hardships and risk their lives.

At dawn on July first, the drummer boys beat *The General* instead of *The Reveille*. *The Reveille* was the drum call that instructed sleeping soldiers to rise, and all sentries to forbear challenging. *The General*, on the other hand, gave notice to prepare to march. An hour after beating *The General*, the drummers beat *The Assembly*, instructing the different regiments to repair to their respective rendezvous points. The horseless German dragoons would be left behind at Crown Point, and at Chimney Point on the opposite shore, to guard the camps. Lieutenant James Hadden describes the embarkation:

> Tuesday, July 1st. This day the army embarked, the weather being fine and the [lake] ... between Crown Point and Tyconderoga was cover'd with boats or batteaux; some of the armed vessels accompanied us. The music and drums of the different regiments were continually playing and contributed to make the scene

and passage extremely pleasant.

The British brigades came ashore on the west side three miles north of Ti, and the Germans landed the next day opposite them on the east side. From these landing points, each brigade proceeded on foot. The British landing at Three Mile Point was observed from Mount Independence by nineteen-year-old Colonel Henry Brokholst Livingston. Brave, inexperienced, and optimistic, he was an aide-de-camp to Philip Schuyler, head of the Continental Army's Northern Department. Schuyler was at headquarters in Albany, so young Livingston was serving as his "eyes" at Ti, under its commander General Arthur St. Clair. Livingston repeated some of his observations in a letter to his father, the governor of New Jersey:

> We have a fine view of their boats. Many betts are depending, that we shall be attacked in the course of the week.
> July 3. We are daily receiving additions to our strength. Tomorrow we shall give the British a 13-gun salute, a "feu de joi," because it will be the anniversary of the ever-memorable 4th of July, 1776, on which day we broke off connections with slavery and became the free and independent States of America.

* * * * * *

About the same time that Burgoyne was preoccupied with the investment of Ti, one of his colleagues, General Richard Prescott, was involved in a less important but much more sensational event on Rhode Island. Ever since the British had captured Washington's second in command, Charles Lee, in December 1776, Washington had been unable to obtain Lee's release because he did not have a British general to offer in exchange. However, William Barton, a major of Rhode Island militia, formulated a plan to procure one.

It seems that General Prescott had a habit of riding out every evening to visit a lady at a house four and a half miles north of his Newport headquarters. It was fairly safe to venture out with only a couple of bodyguards, because hundreds of British and German troops were encamped at various places on the island, and a squadron of warships surrounded it. After an evening of pleasure and a restful sleep, the refreshed general would ride back to Newport the next morning. Major Barton learned this from a British deserter. In fact, so many soldiers were deserting from the island that summer that American militia would wait for them with boats ready to bring them across from Rhode Island to the mainland.

Knowing General Prescott's nocturnal habits, the exact location of his hideaway, and those of the British camps and pickets, Barton planned his raid, obtained permission to try it, and then hand-picked 38 trusted men. He "told them his design, acknowledged that it was hazardous, and probably could not be executed without the loss of life to some of those engaged in it; that he, for his part, was determined to risk his." All 38 militiamen elected to go with him. After blackening their faces, they set off from the mainland shore in five boats on the evening of July 4th. With muffled oars, they slipped by a British fort, undiscovered. After being delayed by a severe storm, they set out again on July 9th. Finally, in the darkness they rowed between two British men-of-war and landed a mile from their destination.

After leaving a few men to guard the boats and watch for enemy patrols, Barton led the way. Two black soldiers marched right behind him, followed by the rest of the column. The Pennsylvania Evening Post printed one account of what happened when they approached the house:

> A single sentry saw and hailed. [Barton] answered by exclaiming against and inquiring for rebel prisoners, but kept slowly advancing. The sentinel again challenged him, and required the countersign; he said he had not the countersign, but amused the sentry by talking about re-

bel prisoners, and still advancing till he came within reach of the bayonet, which [Barton] suddenly struck aside and seized him. He was immediately secured, and ordered to be silent, on pain of instant death.

As planned, the force divided into five groups: one for each of the three doors, one to guard the line of retreat, and one to stand by in case of emergency. By whispering a few threats to the captured sentry, Barton extracted from him what he wanted to hear - that Prescott was inside. "The party, instantly breaking the doors and entering the house," aroused the owner, who vehemently denied that any British general was on the premises. In no mood to waste time, Barton then announced in a loud voice that he would burn the house down if necessary. At that point, a distinctly English voice could be heard from above, inquiring what the ruckus was about. Barton and his men bounded up the stairs and seized the general, still in his bedclothes.

During the search of the house, one of Prescott's guards escaped through a window in his nightshirt and ran to the nearest British guardhouse. The officer in charge laughed at him and refused to believe so preposterous a tale. So, exasperated, he ran off toward the next post. Meanwhile, Barton gave Prescott only enough time to partially dress himself, then quickly left, with the general carrying the rest of his clothes.

By the time the raiders reached the waiting boats, they heard an alarm cannon boom in the distance far behind them, and flares were illuminating the sky. "But it was too late," as the newspaper story related, "the bird had fled." The men-of-war did not respond to the alarm. Barton's five small boats rowed past them again and reached the mainland.

General Prescott, who two years before had captured Ethan Allen in Montreal and threatened Allen with death, now found himself in a similar predicament. However, the general was well aware that he was more valuable to the rebels alive than dead. He sat in the boat, dumbfounded, and said to Colonel Barton, "And is it possible that I am a prisoner of war! Yes, I see I am; but when you set out with me I had no doubt that I should have been rescued and all of you been made prisoners."

Prescott's capture earned a colonelcy for Barton, and the eventual release of General Lee. It also amused newspaper readers on both continents. The <u>London Chronicle</u> commented in verse:

> What various lures there are to ruin man;
> Woman, the first and foremost, all bewitches!
> A nymph once spoiled a General's mighty play,
> And gave him to the foe - without his breeches.

* * * * *

Returning to Ticonderoga, let us review the circumstances of the Northern Department of the Continental Army during the months leading upReturning to Ticonderoga, let us review the circumstances of the Northern Department of the Continental Army during the months leading up to Burgoyne's arrival. It had been an extremely trying winter at Ticonderoga, a "cold and inhospitable region." Severe weather, smallpox and dysentery, plus a lack of adequate shelter, fuel, clothing, medicines, and food all combined to make life there a living hell.

Added to these privations and the rigors of winter duty were the soldiers' own prejudices. The term "damn'd Yankees" became the common label for anyone from New England. A general from New England described the animosity held by the "southerners":

> It has already risen to such a height that the Pennsylvania and New England troops would as soon fight each other as the enemy. Officers of all ranks are treated in the most contemptible manner, and whole colonies traduced and vilified as cheats, knaves, cowards, poltroons, hypocrites and every term of reproach, for no other reason but because they are [from] New England.

The Pennsylvania officers scorned the "pumpkin gentry" Yankee officers for their lack of dash and style, and especially their "levelling" - that is, their democratic ways of treating their men. The southerners felt that levelling was derogatory to the standing of an officer and a gentleman. The Yankees, in turn, expressed equal disdain for the aristocratic Pennsylvanians.

Hostile feelings reached the boiling point on Christmas night, 1776. In an effort to remedy the shortage of shoes in his regiment, a Colonel Asa Whitcomb, of Massachusetts, drew "the contemptuous sneers of the gentlemen officers" from the southward by letting his son set up a cobbler's bench in his quarters. This incensed the Pennsylvania officers so much that one of them, a Lieutenant-Colonel Thomas Craig, determined that he would teach the Yankees a lesson. In a drunken rage he burst into Whitcomb's quarters, smashed the bench, and struck the elderly Yankee colonel, injuring him seriously. The noise attracted a crowd, and a fight developed which the Pennsylvanian troops were prepared for, as they fired on the Massachusetts men, severely wounding several of them. The next day the volatile situation was defused, and the Yankees appeased, when Craig sent some of his men into the woods to shoot a fat bear, which Craig presented to Colonel Whitcomb. Feelings were soothed as the officers from both regiments shared in the feast.

The fort's commander, Major-General Horatio Gates, had left Ti in November for Philadelphia, to lobby the Congress for an appointment as head of the Northern Department, replacing Philip Schuyler. Schuyler's indecisiveness, and rumors started by Yankees concerning the New York general's honesty and loyalty, made him a popular scapegoat for the disastrous results of the 1775 invasion of Canada. Schuyler did not help himself by writing a series of "ill-advised and highly indecent" letters to Congress during the winter of 1776-77. As was his custom, Schuyler denied any blame and contemptuously faulted the Yankees. Not stopping there, he then scolded Congress for its lack of faith in him.

While Congress was digesting these disagreable letters, Gates was conveniently on hand for frequent detailed consultation with its Board of War, impressing them with his knowledge of every detail of the Northern Department. By March, Gates returned triumphantly to Ti as the new head of the Northern Department.

Then it was Schuyler's turn to leave for Congress, where he demanded a full inquiry into his own conduct. Schuyler was exonerated and restored as the supreme commander of the Northern Department. Gates, of course, refused to serve under him, and again rode away to Philadelphia to see if he could regain the command. While Gates was away, command at Ticonderoga was given to Major General Arthur St. Clair.

Originally from Scotland, Arthur St. Clair had served under Wolfe as a 22-year-old ensign during the British attack on Quebec in 1759. After the war, he married well and settled in Pennsylvania as a gentleman farmer. He soon became active in the political conflict with Parliament, and when the war broke out in 1775 he organized a militia regiment. After serving in Canada, he was sent southward in the fall of 1776 and took part in Washington's Christmas night surprise attack on Trenton. With plans for a much larger army in 1777, Congress had many generalships available and chose St. Clair to fill Pennsylvania's quota.

Having been assured that he would have a peaceful summer at Ticonderoga, St. Clair headed north, bringing his eleven-year-old son with him. He arrived on June 12th and soon learned that a British army was moving up the lake. Despite his son's objections, St. Clair quickly sent him off to the safety of Albany.

Neither the Congress nor the Commander-in-Chief seriously considered the possibility of another British attempt on Ticonderoga. Washington thought a second British "attempt to penetrate the country by way of the lakes against all probability." Therefore, in March, he redirected newly raised regiments from New England (originally destined for Ti) to the lower Hudson River forts and to the main army in New Jersey. He felt that a large force at Ticonderoga would be a "useless body of troops."

Congress and Washington were convinced that Howe's main army at New York would try to pin down Washington in New Jersey. And the Canadian army, they predicted, would take a sea route around New England to New York, then sail up the Hudson to attack the forts south of Albany.

Schuyler had a different theory. He sent reinforcements to the western Mohawk River settlements, anticipating that this time Carleton would advance by way of Lake Ontario and then overland to the Mohawk River, which empties into the Hudson near Albany. Any British movement on Lake Champlain, Schuyler felt, would be merely a feint designed to draw American forces away from the Mohawk and Hudson.

Only Gates argued that the British would mount their major effort of the year - control of the Hudson - by way of Lake Champlain. However, he was unable to convince the Board of War, which had received inaccurate, self-serving reports from Anthony Wayne before he left Ti that "all was well" at the fort and that "it can never be carried without much loss of blood." Evidently, Carleton's retreat the previous October had added to Ticonderoga's myth of invincibility.

But it was far from invincible. Fort Ticonderoga was located on a tapering tongue of land that sloped down to the shore of Lake Champlain on the New York side. The lake continued southward from there, as the narrow, river-like "South Bay" to Skenesborough. Westward from Ti, a creek and short portage led to Lake George. The main stone fort, built by the French in 1755 on the site of earlier ones dating back to 1690, was surrounded on its land approaches - west and northwest - by very extensive trenches and breastworks known as the "Old French Lines." It was here that so many British and Americans had died during Abercrombie's unsuccessful assault on these lines in 1758.

Just as Ticonderoga was on a peninsula that reached into the lake from the west, another peninsula jutted out from the eastern (Vermont) side. Together, they narrowed the lake to just a quarter mile across, explaining one of the translations of the Iroquois word Ti-conderoga as "place where the lake shuts itself." The eastern peninsula included a small hill christened Mount Independence the previous July, when news arrived of the great Declaration. It was an ideal setting for fortifications, as Colonel Trumbull makes clear:

> The land rose to an almost level plateau elevated from fifty to seventy-five feet above the lake, and surrounded on three sides by a natural wall of rock, everywhere steep, and sometimes an absolute precipice sinking to the lake. On the fourth and eastern side of the position ran a morass and deep creek at the front of the rock, which strengthened that front, leaving room only by an easy descent for a [newly cut] road to the east.

Works had been started at Mount Independence in 1776, and now the redoubts and breastworks were extensive, though by July 1777 they were still an estimated six weeks from completion. Ti and Mount Independence together boasted over 100 cannon in place. The army's few boats were now anchored behind a boom of logs linked together by heavy chains stretching from shore to shore - an obstacle designed to stop Burgoyne's ships from getting into the South Bay.

To facilitate movement of men and materiel, a bridge had been constructed from the shore below Ti to the foot of Mount Independence the previous winter. Twenty-two holes, fifty feet apart, had been cut in the ice. Next, log cribs, made of thick tree trunks twenty-five feet long, had been sunk through these holes. The cribs had then been filled with stones from a nearby quarry, so the strong current could not dislodge them. Finally, in between these supports, floating sections of fifty-foot logs had been chained together and then covered with a plank deck twelve feet across. One German officer, after examining the bridge, stated that only in a country fighting for its freedom would soldiers persevere against the obvious hardships involved in building such a structure.

One of the regiments on duty at Mount Independence was that of Colonel Seth Warner, of Green Mountain Boy fame, from the mountainous region east of the lake known recently as the Hampshire Grants. In March of 1777, a convention of the inhabitants had proclaimed these lands the independent republic of New Connecticut. However, they soon learned that pioneers in Pennsylvania's Wyoming Valley were calling that area the same thing. So, on June 4th, they changed it to Vermont, based on two French words meaning "green mountain."

Seth Warner sent numerous letters to the Committees of Safety in the Vermont towns, asking for more men and food to defend Ti.

> If forty or fifty head of cattle could be brought on with the militia they will be paid for by the commissary on their arrival. I should be glad if a few hills of corn unhoed should not be a motive to detain men at home, considering the loss of such an important post can hardly be recovered.

By July first, Dr. James Thacher was noting in his journal that "the militia of New England are daily coming in to increase our strength." But with only a few weeks' worth of provisions in stock, the outlook for withstanding a prolonged siege was not promising. As one man wrote, more militia were available, "but should we call them in, immediate starvation is the consequence."

Yet, to effectively man all the works would require 12,000 men, not the 3000 that St. Clair had at his disposal. Colonel James Wilkinson, Gates's 21-year-old deputy adjutant, had chosen to stay on at Ti after Gates left. Wilkinson wrote to Gates on June 25th, explaining St. Clair's predicament:

> Should we attempt to support this place in our present deficient situation, we lose all, and leave the country defenseless and exposed. What then, will there be to

obstruct their favorite scheme - a junction by the North River?

Schuyler arrived on June 19th to consult with St. Clair and his subordinate generals. Colonel Wilkinson was also at the council of war. Although Schuyler's exact comments were not recorded, Wilkinson did note that Schuyler doubted the wisdom of defending the fort with a "number of troops ... greatly inadequate to the defense." However, Schuyler stopped short of ordering an evacuation: "without orders from Congress, he dare not undertake on himself the responsibility of a measure which would create a great outcry." The council resolved that efforts to improve the posts, especially at Mount Independence, should continue. And the posts on both shores ought "to be maintained as long as possible, consistent with the saftety of the troops and stores."

However, the council of war further resolved that "it would be imprudent to expose the army to be made prisoners by the enemy; and that, therefore, it is prudent to provide for a retreat." If the British attacked in earnest, rather than the predicted feint, the army should retire without delay, so that their retreat would not be cut off. To encourage the men, Schuyler promised that he would ask Washington to forward reinforcements. He then returned to headquarters at Albany, leaving St. Clair in a most unenviable position.

During the spring, American scouts, sent to the northern end of the lake, had been frustrated when they were not able to penetrate the screen of Indians around the British posts there. However, by early June they had captured a British soldier in northern Vermont. He revealed that Burgoyne had 10,000 men and was intent on advancing on Ticonderoga, while a separate, smaller expedition would go by way of Lake Ontario to make a diversion on the Mohawk. The prisoner, one William Amsbury, was brought to the new commander, St. Clair, who didn't believe the story. Judging from the amount of money on his person, and the numerous letters he was carrying addressed to loyalists, St. Clair believed he must be a spy deliberately planted on American soil to spread false information. He sent the man to Schuyler at Albany, where his story received the same reception. Schuyler wrote to Washington, including St. Clair's opinion as well as his own. Washington replied that, even if the story was true, "I cannot conceive it will be within the power of the enemy to execute it."

St. Clair interpreted Burgoyne's slow progress to mean he must have a small force on the lake acting as a decoy. As late as June 26th, St. Clair still "did not imagine" the British "meant a serious attack on Ticonderoga." Perhaps, "this movement of theirs" was "intended to cover an attack on the Mohawk River ... or an attempt to penetrate New Hampshire." Within a few days, though, St. Clair had in hand copies of Burgoyne's *Proclamation* to the inhabitants, and he knew that Burgoyne's army had advanced as far as Crown Point. But still, St. Clair did not realize the magnitude of Burgoyne's forces, as he wrote on June 30 to Schuyler, "should the enemy attack us, they will go back faster than they came."

St. Clair, to prevent his men who manned Ti's walls from throwing away their fire, ordered them to sit down with their backs to the parapet while the officers kept an eye on the enemy. On July 2nd, a lone British soldier crept within 40 yards of the fort, hid behind a stump and fired his musket, then reloaded and kept firing. Young Colonel Wilkinson ordered a sergeant to rise and shoot the sniper. Wilkinson later recorded what, to his surprise, occurred after he gave this order:

> The order was obeyed, and at the discharge of the musket every man arose, mounted the banquette [firing step], and without command fired a volley; the artillery followed the example, as did many of the officers, from the colonels down to the subalterns. Notwithstanding the exertions of the general, his aides, and several other officers, three rounds were discharged before they could stop the firing.
>
> Casting my eyes on the stump where I had perceived the infantryman whom I directed to be shot, I discovered

him lying prostrate on his back, and mentioned the circumstance to General St. Clair, who ... replied to me. "Send out a corporal and a file of men, and let the poor fellow be brought in and buried." But as the corporal approached the supposed dead man, he jumped up, clubbed his musket, and exclaimed, "By Jasus, I killed the man at the sallyport; a fair shot!" The fellow was brought in; he belonged to the 47th Light Infantry, and was intoxicated and insolent, refusing to give a word of information.

To acquire such information as the prisoner might possess, a Captain Johnson of the artillery (a son of Hibernia) was metamorphosed into a Tory, and thrust into the guard-room with him. He soon became acquainted with his countryman, and with the aid of a bottle of rum which Johnson had concealed among his tattered apparel, he before midnight procured from his companion, who happened to be an intelligent old soldier, the number and name of every corps under General Burgoyne, with an estimate of their strength.

This information removed all doubts relative to the force of the enemy, and their movements indicated an "investissement" [rather than an assault]. Still, General St. Clair lacked resolution to give up the place, or in other words to sacrifice his character to the public good: for by several manoeuvres of his adversary on the 3rd and 4th, he was cheered with the hope that General Burgoyne intended to hazard an assault, which he was determined to await at all events.

Thomas Allen, the "fighting parson" of Pittsfield, Mass., addressed the garrison at Ticonderoga on the afternoon of July 5th:

Valiant soldiers, yonder are the enemies of your country who have come to lay waste and destroy this pleasant land. They are mercenaries hired to do the work of death, and have no motive to animate them in their undertaking. You have every consideration to induce you to play the man and act the part of valiant soldiers. Your country looks up to you for its defense. You are contending for your wives, whether you or they shall enjoy them. You are fighting for your children, whether they shall be yours or theirs. - For your houses and lands; - For your flocks and herds; - For your freedom; - For future generations; - For everything that is great and noble, and on account of which only life itself is worth a fig.

CHAPTER EIGHT
TICONDEROGA FALLS
JULY 1777

"Where a goat can go a man can go, and where a man can go he can drag a gun."

> *- General Phillips, placing his artillery above Ticonderoga.*

While St. Clair and the northern army celebrated July 4th as best they could, the British were preparing some unfriendly fireworks for them. On July 3rd, General William Phillips, a former artillery officer himself, cast his eyes upon the most prominent hill in the area, Sugar Loaf Hill, just across the creek that connected Lakes George and Champlain. Because of its proximity and its elevation - 660 feet higher than Fort Ti and 550 feet higher than Fort Independence - it was the obvious place to mount a battery of guns, if its steep slopes could be mastered. Burgoyne later remarked that the Americans' failure to do this indicated "they have no men of military science." Phillips asked Lieutenant William Twiss to reconnoiter the site. Burgoyne's journal tells us what Twiss found on his hike:

> Lieutenant Twiss reported this hill to have the entire command of the works and buildings both Ticonderoga and Mount Independence, at the distance of about 1400 yards from the former and 1500 from the latter; that the ground might be leveled so as to receive cannon; and that a road to convey them, though difficult, might be made practicable in twenty-four hours.

Fourteen hundred yards, nearly a mile, was a very long shot, but the starting elevation being several hundred feet above the targets effectively reduced the distance to within accurate range. Of course, the rebel boats in the South Bay would now be sitting ducks, too, making a daytime evacuation of Ti extremely hazardous in that direction. The last sure escape route left to the rebels would be a recently cut wagon path, called the Military Road, from Mount Independence to Castleton, Vermont. And even this route would soon be cut off by Riedesel's Germans, who were slowly working their way around the swamps that protected Mount Independence on the north and east.

After hearing what he had hoped to hear from Lieutenant Twiss, General Phillips gave the order for a battery to be mounted as close to the top of Sugar Loaf Hill as possible. He declared, with a laugh: "Where a goat can go, a man can go, and where a man can go, he can drag a gun." Germans were borrowed from Riedesel for the working party of 700, which cut a winding road through the forest's dense underbrush on the west slope of Sugar Loaf, out of sight of the rebels.

To avoid discovery by the rebels, the work was done during the nights of July 3 and 4. It was done with so much secrecy that not even the British pickets were told that a party of men and oxen would be bringing cannon past their outposts near the Old French Lines. For a few tense minutes, the sentries almost fired upon the working party when they did not give the password. With the light of a full moon as their guide, Twiss directed the men in using rope cradles and pulleys fastened to trees near the summit to hoist up the disassembled guns. In some places the "ascent was almost perpendicular." Six cannon were brought up the night of July 4th. They were reassembled and put in place by the morning of the 5th. When the battery of six guns was complete the British named it Fort Defiance, and since that day the hill has been known as Mount Defiance.

The British presence there was soon detected. Someone had foolishly lit a campfire near the summit during the early morning hours of July 5th. At dawn "the smoak was discovered by the enemy in the fort." Psychologically, this was a great shock to the Americans. St. Clair called a council of war for 3 o'clock that afternoon to reconsider making an evacuation.

Their current predicament reminded some of them of the previous September, when Colonel Trumbull, at the officers' mess, had advocated mounting a few guns on Sugar Loaf. Gates and the other officers had ridiculed him "for advancing such an extravagant idea," so convinced were they that the British could not possibly bring guns up those steep slopes. They still rejected the proposal, even after Trumbull and some other officers got off their horses and "clambered to the summit" to prove its accessibility.

Eight months later, in May, 1777, a Polish engineer, Tadeusz Kosciuszko, arrived and he, too, suggested placing a battery on Sugar Loaf. He had nearly persuaded Gates when, in June, the command was taken over by Schuyler, who said he "was not disposed to embarass himself or his means of defense by making the experiment." Colonel Wilkinson, observing the conversation, "detected, under his [Kosciuszko's] placid silence, more than a little anguish and mortification." Kosciuszko proved useful, though, as he oversaw construction of the Horseshoe Battery on Mount Independence, which was praised later by British and German officers as first class. In the coming weeks, he would prove invaluable to Schuyler in his attempts to first delay, and then stop Burgoyne on the way to Albany.

St. Clair's July 5th council of war resolved that as soon as darkness fell a "retreat ought to be undertaken as soon as possible, and that we shall be fortunate to effect it." By the next day, Lieutenant William Digby was writing in his diary, with pleasure:

> They no sooner perceived us in possession of a post which they thought quite impossible to bring cannon up to, than all their pretended boastings of holding out to the last, and choosing rather to die in their works than give them up, failed them.

Fearful that deserters would alert Burgoyne, St. Clair ordered his generals to not even mention the planned evacuation to subordinate officers until after dark. As a consequence, the men had to be awakened and, in utmost haste and confusion, prepare to march. Tons of provisions, eighty pieces of artillery, even paper currency, were left behind. The lightest field pieces, some barrels of powder and provisions, and the invalids were loaded into the boats. They set out, with 600 men on board as an escort, about 2 a.m., heading up the lake's South Bay toward Skenesborough.

Meanwhile, the main force, led by St. Clair, marched across the bridge and up Mount Independence. The garrison there joined the column, making a total of about 4000 men (including 1000 militia who had just arrived two days before). St. Clair planned to march down the new Military Road to Castleton, then continue on and join the boat party at Skenesborough.

Ebenezer Fletcher, a sixteen-year-old fifer, recalled that night: "Early on the morning of the 6th of July, orders came to strike our tents and swing our packs. It was generally conjectured that we were going to battle, but orders came immediately to march." As he and some of the others in the tail end of the long column made their way up Mount Independence, they suddenly found themselves illuminated. In a drunken stupor, the Frenchman, General Roche de Fermoy, had set his headquarters afire.

This unfortunate occurrence alerted British sentries on the west side and Germans on the east. General Simon Fraser, in charge of the British advance guard, ordered his pickets and the closest light infantry companies to "march and take possession" of Fort Ticonderoga "and hoist the King's colors." Then he led the pursuit of the retreating rebels into Vermont. Sergeant Roger Lamb recalls crossing the bridge:

> In passing the bridge we found four men lying intoxicated with drinking, who had been left to fire the guns of a large battery on our approach. Had the men obeyed the commands they received, we must have suffered

great injury; but they were allured by the opportunity of a cask of madeira to forget their instructions, and drown their cares in wine. Matches were found lighted, the ground was strewed with powder, and the heads of some powder-casks were knocked off in order, no doubt, to injure our men on their gaining the works. An Indian, from his curiosity, holding a lighted match near one of the guns, it exploded. But being elevated, it discharged without harm.

Fraser wanted to bring over more regiments for the chase, but he found that the British ships had wasted no time in destroying the bridge and boom. "A few well directed cannon-shots broke in two the collosal chain upon which so many hopes had hung." A messenger soon arrived from Burgoyne, giving Fraser permission to set out with what men he already had on the Vermont side, and "to attack any body of rebels that he might come up with." Burgoyne also directed Riedesel, making his way around the swamps east of the Military Road, to follow and support Fraser, then push on to Skenesborough.

While Fraser, and Riedesel a few miles behind, were chasing St. Clair's land party, Burgoyne personally led the pursuit of the rebel boat party up South Bay. The Americans, on their way to Skenesborough, felt safe from pursuit - not expecting the enemy could very quickly break through the boom. In the boat party was Dr. James Thacher, serving in the Continental Army as a surgeon. For several days he did not have time to write. He finally caught up with his diary on July 14th, when he wrote of this "extraordinary and unexpected event":

Having with all possible despatch completed our embarkation at 3 o'clock in the morning of the 6th, we commenced our voyage up the South Bay. We could look back with regret, and forward with apprehension. We availed ourselves, however, of the means of enlivening our spirits. The drum and fife afforded us a favorite music; among the hospital stores we found many dozens of choice wine, we cheered our hearts with the nectareous contents.

At 3 o'clock in the afternoon, we reached our destined port at Skenesborough, being the head of navigation for our gallies. Here we were unsuspicious of danger, but behold! Burgoyne himself was at our heels. We were struck with surprise and consternation by a discharge of cannon from the enemy's fleet on our gallies and batteaux lying at the wharf.

A number of their troops and savages had landed and were rapidly advancing towards our little party. The officers now attempted to rally the men and form them in battle array; but in the utmost panic they were seen to fly in every direction for personal safety. In this desperate situation I perceived our officers scampering for their baggage; I ran to the batteau, seized my [medical] chest, carried it a short distance, took from it a few articles, and instantly followed in the train of our retreating party.

We took the route to Fort Ann through a narrow defile in the woods, and were so closely pressed by the pursuing enemy that we frequently heard calls from the rear to "march on, the Indians are at our heels." Having marched all night, we reached Fort Ann at 5 o'clock in the morning, where we found provisions for our refreshment. A small rivulet called Wood Creek is navigable from Skenesborough to Fort Ann, by which means some of our invalids and baggage made their escape; but all our cannon and provisions and the bulk of our baggage [including 300 barrels of gunpowder], with several invalids, fell into the enemy's hands.

Help was coming, though. Schuyler was on the way from Albany with a few regiments that Washington had ordered forward from the lower Hudson forts. The first of these, 400 militia under Colonel Van Rensselaer, arrived and were soon put to use the morning of July 7th. During the previous day's pursuit, a British detachment of 190 men had outpaced the three other regiments Burgoyne had sent forward from Skenesborough. This small force had camped less than a mile short of Fort Ann, and received a visitor from the fort that evening. Claiming to be a deserter, the American lied and told the British Colonel Hill that about one thousand men were in Fort Ann. Hill sent back word to Burgoyne to hurry up reinforcements while he held his position. Before dawn, the "deserter" snuck out of the British camp and returned to Fort Ann to advise Colonel Long of the strength and isolated position of the British detachment. With Van Rensselaer's 400 added to his own 150 effectives, Long quietly advanced in the morning against the enemy.

While part of Long's forces attacked the British front, another party gave them a "heavy and well directed fire" on their flank, and still others sifted through the woods trying to get in the rear. Outnumbered three to one, and in danger of being surrounded, the British colonel withdrew to a high knoll, but was again pressed by "a very vigorous attack." Musket balls "poured down upon them like a mighty torrent."

One British officer noted that at this point "they certainly would have forced us, had it not been for some Indians that arrived and gave the Indian whoop." A party of Indians had been ordered to come to Hill's aid. But they refused to join the battle. Being content to let the British fight while they waited for the chance to scalp the wounded and dead Americans, they "either stood still or advanced very slow." Finally, in desperation, the British captain escorting them gave his imitation of an Indian war whoop. The ruse had the intended effect, as "being followed by three cheers from the English, the Americans were induced to give way." The resulting pause in the action allowed Hill's party time to make their escape.

The British Sergeant Roger Lamb had been in the thick of the fight, and saw two men killed near him. One was shot through the heart, while the other received a ball in the forehead which tore off the roof of his skull. "He reeled round," Lamb wrote, "turned up his eyes, muttered some words, and fell dead at my feet." Altogether, there were about fifty British casualties in this action near Fort Ann. Sergeant Lamb continues his account:

> It was a distressing sight to see the wounded men bleeding on the ground, and what made it more so, the rain came pouring down like a deluge upon us. The poor fellows earnestly entreated me to tie up their wounds. Immediately I took off my shirt, tore it up, and with the help of a soldier's wife (the only woman that was with us, and who kept close by her husband's side during the engagement) made some bandages, stopped the bleeding of their wounds and conveyed them in blankets to a small hut about two miles in our rear.

The British captured a curious rebel flag during the fight. Lieutenant James Hadden noted that it had thirteen red and white stripes, as well as a "constellation." This is believed to be the first time that Americans carried the Stars and Stripes into battle.

Dr. Thacher had a most unexpected and welcome surprise when the victorious American party returned to Fort Ann:

> One [British] surgeon, with a wounded captain and twelve or fifteen privates, were taken and brought into our fort. The surgeon informed me that he was in possession of books, etc., taken from my chest at Skenesborough. Some of the British prisoners obtained in the same manner had in their pockets a number of private letters which I had received from a friend in Massachusetts, and which were now returned to me.

General Schuyler was on his way from Albany to Fort Edward, a few miles south of Fort Ann. He sent ahead an order to burn the stockade Fort Ann, and fall back to Fort Edward. There the boat party should await the arrival of St. Clair's division.

* * * * *

While Burgoyne had been pursuing the American boat party up South Bay on July 6th, St. Clair and the main body of Americans were marching eastward on the Military Road from Mount Independence into Vermont. In an effort "to harass their rear," General Simon Fraser was pursuing them with 800 British troops and a handful of Tories and Indians, followed by 1100 Germans under Baron Riedesel. Fraser had tried to bring along artillery but soon found the newly cut Military Road, with its countless roots and stumps, was "impassable for any sort of carriage." He marched his men at a fast pace from 4 a.m. to 1 p.m. on a "very hot and sultry day, over a continued succession of steep and woody hills." The dense foliage of the forest cut off all air circulation, making the heat and humidity almost unbearable.

After consulting with Riedesel, Fraser pushed on again at 3 p.m., not stopping until dark, when the exhausted troops finally made camp, nearly twenty miles from Ticonderoga. The Germans, slowed by their heavier equipment, camped a few miles behind the British. Fraser had refused to wait for provisions to be sent across the lake before he set out from Mount Independence, so Lieutenant Digby remembered that day's march as a hungry one: "We continued the pursuit the whole day without any sort of provisions, excepting one cow we happened to kill in the woods, which, without bread, was next to nothing among so many."

Three miles ahead of Fraser's camp, St. Clair had halted briefly at a point where the Military Road joined the older road from Crown Point to Castleton. This was Hubbardton, a hamlet of just nine families. There he learned that Tories and Indians had been in the area that day, and carried off a few settlers before moving on toward Castleton. St. Clair wondered if they were the vanguard of a larger force of British or Germans coming down the road from Crown Point.

The militia regiments' officers made it clear to St. Clair that, despite their weariness, they wanted to put as many miles as possible between themselves and the known enemy pursuing them on the Military Road. So St. Clair set most of the column in motion again, heading for Castleton. But he ordered Seth Warner to stay at the Hubbardton crossroads with his Green Mountain Boys regiment. He told Warner to wait for Nathan Hale's New Hampshire regiment to come up with the sick and other stragglers; and also for Ebenezer Francis's Massachusetts regiment, which had been the rear guard until now. Seth Warner, familiar with the territory, would be in charge of this new enlarged rear guard of about 1100 men. When the others came up, Warner was to immediately continue the march to Castleton.

However, when Francis and Hale arrived and held a council with Warner in the lone farmhouse at the crossroads, a decision was made to disobey St. Clair's order. They would let their exhausted men - many of them too sick to continue - encamp for the night. The three continental regiments spread out atop the low hill where the roads crossed, Hale on the right facing the enemy's approach, Francis in the middle, and Warner on the left. One company, detached from Hale's New Hampshire regiment, guarded the 300 stragglers, camped in the hollow between the foot of the hill and Sucker Brook. Before bedding down, Warner ordered sentries to post themselves back on the Military Road a half mile from camp to watch for the approach of the enemy on the Military Road. He also sent a party of 200 men up the Crown Point Road "to bring off settlers" and watch for any enemy forces coming from that direction.

General Fraser had his Regulars awake and marching again by 3 a.m. Shortly before 5 a.m. his platoon of Tories and Indians "descryed the enemy's centrys, who fired and joined the main body." Fraser halted his force of 850 to gather intelligence, sending scouting parties wide to the left of the rebel camp. By the time they reported back, about 6:30, the rebel detachment had returned from their scout of the Crown Point Road. Their arrival was interpreted by Fraser as the forerunner of even more reinforcements from this, "the most disaffected part of America." This was the reason, he explained in a letter to a friend, that he decided to reject the prudent approach of waiting for Riedesel to come up. Perhaps another factor in Fraser's decision to initiate the combat right away was his desire to fight his own battle, for he wrote that he "felt much hurt and embarrased by a senior officer" being sent to support him.

So Fraser deployed his forces to the left and right and marched down to Sucker Brook, where a small party of Hale's men were manning a crude abatis - trees felled in such a way that their branches pointed toward the approaching enemy.

Major Robert Grant had command of Fraser's vanguard that made the inital charge across Sucker Brook. Twenty years before, as an American militia officer, Grant had marched over virtually the same ground on his way to fight alongside the British against the French at Crown Point. Thomas Anburey explains:

> This gallant and brave officer fell victim to the great disadvantages we experience peculiar to this unfortunate contest, opposing expert riflemen. Upon his coming up with the enemy, he got upon the stump of a tree to reconnoitre, and had hardly given the men orders to fire when he was struck by a rifle ball, fell off the tree, and never uttered another syllable.

After this initial skirmish, the defenders retreated up the slope to join their main body on the American right. This left only the 300 sick and stragglers in the hollow below the American left, guarded by Captain Carr's company from Hale's regiment. Among the stragglers was Ebenezer Fletcher, the sixteen-year-old fifer from New Hampshire, who was recovering from the measles. He later recalled the surprise attack:

> The morning after the retreat, orders came very early for the troops to refresh and be ready for marching.

Some were eating, some were cooking and all in a very unfit posture for battle. Just as the sun rose there was a cry, "The enemy are upon us." Looking around, I saw the enemy in line of battle.

Orders came to lay down our packs and be ready for action. The fire instantly began. We were but few in number compared to the enemy at the commencement of the battle, and many of our party retreated into the woods. Captain Carr came up and says, "My lads, advance, we shall beat them yet." A few of us followed him in view of the enemy. Every man was trying to secure himself behind girdled trees which were standing on the place of action.

Like the others, young Fletcher "made shelter" for himself and fired his musket at the oncoming enemy. He reloaded and took aim again, but this time it misfired. Before he could attempt a third try he "received a ball" in the small of his back. He was carried back some distance and laid down behind a large tree.

By this time I had bled so freely I was very weak and faint. I observed the enemy were likely to gain the ground. Our men began to retreat and the enemy to advance. Having no friend to help me, and everyone taking care of himself, all things looked very shocking to me. To remain where I was and fall into the hands of the enemy, especially in the condition I was in, I expected no mercy. It came into my mind to conceal myself from them. I crawled about two rods among some small brush and hid myself under a log.

Here I lay concealed from the enemy, who came instantly to the place where I lay. Two of the enemy came so nigh I heard one of them say, "Here is one of the Rebels." They pulled off my shoes, supposing me to be dead. I looked up and spoke, telling them I was their prisoner, and begged to be used well. "Damn you," says one, "you deserve to be used well, don't you? What's such a young rebel as you fighting for?"

One of these men was an officer, who appeared to be a pretty sort of man. He spoke to the soldier who had taken my shoes, and said, "Give back the shoes and help the men into camp." ... Here [behind the British lines] I found a number of my brother soldiers in the same situation as myself.

When the British had burst out of the woods, Warner, Francis and Hale had just ordered their respective regiments to form for the day's march. So when the British infantry reached the crest of the slope they found, to their surprise, their enemy already formed and ready for them. These troops presented the British with such a concentrated volley that twenty-one men fell and the rest fled back down the slope, not stopping until they had recrossed the brook. One unfortunate officer named Douglas "as he was carried off the field wounded, received a ball directly through his heart."

Lieutenant William Digby was one of the Regulars who had charged the hill:

> With the greatest steadiness and resolution, [we] mounted the hill amidst showers of balls mixed with buck shot, which they plentifully bestowed amongst us. This being the first serious engagement I had ever been in, I must own, when we received orders to prime and load, which we had barely time to do before we received a heavy fire, the idea of perhaps a few moments conveying me before the presence of my Creator had its force; but ... [I did] my duty as a soldier, as I have always made it a rule that a proper resignation to the will of the Divine Being is the certain foundation for true bravery.

Just after the battle began, a courier from St. Clair reined in his horse and informed Warner that the British had taken Skenesborough, so the rendezvous site must be changed. St. Clair's new route would be much longer, as he would have to swing further east, to Rutland, before heading south through Manchester and finally west to Fort Edward. For the moment, though, Warner had enough on his mind.

Fraser soon realized he was in for a tough fight. The Americans' position on higher ground, and their officers' ability to rally and lead their men, had neutralized his initial advantage of surprise. He decided to try flanking them. He detached about half his entire force - his light infantry company, and the grenadier regiment under Major John Dyke Acland. They moved off through the woods to the right. To make the maneuver less noticeable, only one company was detached at a time. If they succeeded, they would be in a position to bring "enfilade" (from the side) fire down upon the entire American line. And they would prevent the Americans from escaping to join their main army by "gaining the road, which leads to Castleton and Skenesborough."

The flanking party reached the road without being seen. But, as they formed there, part of Warner's Vermont regiment came running to meet them. For Fraser had inadvertently caused Warner to shift part of his forces: Fraser had moved two of his own companies in the hollow slightly to the right, to keep Warner from flanking him. Warner had observed this and suspected it was a flanking maneuver, so he had moved part of his own forces further to his left to counter it. It was these troops who soon discovered the real flanking party - Acland's grenadiers.

The grenadiers formed and charged with bayonets fixed. Refusing to panic, the Vermonters repelled the first charge. When the second charge came, they fell back into the woods. Now the Green Mountain Boys were in their element. Each man acted on his own, firing from behind a tree and, when necessary, retreating to another tree to reload. They darted in and out of the trees so much that some of the British officers thought their numbers were twice what they really were. By contrast, for the British, who were not used to woods fighting, "the woods were so thick that no order could be observed in advancing upon the enemy, it being totally impossible to form a regular line." Their training in formation maneuvers, mass volleying, etc., was useless in the woods, and Warner was able to successfully counter this attempt to turn his position.

Our "gentleman volunteer," Thomas Anburey, was with the grenadiers, and later reflected on the art of warfare with small arms:

> In this action I found all manual exercise is but an ornament, and the only object of importance was loading, firing, and charging with bayonets. As soon as they had primed their pieces and put the cartridges into the barrel, instead of ramming it down with their rods, they struck the butt end of their piece upon the ground, and bringing it to the present, fired it off.
>
> The confusion of a man's ideas during the time of action, brave as he may be, is undoubtedly great; several of the men, after all was over, found ... [in their muskets] cartridges which they were positive to the having discharged.

The battle raged back and forth for an hour and a half, with Riedesel's 1100 Germans still nowhere in sight. Fraser's men were suffering heavy casualties and found themselves in danger of being outflanked, for Colonel Francis had decided the time was ripe to take the offensive. He sent part of his own regiment circling around to the right in an effort to flank Fraser's line of infantry. This attempt looked like it would succeed, until the Germans began arriving.

Riedesel had earlier sent back word to his grenadiers to quicken their pace, while he personally led the "jager" (rifle) company and 80 light infantry upon "a rapid march of a quarter of an hour." They "arrived, terribly heated, upon an eminence from which could be seen the contending forces." Now he received another message from

205

Fraser, "that he feared his left wing would be surrounded." Riedesel sent a return message, informing Fraser "that he was about to attack the enemy's right wing." He sent his 80 light infantry into the woods to circle wide to the left and flank the American flankers. He also ordered his 100 jagers to move forward and support the British infantry on the slope at the center of the battle.

Riedesel, furious over the slow progress of the main body of his troops, was heard "pouring forth every imprecation against his troops for not arriving." Riedesel "ordered a band of music to lead the jaegers," so that the Americans would think a much larger column was arriving. The Germans also "began singing hymns on their advance." According to a British officer, the jagers kept on coming, singing and firing by platoons. He was generous enough to credit them with "keeping up an incessant fire which totally decided the fate of the day."

By now, Francis and Hale had fallen back behind a log fence just beyond the Crown Point Road and their men stopped there to reload. While the American and German flanking parties were running into each other in the nearby woods, Francis and Hale repelled two advances by the British infantry, under Major Alexander Leslie, the Earl of Balcarres. "We drove them back twice," wrote Joseph Bird, an American private, "by cutting them down so fast. We didn't leave the log fence or charge them. They couldn't drive us from the fence until they charged us" with bayonets. This was after the American right - the flanking party - "gave way."

In the face of the united British-German bayonet charge, Francis and Hale had their men fall back through a wheatfield, then up the slopes of Pittsford Ridge, toward Rutland. After crossing the wheatfield, each man "took a tree and waited for them to come within shot. We fought through the woods, all the way to the ridge of Pittsford mountain, popping away from behind trees." By now, Acland's grenadiers had enveloped Warner on the American left and forced him to retreat up the ridge, too. The grenadiers "slung their firelocks" over their shoulders and used both hands to climb up the steep ascent in order to gain the summit before the Americans. The battle continued for another hour along the ridge.

Two-thirds of the Americans reached Rutland, and eventually joined St. Clair south of Skenesborough a week later. Colonel Francis would not make it, though, as Joseph Bird explains:

> Col Francis told me to take off my pack. I replied that I could fight with it on. He said, "I tell you to take it off." At this time smoke was so thick we did not see the enemy until they fired. There being some scattering firing, Francis told the soldiers not to fire, they were firing on their own men. Then came a British volley and Francis fell dead.

During the confused retreat up the ridge, Colonel Hale and 70 of his men were captured when a small party of the enemy, pretending to be bigger than their numbers, tricked them into surrendering. While a prisoner of war, Hale learned that accounts published in the newspapers accused him of cowardice in being taken. Hale wrote to Washington, asking to be exchanged, so he could vindicate himself at a court-martial. But before it could be arranged he died on a British prison ship in 1780.

From his bivouac outside Castleton, St. Clair had faintly heard the firing. He set out to aid Warner, after much wrangling with some of his officers, who objected that he would be playing into the hands of an enemy force of unknown strength. According to Major Wilkinson, there was "a manifest repugnance in the corps to turn about and march upon the enemy; even one of the Brigadiers was open in his opposition to the measure."

Two militia regiments had fallen behind the night before and were camped only two miles south of the battle site. St. Clair dispatched two aides on horses with an order for those regiments to start back toward Hubbardton and join the battle, assuring them that the main body was on the way. The aides, approaching the militia, saw that they were already on the move. But they were going away, rather than toward, the sounds of battle, as fast as they could go. They refused to listen to St. Clair's aides or even their own officers. The two aides rode on toward the battle alone, determined to at least gather intelligence.

Marching north toward Hubbardton, St. Clair met the militia. They spread their panic to his main body of troops, as did some early refugees from the battle. Soon the two aides returned to announce that the battle was over and the rear guard had scattered. With no choice left now, St. Clair headed for Rutland, eventually joining Schuyler at Fort Edward five days later. It was a difficult trek, as one of the New Hampshire men a week later related in a letter to Colonel John Stark:

> Indians took & killed a vast number of our men on their retreats; then [we] was hurried at an unmerciful rate thro' the woods at the rate of thirty five miles a day, obliged to kill oxen belonging to the inhabitants wherever we got them; before they were half-skinned every soldier was obliged to take a bit and half roast it over the fire, then before half done was oblidged to march - it is thought we went 100 miles for fear of seeing a Regular.

Hubbardton had been a bitterly contested battle, and a bloody one. The Americans suffered 12 percent in killed and wounded, and another 20 percent in captured. British and German killed and wounded totaled about 20 percent, with none captured. Their heavy losses convinced Fraser and Riedesel to temporarily call off the chase.

Ebenezer Fletcher, the fifer from New Hampshire captured in the early action, had the musket ball taken out of his back by a British surgeon and his mate.

> They pulled several pieces of my clothing from my wound, which were forced in by the ball I received. Some of the enemy were very kind, while others were very spiteful and malicious. One of them came and took

my silver shoe-buckles and left me an old pair of brass ones, and said, "Exchange is no robbery." But I thought robbery at a high rate. Another one came and took off my neck handkerchief. An old Negro came and took my fife, which I considered as the greatest insult I had received while with the enemy. The Indians came and often abused me with their language, calling us Yankees and rebels; but they were not allowed to injure us. The officers would flatter me to 'list in their service; telling me they were very sure to conquer the country, since they had got our strongest post. I told them I should not 'list.

Fletcher, and the other wounded from both sides who were too weak to march, remained with a small British guard near the battlefield for over two weeks, before horses and carts finally arrived from Ticonderoga. This period of waiting was an anxious one for the British soldiers, who constantly expected to be attacked by rebels they thought might be lurking in the area. The night after the battle was especially terrifying, since they were kept awake by the sounds of a large pack of wolves devouring the dead on the battlefield. Their bones were left to bleach in the sun until, seven years later, they were collected and ceremoniously interred by the local inhabitants.

On a dark night two weeks later, Ebenezer Fletcher made his escape. After wandering, lost in the wilderness, and barely avoiding being turned over to the British by local Tories, he finally reached his home in Ipswich, New Hampshire. On his arrival, he was promptly accused of desertion and sent back to his regiment.

The British volunteer, Thomas Anburey later reflected on the battle, and concluded, "This was a strange sort of war." Anburey had been shocked by an incident that occurred on Pittsford Ridge almost two hours after the battle had ended:

A number of officers were collected to read the papers taken out of the pocket-book of Colonel Francis, when Captain Shrimpton of the 62nd Regiment, who had the papers in his hand, jumped up and fell, exclaiming he was severely wounded. We all heard the ball whiz by us, and turning to the place from whence the report came, saw the smoke from some tree. A party of men were instantly detached, but could find no person; the fellow, no doubt, as soon as he had fired had slipped down and made his escape.

Ten months later, while prisoners of war in Massachusetts, Anburey and some other officers who had been at Hubbardton experienced one of those strange twists of fate that sometimes happen in wartime.

Walking out with some officers, we stopped at a house to purchase vegetables. Whilst the other officers were bargaining with the woman of the house, I observed an elderly woman sitting by the fire, who was continually eyeing us, and every now and then shedding a tear. Just as we were quitting the house she got up, and bursting into tears, said: "Gentlemen, will you let a poor distracted woman speak a word to you before you go?" Upon inquiring what she wanted, with the most poignant grief and sobbing as if her heart was on the point of breaking, [she] asked if any of us knew her son, who was killed at the battle of Huberton, a Colonel Francis. Serveral of us informed her, that we had seen him after he was dead. She then inquired about his pocket-book, and if any of his papers were safe, as some related to his estates, and if any of the soldiers had got his watch; if she could but obtain that in remembrance of her dear, dear son, she should be happy. Captain Ferguson told her, as to the colonel's papers and pocket-book he was fearful that they were either lost or destroyed, but pulling a watch from his fob, said, "There, good woman, if that can make you happy, take it and God bless you!"

We were all much surprised, as unacquainted [that] he had made a purchase of it from a drum boy. On seeing it, it is impossible to describe the joy and grief that was depicted in her countenance; I never in all my life beheld such a strength of passion. She kissed it, looked unutterable gratitude at Captain Ferguson, then kissed it again; her feelings were inexpressible. She could only sob her thanks. Our feelings were lifted up to an inexpressible height. We promised to search after the papers, and I believe, at that moment, could have hazarded life itself to procure them.

* * * * *

The news of Ticonderoga's capture reached London in early September. An exuberant King George III burst into the Queen's apartment, yelling, "I have beat them - beat all the Americans!" It was reported that "Lord George Germain announced the event in Parliament as if it had been decisive of the campaign and of the fate of the colonies." What could possibly stop Burgoyne from reaching the Hudson now? By contrast, in Paris the news was a setback to Benjamin Franklin's ongoing efforts to coax the French into an alliance against Great Britain.

Back in America, meanwhile, Burgoyne had celebrated his victories on July 10th with a *feu de joie* from his artillery at Crown Point, Ticonderoga, Skenesborough and Castleton. But fire of a different sort was being spoken in Philadelphia, where angry congressmen were seeking scapegoats. One blamed the "shameful business" upon placing the New England troops under the command of "Scotch officers [St. Clair] and others in whom even less confidence is to be placed." A New Hampshire congressman declared that Yankees "can do better with oak saplings under officers in whom we can confide, than with the best arms when commanded by cowards and traitors." John Adams expressed his disgust privately in a letter to his wife, "I think we shall never be able to defend a post until we shoot a general."

On July 14th, St. Clair gave his side of the story in a letter he sent to his father-in-law in Boston. In an excerpt from it, published in the Boston Gazette, he predicted that "by abandoning a post I [will] eventually save a state." The publisher added in italics "Believe it who may." Newspaper editors felt the public wanted either heroes or martyrs, not pragmatists. The Connecticut Courant published extracts from the journal of Pittsfield's Reverend Thomas Allen. He had preached, just five hours before the evacuation, an ardent call for the garrison at Ti to fight to the last man. While on the discouraging retreat through Vermont he wrote, "Oh how happy had these states been [compared] to what they now are, had we been half slain in a glorious defence of that fortress, and the other half captivated."

A writer declared, in the New York Journal, that "fear was treason," and if St. Clair had possessed "a noble and heroic soul" he would have preferred to be "gloriously unfortunate," rather than "spin out the remainder of his life in obscurity, derision and contempt." St. Clair, however, had no intention of spinning out his life that way. He wrote to General Washington, requesting a court-martial. St. Clair eventually was granted his wish and was exonerated. Ten years later, he would become president of Congress, and after that would be the first governor of the Northwest Territories.

Though St. Clair was the most convenient scapegoat, Schuyler was also blamed for the disaster. The bad news from the north resurrected the Gates faction in Congress, and before long that body was again debating whether Gates should be sent north to command the Northern Department. A popular rumor said that St. Clair and Schuyler had sold their loyalty to Burgoyne and arranged for the British to fire silver bullets into the fort, which St. Clair collected and shared with Schuyler. Some people accused Schuyler of not supplying the fort with enough men and materials; others accused him of supplying it too well, so there would be that much more to lose upon evacuation.

Schuyler, of course, blamed the loss of Ticonderoga and Mount Independence on the New England states. Typically, he refused to accept any responsibility, pointing out that he had never given St. Clair written instructions to evacuate the fort. He naturally kept quiet about his June 20 council where the contingency plans to retreat were formulated. Schuyler even wrote confidently to Washington that he would "go on smiling with contempt on the malice of my enemies, and attempt to deserve your esteem, which will console me for the abuse which thousands may unjustly throw out against me."

Hurrying to Fort Edward to take personal command of the army, the much maligned Philip Schuyler was determined to try his best to prevent Burgoyne from reaching Albany. But could he do it? That was now the question on everyone's mind. As one officer put it, "Without speedy and effectual support [the army] will not be able to maintain themselves, & if running comes in vogue I know not where they may stop."

CHAPTER NINE
DRUMS ALONG THE MOHAWK,
JULY - AUGUST 1777

"Tell the garrison not to make a Ticonderoga of it, but be courageous."

> *- Oneida Indian chiefs, to the*
> *Committee of Safety.*

The reader may recall that General Burgoyne's plan for seizing the Hudson River included a diversion along the Mohawk River. While Burgoyne was concentrating on Ticonderoga, a separate force was to row up the St. Lawrence River to the fur trading post of Oswego, on Lake Ontario's southern shore. Reinforced by Indians, they would march eastward, through the Iroquois country west of New York's frontier settlements, to the Mohawk River. After overcoming any rebel opposition thrown in their way, they would move downriver to the Hudson and cut off Ticonderoga's supply line. Along the way, they would encourage the substantial loyalist population of the Mohawk Valley to rise up and secure that part of the country for the King. Once this second British army reached the Hudson, the rebel northern army would be caught between two British armies.

Chosen to lead the expedition was 40-year-old Lieutenant-Colonel Barry St. Leger, a personal friend of Burgoyne's from previous campaigns. Eager to execute his part of Burgoyne's grand plan, he set out from Montreal on June 23rd with what troops and light field pieces were available, not waiting for the 200 additional Germans and several heavier guns that were delayed. They would follow as soon as they could.

St. Leger arrived at Oswego on July 15 with the non-Indian half of his army: 200 British infantrymen, 80 German jagers, 400 American Tories, and 30 artillerists to serve the two 6-pounders, two 3-pounders and four 4-inch mortars (known as "cohorns" or "royals"). Also along for the march were about 100 French Canadian "batmen" and "sappers" to help row and pole the bateaux, haul supplies, and "sap" (dig trenches) if necessary.

The 400 Tories were nearly all refugees from the Mohawk Valley. A year or two earlier they had left their homes and, in many cases, their families, and enlisted in the new loyalist, or Tory, regiments then being formed in Canada: the "Royal Greens" under Sir John Johnson, and the "King's Rangers" under John Butler. Johnson was the son of the late Indian Superintendent, Sir William Johnson, who had kept the Iroquois on the British side during the last war. Johnson, Butler and these other loyalists from the Mohawk Valley were even more eager than St. Leger. This expedition offered them the chance to avenge their former neighbors and take back their homes, restoring their lives to what they had been before the war.

Close to a thousand Iroquois warriors joined St. Leger at Oswego, swelling his total fighting force to 1700. They were given muskets, new tomahawks, and brass kettles by the hundreds as gifts, and promised eight dollars for each scalp taken.

St. Leger's first objective - the only serious obstacle in his path to the Hudson - was Fort Stanwix (present city of Rome, New York). Located about thirty miles west of the German Flats, in 1777 it was the western-most white settlement in the Mohawk Valley. At Oswego, St. Leger learned that earlier reports, saying the fort was in disrepair and defended by only sixty men, were no longer true. He had hoped for a quick march which would catch the American garrison by surprise before news of his arrival at Oswego could reach Albany and spur American reinforcements.

At this critical point, St. Leger had two choices: wait for the additional troops and heavier artillery to come up from Montreal, or order the advance without them. Having received word that Ticonderoga had already fallen, St. Leger did not want to risk any delay that might allow Burgoyne to reach Albany without him. Also, like most British officers, he was filled with contempt for the fighting ability of an un-professional army of provincials; he was confident Fort Stanwix's defenders would either surrender to him or evacuate before he arrived. He therefore set out immediately from Owsego. Complete with flank-ers plus advance and rear guards, the army marched cautiously but swiftly through the virgin forests and swamps, averaging over ten miles a day, and steadily approaching its objective.

Fort Stanwix was a square fortress of logs and earth, with 15-foot thick walls surrounded by a 10-foot deep trench. Built in 1758 by a British general named Stanwix, it guarded a portage between the Mohawk River and Wood Creek. Wood Creek flowed west into Lake Oneida, from which the Onondaga River led to Lake Ontario. This had been one of the routes used by the British in their attack on Canada in 1759. In 1776, it was renamed Fort Schuyler, but over the years the former name has regained popular usage to distinguish it from another Fort Schuyler (on the site of present day Utica).

Despite rumors of a British expedition into the region, a general apathy (or, in Schuyler's words, a "pusillanimous spirit") prevailed in the Mohawk Valley. Calls for the Tryon County (western Mohawk Valley) militia to turn out and reinforce the continentals at the fort met with minimal success. Schuyler feared that the inhabitants would be "inclined to lay down their arms and take whatever terms the enemy may please to afford them."

Fortunately, the garrison was replaced in May by Colonel Peter Gansevoort's regiment. Gansevoort, a relatively inexperienced aristo-crat from Albany, and his second in command, Lt.-Colonel Marinus Willett, a poor but fiery young New Yorker, brought a refreshing spirit and determination. All during the hot days of June and July they pushed their troops hard to make the fort capable of withstanding a siege. At first they were hampered by their engineer, yet another vol-unteer from France who Congress had commissioned and forced upon the army. Instead of improving the fort itself, he wasted much time and manpower constructing useless outworks, including barracks over a hundred yards from the fort. Finally, Gansevoort had him arrested and sent back to General Schuyler at Albany.

Besides improving the fort, Gansevoort took Schuyler's advice and sent detachments west to fell trees and in other ways block up Wood Creek so that St. Leger would have difficulty bringing up his artillery and supplies. Schuyler was doing the same thing about 110 miles to the east to slow Burgoyne's advance.

Evidence of St. Leger's approach became more common as July progressed. Anyone outside the fort became susceptible to attack by his Indian scouts. Incidents like the one here related in a Gansevoort letter demonstrated to the garrison and the people of Tryon County what might happen to them if they did not stop St. Leger.

> Yesterday at 3 o'clock in the afternoon, our garrison was alarmed with the firing of four guns. A party of men was instantly dispatched to the place where the guns were fired, which was in the edge of the woods, about 500 yards from the fort; but they were too late. The villains were fled, after having shot three girls who were out picking raspberries, two of whom were lying scalped and tomahawked, one dead, the other expiring, who died in about half an hour after she was brought home. The third had two balls through her shoulder, but made her escape; her wounds are not thought danger- ous. By the best discoveries we have made, there were four Indians who perpetuated these murders. I had four men with arms just passed that place, but these merce- naries of Britain came not to fight but to lie in wait to murder. It is equally the same to them, if they can get a scalp, whether it is from a soldier or an innocent babe.

One of the girls was the daughter of a recently retired British artil- lery officer who had been stationed as a guard and caretaker at the fort for many years. In a similar incident the week before, Corporal Madison and Captain Gregg, desiring fresh venison, "went out a gunning, contrary to orders." Surprised by two Indians, they were each shot, Madison fatally, and both scalped. Gregg had the presence of mind and fortitude to feign death and not utter a sound while he was being scalped. Several hours later his dog led some men who were fishing in the vicinity to him and he was carried into the fort. He was later sent downriver with the wives, children and other men too sick for duty. Incredibly, he recovered and led his company against the Iroquois during many a campaign later in the war, causing quite a commotion whenever he doffed his cap for the benefit of new recruits.

Because of the influence of a missionary, Samuel Kirkland, the Oneidas - one of the six nations of the Iroquois Confederacy - had given a pledge of neutrality to Schuyler. Now they were risking the wrath of their fellow Iroquois by scouting and providing intelligence to Gansevoort and the Tryon County Committee of Safety. Thomas Spencer, a half-breed Oneida blacksmith, wrote to the Committee on July 29, informing them that St. Leger's main force would likely reach the fort within four days.

Spencer also brought word from the Oneida chiefs: "Tell the garrison not to make a Ticonderoga of it, but be courageous," and tell the committee to "let the militia rise up and come." But Spencer also warned the committee that the militia should "take care on their march, as there is a party of Indians to stop the road below the fort, about 80 or 100."

Indeed, St. Leger had sent out a party of Indians, for his own scouts had informed him that a convoy of rebel bateaux, loaded with supplies and reinforcements, was making its way upriver. He had sent forth a lieutenant with a handful of Regulars and 100 Indians to push ahead and intercept them. Inside the fort, Lieutenant William Colbrath recorded in his journal that night the almost simultaneous arrival of the boat party and the enemy's advance party:

Aug 2d. Four batteaus arrived, having a guard of 100

men, from Fort Dayton. The lading being brought safe into the fort, the guard marched in; when our centinels on the S.W. bastion discovered the enemy's fire in the woods. The troops ran to their respective alarm posts. In this time we discovered some men running from the landing towards the garrison.

On their coming they informed us that the batteau men who had staid behind when the guard marched into the fort had been fired on by the enemy at the landing, that two of them were wounded, the master of the batteaus taken prisoner and one man missing. A party of 30 men with a field piece was sent out in the evening to set fire to two barns standing a little distance from the fort. Two cannon from the S.W. bastion loaded with grape shott were fired at the barnes to drive off the enemy's Indians that might have been sculking about them.

St. Leger believed that the rebels would surrender on first sight of his forces. So, to prevent the massacre of the rebel garrison by his Indians, he had given his lieutenant in charge of the advance party specific orders: begin the siege, but should the rebel commander "offer to capitulate, you are to tell them that you are sure I am well disposed to listen to them [as soon as I arrive]." St. Leger misjudged Colonel Gansevoort, who had no intention of capitulating.

St. Leger arrived the next day, August third. After marching his entire force of 1700 in full view of the fort, he sent forward a messenger carrying a flag of truce and a proclamation. According to one of the defenders, it offered them "protection if the garrison wou'd surrender." It "was rejected with disdain."

The garrison was in an unreceptive mood. Their spirits had been fortified by the previous day's reinforcements, and by a homemade flag. Pieced together just that morning, it was now proudly flying in the face of the enemy. It had been made "by cutting the white stripes from a shirt, and the red ones from the petticoat of a soldier's wife, using the blue cloak of Captain Abraham Swartout to make a field upon which to display the new constellation." Lieutenant Colbrath noted that when the "Continental Flagg was hoisted" early that morning, "a cannon levelled at the enemies camp was fired on the occasion."

Lieutenant-Colonel Marinus Willett's account of the siege mentions St. Leger's first call for surrender, as well as the hazards the men faced the next day, as they piled strips of sod on top of the fort's ramparts:

[Sunday, August 3] They sent in a flag, who told us of their great power, strength, and determination in such a manner as gave us reason to suppose they were not possessed of strength sufficient to take the fort. Our answer was a determination to support it.

All day on Monday we were much annoyed by a sharp fire of musketry from the Indians and German rifle-men which, as our men were obliged to be exposed on the works, killed one and wounded seven. ... This evening [August 5] indicated something in contemplation by the enemy. The Indians were uncommonly noisy; they made most horrid yellings great part of the night.

The Indians were dancing, drinking and painting themselves in preparation for battle. A runner had arrived from the east, informing St. Leger that the militia had finally been raised and were on the march to relieve the fort. The runner was sent by Molly Brant, Sir William Johnson's widow and sister to the Mohawk war-chief Thayendenagea, known to whites as Joseph Brant.

The intelligence about the approach of rebel reinforcements added to the discouragement St. Leger was feeling. He had been greatly surprised and disappointed that Gansevoort had refused to immediately surrender, and the siege so far had not been going well. The rebel commander's "mulish obstinacy" showed no signs of weakening. Just when St. Leger needed his Regulars on hand to oppose the approaching militia column, they were not available - he had sent them back along Wood Creek to bring up the rest of the light artillery and supplies. Even when the guns arrived, they would be too small to break down the fort's walls, unless he could move them up to point-blank range. And, on top of all this, his Indian allies were giving him problems. They were already disenchanted, and threatened to go home. The chiefs reminded St. Leger that they had come here to watch the Regulars beat the rebels. They were not willing to play the fool (like so many white leaders) and order their warriors to assault a strongly defended fort.

St. Leger was compounding his problems by contemptuously ignoring the advice of his subordinates. And he was rarely sober, according to the leader of the Canadian batmen and sappers, who later wrote an epic comic poem about the expedition. In its foreward, the Canadian explained that "M. St. Leger alienated himself from those whom he commanded, by haughtiness and by the little consideration that he had for them, until he was drunk, and that was nearly continual."

Nevertheless, St. Leger knew he must rise to the occasion somehow. So he called a council of his officers, including "Captain" Joseph Brant, war chief of the Iroquois. He finally settled on a plan to stop the militia's advance, as he explained three weeks later in his offical report to General Burgoyne:

> On the 5th, in the evening, intelligence arrived that a reinforcement of eight hundred militia conducted by General Herkimer were on the march to relieve the garrison and were actually at that instant at Oriska, an Indian settlement twelve miles from the fort. I determined to attack them on the march. At this time I had not two hundred and fifty of the King's troops in camp, and therefore could not send above eighty white men with the Indians.

St. Leger demanded that Joseph Brant persuade the other chiefs in camp to have their warriors help the Tories lay the ambush. Otherwise, he threatened, no more boatloads of gifts would ever again make their way to the tribes. After much persuasion, the chiefs agreed.

Brant selected the site for the ambush, six miles east of the fort. Here the King's Road from Albany descended sharply fifty feet into a wide, heavily wooded ravine that was fairly flat for several hunred yards before rising sharply again at the western end and continuing on to the fort. "The bottom of this ravine was marshy and the road crossed it by means of a causeway" of logs laid crossways, known as a "corduroy" road. Towering hemlocks overhead made even a bright day seem like dusk along the corduroy road.

The 80 Tories and perhaps 800 Indians reached the site before dawn and were ordered by Brant, the other chiefs, and Colonel Butler of the King's Rangers to hide themselves within easy shooting range of the log causeway. They lay down, many of them still drunk from the rum St. Leger had freely provided the evening before, and waited for the approaching column. The Indians were evenly spread out on both sides of the road all the way to the western slope of the ravine, where the Rangers and Mohawks would cover the exit leading to the fort. The other, eastern slope was left open to allow the militia column to march down into the ravine. However, once the whole column was inside, the entrance would be sealed off and the trap sprung.

Colonel Butler, not wanting to see his former neighbors and friends slaughtered needlessly, proposed to Brant, that when the militia column was in the trap, he be allowed to call out to General Herkimer and give him a chance to surrender without bloodshed. Brant and the other chiefs would not listen to such a suggestion. They felt it would take away the advantage of surprise, and they suspected Herkimer would rather fight it out, if given the choice.

Though the residents of Tryon County had been largely apathetic earlier, the arrival of St. Leger's army (especially his Indian allies) had been enough to stir up the militia. Their general, Nicholas Herkimer, was a prosperous local farmer of German descent. He had issued a call to arms for all able-bodied men between the ages of 16 and 60, threatening imprisonment for all "shirkers." By August fourth, over

800 men had collected at Fort Dayton in the community of German Flats (present day city of Herkimer). They had set out at a swift pace and by the evening of the fifth were camped at Oriska, an abandoned Indian village twelve miles from their destination.

At Oriska, Herkimer dispatched four runners, all local men who knew the trails through the woods, to sneak past the enemy and through the "impenetrable swamp" bordering one side of Fort Stanwix. They were to inform Colonel Gansevoort of Herkimer's approach, and ask him to signal receipt of the message by firing three cannon and follow it up with an attack on St. Leger's camp. This would scatter the enemy and increase the militia's chances of making it into the fort.

The morning of August sixth found the strong but normally quiet 56-year-old General Herkimer in a heated argument with his three younger colonels. These subordinates were all hotheads anxious to push on as rapidly as possible and play the hero's part in this drama. Herkimer repeatedly cautioned them that more reinforcements should be coming up shortly, and that it would be wise to wait for the three gun signal from the fort. When they implied that his caution was actually masked cowardice, he calmly predicted that they would be the first to run when the enemy made their appearance. The morning dragged on, and the three impatient officers accused Herkimer of lacking a true spirit for the cause (his brother was known to be a captain in the King's Rangers and serving under St. Leger). Finally, irritated, and perhaps fearing a large scale mutiny, Herkimer responded by shouting the order, "March on!"

The long column quickly formed and rushed forward. Some accounts say they marched in files five deep, preceded by an advanced guard, with flanking parties on each side. Others say they marched without such ordinary precautions. All agree, however, that when they reached the ravine there were no flanking parties, because of the swamp and thick brush.

By ten o'clock, two Oneida scouts, trotting a short distance ahead of the column, reached the eastern slope of the ravine. After momentarily pausing to listen, they plunged into the ravine and passed over the long causeway. However, as they climbed the western slope a dozen Mohawks suddenly leaped out of hiding and silenced them before they could fire a warning shot.

Soon the column, with the mounted General Herkimer at its head, made its way down the eastern slope. As it progressed along the dark corduroy road, many men stopped to drink from the creek, then hurried back to their places in line. On both sides of them lay hundreds of men, cramped from holding the same position for hours, stoically ignoring the buzzing, crawling, stinging insects, intent only on remaining motionless until the attack signal was given. For some of the Tories, this was a critical moment. They were suffering pangs of apprehension, and for many, regret. They realized that the time had finally come when they must kill men they had known for years ... or be killed by them.

Colonel Butler planned to blow his whistle as soon as the head of the column started up the western slope out of the ravine, signaling the Tories and Mohawks on that slope to begin the action. The rebel column would come to a halt, bunching up those behind, and thus improving the firing efficiency of the Senecas, Cayugas, Onondagas and other ambushers along the length of the ravine. Finally, the Missisaugas and Senecas at the eastern end would quickly rush into the road, sealing off that escape route and completing the trap.

Fortunately for the patriot militia, the trap was sprung prematurely. Their rear guard of 200, which trailed the train of supply carts, had not yet reached the ravine's entrance when the Missisaugas and Senecas on the eastern slope, without waiting for the signal, rose up and fired on the militia marching down into the ravine. Butler's and Brant's curses went unheard, as hundreds of Indians and Tories up and down both sides of the causeway rose to their knees and began firing at the terrified militia. Many of them were young farm boys on their very first military expedition.

Over one hundred of the 600 militia in the ravine at that point were killed in that first volley, as well as nearly all the sixty Oneidas who had joined Herkimer that morning. The stunned survivors could not even see the enemy, as the gunsmoke added to the poor visibility in the dark woods. Flashes of fire seemed to be coming from the bushes and trees, not from men.

This moment of panic was the crucial point of the battle. Two more quick volleys like the first one would devastate the militia's ranks sufficiently to force an early surrender. The whole battle could have been over in three minutes, and British control of the Mohawk Valley would have been assured: the loyalists would have seized local control from the patriot party, Gansevoort would have had to capitulate, and St. Leger would be in Albany within a week.

But the blood lust of the Indians was too strong. St. Leger later explained it in his report to Burgoyne:

> The impetuosity of the Indians is not to be described. On the sight of the enemy, forgetting the judicious disposition agreed to, they rushed in, hatchet in hand, and thereby gave the enemy's rear an opportunity to escape.

Not only did this allow the rear guard to escape (running back down the King's Road), but even within the ravine the chance for an easy and complete victory was lost once the Indians left their cover and rushed in after scalps. The militia, now that they could see their charging enemy, raised their muskets, and took a heavy toll on the Indians. The perfect ambuscade quickly degenerated into firing at close quarters and hand-to-hand combat with musket butts, tomahawks, and knives. Almost immediately, without waiting for orders, the more experienced woods fighters among the militia led the rest in forming circles to better face the enemy.

Herkimer was down, having received a ball in the knee. His horse was dead, so he told his men to fetch the saddle. He now sat upon it, propped up against a tree. There he calmly lit his clay pipe, and smoked it while directing the action. When one of his men pointed out the danger of exposing himself to the enemy, he replied in his quiet but firm manner, "I will face the enemy." He had let his upstart colonels goad him into this mess; now he would make the best of it.

Moments after Herkimer was shot, Ebenezer Cox, one of the brash young colonels that had disdained Herkimer's caution, rode up to him shouting, "I'm taking command, sir! You're out of commission. I'm taking command!" Just as soon as the last of these words left his lips, a bullet passed through his head, killing him and making his one of history's shortest commands.

While running toward the circle forming around General Herkimer, Private William Merckley was shot in both legs, almost at the same time, by two different bullets. One was in the calf and not serious, but the other severed the main artery in his thigh. As he lay on the ground, watching blood spurt out of him form a puddle, Merckley realized his fate. A neighbor, Adam Thumb, stopped to help him. Merckley pushed him away violently. "Take care of yourself! Can't you see I'm dead?"

As Herkimer had predicted, the colonel of the rear guard had fled with his panicky men at the start of the battle, rather than leading them to the rescue of their brethren in the ravine. Some Indians spotted the fleeing militia and soon a large number set out after them, preferring the excitement and safer odds of the chase to the close quarters fighting in the woods. Ironically, the rear guard, though not caught in the initial devastating surprise attack, suffered even heavier casualties that day than either of the other two regiments inside the ravine. Their dead bodies were later found up to two miles away.

Some of the confrontations in the ravine were between men who knew each other. Abraham Quackenboss had been a childhood friend of an Indian named Bronkahorse. They had taught each other their respective languages and had served together in the late French war. At the outbreak of the Revolution, Bronkahorse had called upon his white friend, to persuade him to join the Great Father's redcoats. Quackenboss had refused, but they parted as friends and did not see each other again until the Battle of Oriskany.

During the thickest of the fighting, Quackenboss heard his named called, and at once recognized the familiar voice of Bronkahorse.

They were each sheltered by a tree at the time. The Indian asked Quackenboss to surrender to him, promising safety and good treatment. Quackenboss refused, whereupon Bronkahorse made motions to kill him. They each feinted and aimed for several seconds until Bronkahorse got off the first shot, just missing Quackenboss's head and hitting the tree. Quickly springing from his cover, Quackenboss returned fire and shot his Indian friend dead.

Suddenly the battle came to an abrupt halt as a tremendous thunderstorm came crashing down on them, and both white man and red hurried to shelter their muskets' priming. During the suspension of the battle, the militia regrouped under the direction of their wounded general, concentrating in a large oval on some relatively high ground toward the western end of the ravine.

When the rains ceased and the fighting resumed, many showed that they had learned something about woods fighting. Earlier, the Indians, often working in pairs, had been quite successful by remembering Brant's instructions: "Keep under cover until you see a gun fired your way from behind a tree, and then run as swiftly as you can to that place and tomahawk your enemy before he can reload." By now the militia had discovered the Indians' tactic and were themselves pairing off to counter it with one of their own: one man would hide behind a tree while the other fired. If he was charged, he would yell to his hidden partner, who would quickly swing out and shoot one of the charging warriors. Then, together, they would raise their own tomahawks to welcome the other savage.

The militia's concentrated and accurate firepower was also more effective than their previous disorganized fire. So many Indians were being hit that they began to fall back.

A party of whites approached from the direction of Fort Stanwix. They were actually thirty of Johnson's Royal Greens, who had snuck out of sight and turned their green coats inside out to deceive the militia. They boldly marched toward a thinly manned section of the militia's oval perimeter.

It was guarded by Captain Gardenier with only seven men. One of his men saw the advancing "Americans" and joyfully announced the arrival of reinforcements from the fort. The disguised Tories continued to advance until one of Gardenier's men, observing an acquaintance, ran to welcome him and presented his hand. It was taken, but rather firmly, and to his surprise he was yanked into a group of them and hidden from the sight of his comrades. Captain Gardenier saw the struggle and ran up to free him. He hit the Tory with his espontoon (a spear, also used to form the men into lines). Two other Tories sprang toward Gardenier and he quickly ran one of them through, and wounded the other. One of the militia yelled at him, "For God's sake, captain, you are killing your own men!" While fending off the enemy, the exasperated Captain Gardenier shouted, "Goddammit! They're not our men. They're Tories! Shoot!"

A deadly fire commenced, and the rest of Gardenier's men charged the Tories. They bashed each other with musket butts, bayonets, and tomahawks, releasing their pent up hatred. Before the firing started, three more Tories leaped upon Captain Gardenier. One of his spurs became entangled in their clothes and he fell to the ground. A moment later two of them pinned his thighs to the ground with their bayonets. The third held his bayonet above Gardenier's breast, but hesitated to run him through. Gardenier grabbed the blade with his left hand, severely lacerating it, then pulled the man down on top of him and held him there as a shield against the other two. One of Gardenier's men ran up and engaged the two standing above him. Gardenier then seized his own espontoon lying on the ground and pierced the side of the man he held astride him.

Captain Gardenier survived to fight other battles. His bravery inspired the men of his company and others. Captain Dillenback, who had vowed not to be taken alive, was now rushing with his own company to assist Gardenier's outnumbered men. Dillenback himself was confronted by three Tories, one of whom grabbed his musket. He wrenched it out of the Tory's hands and brained him with it. Quickly spinning the piece around, he fired it into the body of the second Tory, then bayoneted the third. As he tried to pull his bayonet free an enemy ball hit him in his spine, and Captain Dillenback fell dead.

The ferocity of the militia was observed by the Indians who had stayed in the ravine. Their own numbers had been depleted by heavy casualties. Two hours after the thunderstorm had stopped, a messenger arrived, informing the chiefs that the rebels had sallied forth from Fort Stanwix to plunder their personal possessions left in the camps. Rumors started spreading among the Indians that the whole affair had been a St. Leger plot to destroy them. Some, believing this, began shooting at their Tory allies. The retreating cry of "Oonah! Oonah!" was soon raised and the Indians began leaving. The Tories, now outnumbered by the militia, had no choice but to follow.

The Battle of Oriskany, in proportion to the numbers engaged, was as bloody as any battle of the entire war. The militia, having suffered over 200 casualties, limped back to their homes. Herkimer's leg turned gangrenous and a Continental Army doctor was the only one available to amputate it. Herkimer asked him if he'd ever done an amputation before. "No, I haven't," he answered. "Well," sighed the general, "we've all got to start somewhere." Herkimer bled to death the next morning while quietly smoking his pipe and reading the 38th Psalm, the prayer of an afflicted sinner. "My wounds stink," the Psalmist wrote, "and are corrupt because of my foolishness."

Herkimer's messengers had finally arrived at Fort Stanwix about eleven a.m. and Gansevoort had promptly fired off three cannon, as requested. He had then assigned Lieutenant-Colonel Marinus Willett to sally forth from the fort with 250 men (one third of the garrison) to make the requested diversion. They did not know Herkimer was still more than five miles from the fort, being ambushed by the enemy. Willett formed the detachment, waited for the thunderstorm to stop, then ventured out of the fort, bringing a three-pounder with him. His journal records his success against St. Leger:

> Nothing could be more fortunate than this enterprise. We totally routed two of the enemy's encampments, destroyed all the provisions that were in them, brought off

upwards of 50 brass kettles, and more than 100 blankets, with a quantity of muskets, tomahawks, spears, ammunition, clothing, deerskins, a variety of Indian affairs, and five colours (the whole of which on our return to the fort were displayed on our flag staff under the continental flag). The number of men lost by the enemy is uncertain. Six lay dead in their encampments, two of which were Indians. I was happy in preventing the men from scalping the Indians, being desirous if possible to teach even the savages humanity.

We were out so long [three wagons were loaded and brought into the fort three times] that a number of British regulars, accompanied by what Indians &c. could be rallied, had marched down to a thicket on the other side of the river, about 50 yards from the road we were to pass on our return. The ambush was not quite formed when we discovered them, and gave them a well directed fire. Here especially Major Bedlow with his field-piece did considerable execution. Here also the enemy were annoyed by the fire of several cannon from the fort, as they marched round to form the ambuscade.

From these prisoners we received the first accounts of General Harkaman's militia being ambushed on their march; and of a severe battle they had with them about two hours before, which gave reason to think they had for the present given up their design of marching to the fort.

The Indians and Tories, after suffering nearly 150 casualties at the Battle of Oriskany, returned to their camps outside Fort Stanwix. The Indians were much enraged at the loss of their personal possessions, but even more at the deaths of over seventy of their warriors and "several of their favorite chiefs." They partly relieved their hurt feelings by torturing and, according to one account, eating some of the prisoners they brought back. St. Leger was barely able to persuade them to stay. The Tory Daniel Claus watched them apprehensively. The disgruntled Indians ominously milled around the camps in only their breechclouts and moccasins, "for they had nothing to cover themselves at night or against the weather, and nothing in our camp to supply them."

The results of the Battle of Oriskany might have destroyed the inhabitants' will to resist, but St. Leger did not try to find out. He refused to take advantage of their panic to bypass the fort and push on down the Mohawk Valley, to rouse up the loyalists to join him and meet Burgoyne. He stubbornly stuck to the book and insisted that Fort Stanwix must be taken first. The rest of his artillery was finally brought up from Wood Creek, but its relatively small projectiles had little effect on the fort. By now, St. Leger was surely wishing he had waited for the heavier guns which had been delayed back in Montreal.

Though his artillery had so far been ineffective, St. Leger felt that the defeat of Herkimer's relief column must inevitably result in the garrison's capitulation. He wrote to Burgoyne that "he would soon join him at Albany." On August 8th, the evening after the shelling began, St. Leger sent Butler and two others to Fort Stanwix with a flag. This was, according to Willett:

> To acquaint us that General St. Leger had with much difficulty prevailed on the Indians to agree that if the commanding officer would deliver up the fort, the garrison should be secured from any kind of harm, that not a hair of their heads should be touched. But if not, the consequence to the garrison, should it afterwards fall into their hands, must be terrible; that the Indians were very much enraged on account of their having a number of their chiefs killed in the late action, and were determined, unless they got possession of the fort, to go down the Mohawk River and fall upon its inhabitants.
>
> Our answer was, that should this be the case, the

blood of those inhabitants would be upon the heads of Mr. Butler and his employers, not upon us, and that such proceedings would ever remain a stigma upon the name of Britain; but for our parts we were determined to defend the fort.

This must have been a very trying time for Colonel Gansevoort. Was St. Leger bluffing? Or would he really allow the Indians to massacre the women and children of Tryon County? And would it be prevented if Gansevoort capitulated? Although the spirits of most of his men remained high, the pyschological effects of the failure of the relief column, and St. Leger's massacre threat, were starting to be reflected in desertions. From Lieutenant Colbrath's journal:

> Augt 7th. Very little firing to day. At 11 o'clock this evening the enemy came near the fort [and] called to our centinels, telling them to come out again with fixed bayonets and they would give us satisfaction for yesterday's work, after which they fired a small cannon at the fort. We laughed at them heartily and they returned to rest. Two men deserted from us to the enemy this night.
>
> Augt 8th. Late this evening a party was sent to get water for the garrison with a guard. One of the guard deserted from us but left his firelock behind; one of our centinels fired at him but missed him. Our guard heard the enemy's centinels challenge him twice and fire on him.

Gansevoort also knew that eventually his food supplies would run out. If St. Leger persevered, the garrison's only chance would lay in General Schuyler's sending a detachment of continentals to raise the siege. So he asked for a volunteer officer and scout to try to make it to Albany, or wherever Schuyler could be found, in order to make a first-hand plea. Lieutenant-Colonel Marinus Willett and Lieutenant

Stockwell, "a good woodsman," stepped forward. Many years later, Willett dictated to his son the difficulties they had in passing the enemy camps:

> They passed privately through the sally port of the fort and, proceeding silently along the marsh, they reached the river, which they crossed by crawling over a log unperceived by the enemy's sentinels, who were not many yards from them. Having thus happily succeeded in crossing the river without being discovered, they advanced cautiously into a swampy wood, where they soon found themselves so enveloped in darkness as to be unable to keep a straight course.
>
> While in a state of uncertainty as to the safest step for them to take, they were alarmed by the barking of a dog at no great distance from them. Knowing that the Indians, after their camp had been broken up on the other side of the river, had removed it to this side, they thought it most advisable to remain where they were, until they should have light sufficient to direct their course. Placing themselves therefore against a large tree, they stood perfectly quiet several hours. At length perceiving the morning star, they again set out.

After "a most severe march of about 50 miles through the wilderness," they reached Fort Dayton, where they borrowed horses and continued on toward Albany. Fortunately, they soon met General Benedict Arnold riding west with another officer and a servant.

* * * * *

Back on August 12th, when Schuyler had received news of Herkimer's retreat, he had been at Stillwater on the Hudson, twenty-four miles south of Burgoyne's advancing army. Outnumbered by

Burgoyne, Schuyler had nevertheless immediately called a council of war, where he proposed to his generals that part of the army be detached to march the 110 miles to relieve Fort Stanwix. He argued that, should a Tory uprising assist St. Leger, the example might spread to the east and their attempt to hold the Hudson River against the combined forces of Burgoyne and St. Leger would be hopeless. Despite the immediate threat of Burgoyne, the Mohawk Valley must be held, too.

Those who spoke up were all strongly opposed to the idea. While they spoke, Schuyler paced back and forth, a clay pipe in his mouth. After he heard one of them mutter to another, "He means to weaken the army," he found that he had bitten the pipestem clean through. He knew what they were thinking, having heard, ever since Ticonderoga fell, the rumors questioning his loyalty. Controlling his temper, Schuyler turned to his generals and said simply, "Gentlemen, I shall take the responsibility upon myself. Where is the brigadier that will take command of the relief column? I shall beat up for volunteers tomorrow."

The man who stood up and offered to lead the expedition was Benedict Arnold, newly promoted by Congress from brigadier-general to major-general. He had recently arrived in camp from Connecticut, where he had helped fight off a British raid on a supply depot at Danbury. Congress had sent him to serve under Schuyler, acting on a suggestion from Washington, who was confident that Arnold's "presence and activity will animate the militia greatly." His prediction proved true, for as soon as word went around camp that Benedict Arnold would lead an expedition, General Enoch Poor's brigade of over 900 men quickly volunteered.

Arnold rode ahead and, after meeting Willett, returned with him to Fort Dayton, where he stopped to recruit militia and wait for his 900 continentals to come up. While there, he and Willett served together on a court-martial for the Tory Colonel Butler's son, Ensign Walter Butler, who had been captured at a nearby tavern trying to recruit for St. Leger. Young Butler and the others were found guilty of treason and sentenced to hang. However, the next day a wave of sympathy came over the local officers for Butler, who had been their childhood friend. They convinced Arnold to keep him alive, imprisoned in Albany. They pointed out that this course might have a restraining effect on his father, especially in his control over the Indians. Unfortunately, the next winter Walter Butler would escape and make his way to Canada, there to become infamous during the rest of the war as the scourge of the New York frontier.

Governor Clinton had issued a call to the Tryon County militia to join Arnold. However, by August 22nd only about one hundred men had responded. The losses at Oriskany, plus a new proclamation from St. Leger to the inhabitants, threatening massacre if opposition continued, kept most of them at home this time. Then a messenger from Fort Stanwix arrived, informing Arnold that St. Leger's Canadian sappers were making progress digging "regular approaches" during the nights. Though earlier, at longer range, his cannon "had not the least effect upon the sodwork of the fort," the steady advance of these trenches would soon move those guns up to point-blank range. The messenger also told Arnold that several of Gansevoort's officers were trying to coax him into accepting St. Leger's terms, so that their families would not be massacred.

Arnold therefore decided to set out at once with the troops he now had, nearly one thousand. However, before he left, an old woman threw herself at his feet asking that he spare the life of her son, Hon Yost Schuyler, one of Butler's Tories captured during the recruiting mission. Hon Yost and his family lived in poverty on the fringe of the local white society, befriended primarily by the Indians. He was much respected by them as one touched by the Great Spirit, because he suffered fits when his body became uncontrollable and he spoke in unknown tongues. Arnold promised to spare Hon Yost's life if he would use his influence with the Indians to persuade them to leave St. Leger. To ensure his trustworthiness, Arnold decided to hold Hon Yost's brother hostage until he returned. To make his claim of having escaped from the rebels seem plausible to the Indians, Hon Yost's coat was removed and shot through a few times.

When Hon Yost reached the Indian camps, their great war leader, Joseph Brant, was not there. He had taken fifty warriors to destroy an Oneida village, in retaliation for their having helped the rebels. So Hon Yost talked to the other chiefs. He told them of his capture and escape, showing them his coat, and warned them that the famed Dark Eagle (Arnold) was on the march with a vast number of soldiers.

When the Indians asked how many soldiers, Hon Yost looked confused and just pointed at the leaves on the trees above them. An hour later, an Oneida arrived claiming Arnold was coming with two thousand Yankees. Soon after, another arrived saying "Burgoyne's army was cut to pieces and that Arnold was advancing by rapid and forced marches with 3,000 men." James Thacher later learned some details about the effect Hon Yost had:

> The Indians instantly determined to quit their ground and make their escape. When St. Leger remonstrated with them, the reply of the chiefs was, "When we marched down, you told us there would be no fighting for us Indians; we might go down and smoke our pipes; but now a number of our warriors have been killed, and you mean to sacrifice us." The consequence was that St. Leger, finding himself deserted, deemed his situation so hazardous that he decamped in the greatest hurry and confusion, leaving his tents with most of his artillery and stores in the field.
>
> In the evening, while on their retreat, St. Leger and Sir John [Johnson] got into a warm altercation, criminating each other for the ill success of their expedition. Two sachems, observing this, resolved to have a laugh at their expense. In their front was a bog of clay and mud; they directed a young warrior to loiter in the rear and then, on a sudden run as if alarmed, call out, "They are coming, they are coming!" On hearing this, the two

commanders in a fright took to their heels, rushing into the bog, frequently falling and sticking in the mud, and the men threw away their packs and hurried off. This and other jokes were several times repeated during the night for many miles.

St. Leger's two hundred German reinforcements, along with the sorely missed heavy artillery, finally arrived at Oswego on August 26th. The Germans were stunned to learn that St. Leger had given up the expedition and had returned in utmost haste in his bateaux just two days before. Cursing this stupid American war, they took up their oars again and headed back to Montreal.

After stopping momentarily at Fort Stanwix, Arnold had pursued St. Leger but had not been fast enough to catch him. Nevertheless, General Schuyler was very pleased when he learned that his gamble had paid off, thanks to his pitiful cousin, Hon Yost Schuyler. Dr. Thacher concludes the story of the gallant Barry St. Leger's expedition:

General Arnold with his detachment was now at liberty to return to the main army at Stillwater; and thus have we clipped the right wing of General Burgoyne.

CHAPTER TEN
BURGOYNE FALTERS AT BENNINGTON
JULY - AUGUST 1777

"There are your enemies, Hessians and Tories! We'll beat them today, or Molly Stark's a widow!"

> *- New Hampshire's General John Stark, August 16, 1777.*

Having taken Fort Ticonderoga and dispersed its defenders, Burgoyne now had to decide on the best route to the Hudson River and, ultimately, to Albany. There he planned to meet St. Leger coming down the Mohawk, and possibly Howe coming up from New York as well. Burgoyne's original Thoughts on Conducting the War from the Side of Canada had called for his army to empty its bateaux at Ti and carry them, along with the artillery and supplies, up the difficult three mile portage to Lake George, then to float its 36-mile length to Fort George. From there, "a good road for cannon" for about ten miles would bring him to the Hudson. This, Burgoyne had pointed out, was "the most expeditious and commodious route to Albany."

However, to follow that path - now that his army was already at Skenesborough and Castleton - would have required backtracking 25 miles to Ti, giving "the appearance of a retreat." This was the official reason he gave for rejecting the Lake George route, for he feared the harmful impression that any "retrograde motion [would] make upon the minds both of enemies and friends." After all, Burgoyne had dramatically ended his general orders for the army, when at Crown Point, with the ringing pronouncement, "This army must not retreat!"

Instead, Burgoyne decided to have a modest escort take just the heavier artillery and stores south by way of Lake George. The bulk of the army, the light artillery, and all other supplies would be marched overland from Skenesborough on a 23-mile frontier road through the forests to the Hudson River.

Philip Skene, founder of Skenesborough, has been credited by most historians with persuading Burgoyne to take the land route. After all, Skene must have clearly seen the benefit of having the army plow through the woods and swamps separating the Hudson settlements from his partially developed estate. The army would have to improve the rough road for it to handle all the carts and artillery.

Originally from England, Skene had served with the British Army in this sparsely settled region during the last war. He had retired from the army and returned here with a land grant of 34,000 acres for his military service. Skene had promised to populate it by selling small parcels of land to immigrants. Instead, he had set up a semi-feudal manor, with himself as lord, renting the land to impoverished tenant farmers and making sure they remained perpetually indebted to him. Skene also owned many slaves who worked his iron mine, sawmill, foundry and shipyard. He was a man who valued a dollar saved, by whatever means. When the rebel army first arrived and searched his stone mansion, they were surprised.

> [They] found the dead body of a female deposited in the cellar, where it had been preserved for many years. This was the body of Mrs. Skene, the deceased wife of Skene, who was then in Europe and in receipt of an annuity which had been devised to his wife 'while she remained above ground.'

In 1775, when Philip Skene had returned from England with an appointment as "Lt. Governor of Ticonderoga and Crown Point and Keeper of His Majesty's Forests," he went directly to Philadelphia, carrying British money to bribe members of Congress to end the rebellion. Congress had him arrested, and after a period of confinement he was released on parole. He promptly broke the parole and fled to Canada to enlist in the British Army. He was commissioned a colonel, but not given any troops to command. Instead, he became Burgoyne's political advisor and enroller of any Tories who would come forward to serve in the army.

Thus Skene almost surely had Burgoyne's ear. Yet the general had strategic reasons for having most of his army traverse the wilderness south of Skenesborough. First, he lacked sufficient bateaux to transport his entire army on Lake George at once. Too much time would have been consumed in going back and forth on the lake. And he felt that sending the army via the lake would have hurt his chances of keeping the New England militia at home. In May he had written to another general, "If I can by maneouvre make them suspect that after the reduction of Ticonderoga my views are pointed that way, it may make the Connecticut forces very cautious of leaving their own frontiers, and much facilitate my progress to Albany." It was for this very reason that Burgoyne kept the German division under Riedesel at Castleton for more than two weeks before having them rejoin the British division for the march south.

On July seventh, the day after Ti's evacuation, Burgoyne consolidated his British division by recalling to Skenesborough his advance troops that had gone as far as Fort Anne during the initial chase. He then set his Canadian sappers and some soldiers to work clearing the forest road while he waited for sufficient horses and wagons to arrive from Canada. Gratefully accepting Skene's hospitality, Burgoyne moved into the stone mansion at Skenesborough with his new mistress, "the wife of a commissary." Both men were pleased to see that, although Skene's mill had been destroyed by the retreating rebels, at least his fine furniture remained intact, thanks to General Schuyler's strict ban on plundering the inhabitants.

Historians usually label Burgoyne's choice of routes as the greatest blunder of his campaign. However, it might have worked to his advantage if, in the words of one of his officers, he had chosen "to follow that great military maxim, 'in good success push the advantage as far as you can.'" By the end of July, many of his junior officers felt "that after the late actions [of July 6 and 7] the enemy were struck with such a panic and so dispersed that we should not have given them time to collect." Burgoyne could have pushed the light infantry ahead to chase the demoralized remnant of Schuyler's army across the Hudson and then take post at Fort Edward. Instead, he had called off the chase and concentrated his forces at Skenesborough.

This indeed gave Schuyler "time to collect" his forces. First, St. Clair's Ticonderoga troops made a wide circuit in Vermont and rendezvoused with him at Fort Edward on July 12th. (At least some of them did, many others having "steared for home" during the retreat.) A few days later, two Continental brigades - Nixon's and Glover's Massachusetts - arrived, having been ordered north by Washington. That brought Schuyler's total strength up to 4500, though desertion was still a problem and would continue to be as long as the army kept retreating. One of the new arrivals, upon reaching the army, observed a Connecticut man "throwing away his musket in disgust and saying he would not serve under generals who abandoned forts such as Ti."

Schuyler would try his best to retard Burgoyne's progress toward Albany, while he awaited additional reinforcements (for which he continued to petition Washington and the governors of New York and New England). Thus, even as he was slowly falling back with most of the army, Schuyler sent forward one thousand men with axes, picks and shovels, plus an escort of musketmen. This force was led by the Polish engineer, Tadeusz Kosciuszko, who was told to do everything possible to impede the enemy's advance.

The "road" from Skenesborough was actually nothing more than an unfinished frontier cart path, barely wider than an axle. The previous year a traveller from New Jersey called it "the meanest, worst and most desolate road I ever saw." It continually wound its way back and forth around huge pine and hemlock trunks while keeping to what little relatively high ground could be found in the flat, swampy wilderness. Abnormally high rainfall made the bogs even more widespread than usual. Rainy days seemed to alternate with hot, humid ones, bringing out thousands of "moschetoes" and gnats, known locally as "punkies."

Despite these conditions, Kosciuszko's men worked hard. They dug trenches and built dams to flood the road. They cut down huge trees over both sides of the road so their branches intertwined, forcing the British to hack through them rather than simply pull them off the road. It impressed one British officer, who was surprised the rebels stopped their flight and returned to put such obstacles in his path. He wrote, "one would think it almost impossible, but every ten or twelve yards great trees are laid across the road."

It was twenty-three miles from Skenesborough to Fort Edward. It took the same number of days for the first units of Burgoyne's army to travel that distance. Six hundred loyalists who enlisted at Skenesborough were immediately put to work with the Canadian sappers to clear the road to Fort Edward. Lieutenant Thomas Anburey describes their ordeal:

> It was with the utmost pains and fatigue we could work our way through [the trees]. Exclusive of these, the watery grounds and marshes were so numerous that we were under the necessity of constructing no less than forty bridges to pass them, and over one morass there was a bridge of near two miles in length. The Americans sometimes, when our people were removing the obstructions, would attack them.

On July 30th, the Regulars finally sighted the Hudson, and it "appeared doubly pleasing to us who were so long buried in woods." When the first unit reached the Hudson they found a letter, nailed to a tree and addressed to General Burgoyne, "Thus far shalt thou go and no farther." The unsigned letter was "thought to be wrote by Arnold."

Burgoyne kept his army at Fort Edward from July 30th to August 13th, collecting artillery, munitions, provisions, and bateaux before crossing the Hudson. Again he chose not to push forward part of his forces and catch up with the rebel army, only one day's march in his front, and force a battle or harass their retreat.

The Americans at this time were still demoralized, extremely short on powder, and in no condition to make a stand. In a desperate effort to halt the continuing desertions, and persuade at least some of the militia to stay, Schuyler issued furloughs to half the men of each regiment. He let them go home for harvest time, after receiving their solemn promises to quickly return so the other half could have their turn. Schuyler's deputy quartermaster, Colonel Udney Hay, wrote to New York's governor on August 13:

> Misfortune and fatigues have broken down the disci-
> pline and spirits of the [Continental] troops and
> converted them in a great degree into a rabble. They
> seem to have lost all confidence in themselves and their
> leaders. The militia seem to be infected with the same
> spirit. Such as are with us are good for nothing but to
> eat and waste and grumble, and those at home think
> home safest. When I tell you that the sight of twenty or
> thirty Indians on our flank or rear fills the whole camp
> with alarm and that the act of shooting one from behind
> the walls of a cabin has been commemorated in General
> Orders as a proof of great gallantry, your Excellency will
> be able to judge of what will probably happen if by acci-
> dent we are brought into close contact with Burgoyne's
> veterans.

However, Burgoyne's veterans at that moment were more concerned with where their next meal was going to come from. Burgoyne
later wrote of these days, that "for one hour he [could] find to
contemplate how he shall fight his army, he must allot twenty hours
how to feed it." His second proclamation, this one issued back on July
15th from Skenesborough, had called for all loyalists to come forward
with livestock and vegetables to sell, and for the men to enlist.

The American commander had responded with one of his own.

Schuyler warned the inhabitants that "to give aid and comfort to the enemy would be punished as treason to the United States." Schuyler decided that, regardless of loyalty, any inhabitants within reach of the invading army must be compelled to "drive away their cattle and burn their corn" and other grains. A German lieutenant describes General Schuyler's scorched earth policy:

> Pains were taken, and unfortunately with too great success, to sweep its few cultivated spots of all articles likely to benefit the invaders. In doing this the enemy showed no decency either to friend or foe. All the fields of standing corn were laid waste, the cattle were driven away, and every particle carefully removed; so that we could depend for subsistence, both for men and horses, only upon the magazines which we might ourselves establish.

Moving a large army, complete with equipment and provisions for an extensive campaign, in 18th century North America required almost optimum transport conditions. All had gone smoothly for Burgoyne's army until it gave up the waterways and plunged into the wilderness. He had nowhere near enough horses and oxen. The army, Burgoyne wrote, "is unable to advance three miles without waiting about eight or ten days for our necessary supplies to be brought up."

By early August, word arrived from St. Leger that his forces were already laying siege to Fort Stanwix, and he expected to meet Burgoyne soon in Albany. Burgoyne knew now that if he did not speed up his own advance against Schuyler, the rebel general might feel safe enough to send a column west to oppose St. Leger. So he belatedly acted upon a proposal which Baron von Riedesel had submitted back on July 22.

The German general had written a detailed memorandum to his British commander-in-chief while stationed at Castleton, suggesting a quick raid upon the settlements east of there. Riedesel considered it

foolish to attempt to travel through the wilderness while relying primarily on two-wheeled carts, since they "spoil the road" with ruts and
"cannot get through bad roads without difficulty." Instead, he
suggested that most of these carts be abandoned in favor of "bat
horses" (a military term derived from a French word meaning pack
saddle). Bat horses, Riedesel wrote, "go through everything."

Riedesel had received erroneous intelligence stating that the Connecticut River settlements were "full of good horses." "There is
scarcely an inhabitant," Riedesel wrote to Burgoyne, "who has fewer
than two or three horses," and they could get along without them,
since they use oxen for farm work, and the horses "only to carry grain
to the mill or to take a ride." Besides, "lacking horses they will not be
able to carry news to the rebels so fast and so frequently. ... This small
bleeding is less punitive than they deserve for their treason and bad
conduct toward the King." Riedesel suggested that a detachment of
Germans and Tories, "under a good officer of the rank of major,"
could bring into Castleton 1147 horses (the army's shortage, according
to his calculation).

Burgoyne had liked Riedesel's idea, but back on July 22 had been
preoccupied with moving his army forward. He had therefore gra-
ciously declined the offer (sending along two dozen bottles of madeira
to appease his German ally, and apologizing for the poor quality and
quantity). By August 8, however, the need for horses had become so
paramount that Burgoyne not only reconsidered Riedesel's original
plan, but actually enlarged its scope to cover more territory further to
the south.

Lieutenant-Colonel Friedrich Baum, a stout blond officer with a
good record in Europe, was selected to lead the raid, even though he
could not "utter a word of English." The route was to start at Fort
Miller (a recently burned stockade fort, seven miles south of Fort Edward), and proceed east through Arlington and Manchester to
Rockingham on the Connecticut River. Then south to Brattlebury,
and west from there along "the great road to Albany," passing through
Bennington. They would catch up with the rest of the army before it

246

reached Albany, since Baum's whole route should not take more than "a fortnight" to complete.

Baum's first objective was to find mounts for his 200 horseless dragoons and 150 Tories, then begin collecting an additional 1300 bat horses for the army. ("If you can bring more," Burgoyne added, "so much the better.") The following excerpts are taken from Riedesel's lengthy instructions to Lieutenant-Colonel Baum:

> Your parties are likewise to bring in waggons and other convenient carriages, with as many draft oxen as will be necessary to draw them; and all cattle fit for slaughter, milch cows excepted, which are to be left for the use of the inhabitants. Regular receipts are to be given to such persons as have complied with General Burgoyne's manifesto, but no receipts to be given to such as are known to be acting in the service of the rebels.
>
> Colonel Skene will be with you to help distinguish the good subjects from the bad. You will use all possible means to make the country believe that the troops under your command are the advanced corps of the army, and that it is intended to pass the Connecticut on the road to Boston. You will likewise insinuate that ... [your force] is to be joined at Springfield by a corps of troops from Rhode Island.
>
> It is highly probable that the corps under Mr Warner, now supposed to be at Manchester, will retreat before you; but should they, contrary to expectation, be able to collect in great force, it is left to your discretion to attack them or not.

Though Riedesel drew up the revised plan as requested, he voiced his reservations about the much enlarged risk of the operation, contending that the proposed route was too far south and too extensive.

Burgoyne tried to assuage him by promising that he would detach British light infantry if Schuyler sent any forces from the rebel army to intercept Baum's corps. He also reminded Riedesel that the supplies would be invaluable and that the main army must move forward quickly to prevent Schuyler from sending any forces against St. Leger.

Riedesel was not the only officer who thought the new plan too risky. Lt.-Colonel John Peters, head of a Tory regiment and for years a Bennington resident, disliked having the Englishman, Skene, be the only "local expert" to whom Burgoyne listened. Skene had assured the general and Baum "that in Bennington a large majority of the populace were our friends." Peters, however, "knew the certain danger & the mountains between which they must pass." He later testified regarding a meeting in which his views were presented to Burgoyne by Peters' immediate commander, General Simon Fraser:

> General Fraizer gave countenance to the provincial colonels, for which Gen'l Burgoine told Gen'l Frazier, "when I want your advice I shall ask for it." The General added that the Americans were cowards and disobedient. At this Colonel Peters told the General that he was ready to obey his orders, but "we shall not return."

On the morning of August 13, Burgoyne rode up to the departing Colonel Baum and gave him a last minute verbal change in orders. A Tory captain had just come in and informed the general of "a considerable depot of cattle, cows, horses, and wheel carriages" located in Bennington. It was reportedly "guarded by a party of militia only," to the number of three or four hundred. General Burgoyne therefore instructed Baum to cancel the Connecticut River route, and instead go directly to Bennington, then quickly return and rejoin the army along the Hudson.

Colonel Baum's force, supplemented by two 3-pounders, consisted of about 675 men: 50 Indians; 50 Canadian volunteers; Peters' undermanned regiment of 150 Tories (to be completed on the march by recruits); 50 British "marksmen"; and 375 Germans. Included in the German total were a company of riflemen ("jagers"), a company of musicians, and several wives or "camp followers" who insisted on accompanying their men.

Each soldier was fully equipped, as if he was marching in the more hospitable climate and terrain of the European plains. Sergeant Roger Lamb explains the typical British soldier's burden:

> He carried a knapsack, blanket, a haversack containing four days provisions, a canteen for water, and a proportion of his tent furniture [cast iron kettle, etc.], which superadded to his accoutrement, arms and sixty rounds of ammunition, made a great load and large baggage, weighing about sixty pounds.

A few minor alterations had been made to the British uniforms for hot weather campaigning. Since their uniforms were from the previous year's campaign, in most cases they were badly in need of repair. Therefore, before leaving Canada the British generals had allowed the men to cut off the long tails of their greatcoats and use them for patching material. The hats were also trimmed down to small caps, with regimental facings now indicated by dyed hair (many a Canadian cow was now missing the tuft of white hair at the end of its tail).

The Germans, however, made no accomodations. The horseless dragoons had been the army's laughingstock for marching in their riding outfits: "leather pantaloons, high boots, immensely heavy hats, huge sabers, and jack-boots 12 lbs. the pair" reaching to mid-thigh. Marching thus encumbered in the heat and humidity was pure torture for these men. The sweat poured off them like rain, and something seemed to always be catching the undergrowth - a spur, a sword, or the outrageously long plume sticking out of their huge hats.

Despite these handicaps, the dragoons, like the rest of Baum's raiding party, made 16 miles on the first day. After wading across the

Batten Kill three times, then struggling up and across a steep ridge, they marched down into the hamlet of Cambridge, New York, at 4 p.m.

Baum was already having trouble with his Indian allies, who wanted payment for all horses and cattle they collected. When Baum told them he could not pay them, they slit the animals' throats and took the cow bells, which they highly prized. Baum sent a dispatch to General Burgoyne, informing him that "neither officers nor interpreters can control them," and asking for "authority to pay the savages." He also reported that he had skirmished with forty or fifty militia, and had been told by a captive that rebel forces were gathering in large numbers at Bennington.

The Indians' behavior was a constant problem throughout the whole campaign that summer, as a German diarist noted:

> The farmers had plenty of horses, and we probably could have had all we needed from those who were still loyal to the king, had it not been for the Indians in the army, who by marauding and cruelties forced the farmers to leave their homesteads. It did not make any difference to the Indians if they attacked a subject loyal to the king, or one friendly to the rebels; they set fire to all their homes, took away everything, killed the cattle, leaving them dead on the spot. It would certainly have been better if we had not had any Indians with us.

The next morning, August 14, found Baum "being fired on by the Rebels in their usual way from the bushes," this time at a junction of two creeks. Here, at San Coick's Mill, he dispersed them and captured some flour and salt before continuing on. The Americans were a party of 200 militia which had been sent from Bennington to investigate a report of Indians near Cambridge. A local resident recorded the incident:

They were met and driven back by Col Baum's advancing troops. Some of the party were taken prisoners. But most of them escaped. Being on foot and well acquainted with the country, they took to the fields and made a safe retreat to Bennington.

As our [retreating] Yankee boys were crossing the bridge, they wished they could destroy it to embarass the invading foe; but they did not dare stop to do it because British guns were close to their heels. They hurried forward. At this critical juncture, one man more heroic than the rest, Eleazur Edgerton, declared that the bridge ought to be destroyed, and he would go back and burn it, if any one would join him. Two of his associates volunteered. Those three returned, threw the planks off into the chasm below and set fire to the timbers. Whilst they were doing the heroic work, British balls were whizzing about their ears; but all three safely escaped, and soon rejoined their more discreet fellows.

After repairing and passing over the bridge, Baum's corps was soon within ten miles of Bennington. Numerous inhabitants were now being recruited by Skene, who was providing them with arms and ammunition. However, they quickly became a problem for this "secret expedition," as a German diarist later wrote:

Some of the colonists, pretending loyalty to the king, had joined the corps. The rebels could always get all the information wanted about the movements of this corps through these people, who merely had to pretend to be friends of the English to be received by the corps. Governor Skene, who was to persuade the people to take up the king's cause, seems to have made grave mistakes, particularly by sending them out to levy more men for the army, or to get news from the enemy.

After the skirmish at San Coick's Mill on the morning of August 14, Baum sent another dispatch to Burgoyne:

> Five prisoners agree that from fifteen to eighteen hundred men are at Bennington, but are supposed to leave on our approach. I will proceed so far to-day as to fall on the enemy to-morrow early. ... Beg your excellency to pardon the hurry of this letter, as it is written on the head of a barrel.

Though Baum still had not asked for reinforcements, Burgoyne was concerned enough to immediately order out 643 Germans with two 6-pounders. He must have wondered what would happen to Baum before the reinforcements caught up. Burgoyne would later learn that Baum never did have the opportunity to "fall on the enemy."

* * * * *

John Stark was the man who would block Baum's path. As first captain in Rogers' Rangers during the French and Indian War, Stark had proven his leadership abilities many times. More recently, as colonel of a New Hampshire regiment, he had enhanced his reputation by being instrumental in the actions at Bunker Hill and Trenton, as well as serving in the Canadian campaign. Despite his achievements, however, Stark had been passed over when Congress appointed several new brigadiers early in 1777. This move had justly upset Stark, for two reasons: 1) the New Hampshire appointee, Enoch Poor, was much less qualified; and 2) since New Hampshire was less populous than most states, it was unlikely that Congress would appoint another general from that state in the foreseeable future.

When word of Congress's action arrived in early April, Startk was at home recruiting, as were both New Hampshire's generals, John Sullivan and Enoch Poor. Stark immediately went to see them.

He wished them all possible success and surrendered his commission. They endeavored to dissuade him from this course, but he answered that "an officer who would not maintain his [proper] rank and assert his rights was not worthy of serving his country."

So John Stark retired to his farm in Derryfield (present day Manchester). On July 18th, a special session of the New Hampshire legislature convened to discuss "the news of the fall of Ticonderoga" and an appeal from Ira Allen of Vermont to help "the defenceless inhabitants on the frontier who are heartily disposed to defend their liberties [and] make a frontier for our State with their own."

> John Langdon, the Speaker, seeing the public credit exhausted and his compatriots discouraged, rose and said: "I have a thousand dollars in hard money; I will pledge my plate for three thousand more. I have seventy hogsheads of Tobago rum which will be sold for the most they will bring. They are at the service of the state. If we succeed in defending our firesides and our homes I may be remunerated; if we do not then the property will be of no value to me. Our friend, John Stark, who so nobly maintained the honor of our state at Bunker Hill, may safely be entrusted with the honor of the enterprise, and we will check the progress of Burgoyne.

A messenger was sent to Derryfield with the offer of a commission as militia general. John Stark returned with the messenger, for he wanted to make it clear that he would only serve if his command was independent of the Continental Army.

> He informed them he had little confidence in the then Commander at the North [Schuyler]; but, if they would

raise a body of troops to hang upon the Vermont wing and rear of the enemy and allow him to use his own discretion in directing their operations without being accountable to any other power than their own body, he would again take the field.

The legislature readily agreed to Stark's conditions. Many of the legislators, too, distrusted the Northern Department's generals. If Stark had to subordinate himself to them, it was feared, those generals might draw off the New Hampshire militia to New York, leaving their wives and families "a prey to the enemy." The legislature did not notify Congress, and was later reprimanded by that body for taking independent action "destructive of military subordination." After the legislature issued written instructions to their new general, a vote was taken to adjourn until September, and they dispersed with the Speaker's final words ringing in their ears: "God save the United States." One member immediately mounted his horse and, after traveling all night, reached his home town of Concord on the Sabbath afternoon.

Dismounting at the meeting house door, he walked up the aisle. Mr. Walker paused in his sermon and said, "Col. Hutchins, are you the bearer of any message?"

"Yes," replied the Colonel, "General Burgoyne with his army is on the march to Albany. General Stark has offered to take command of the New Hampshire men and if we all turn out we can cut off Burgoyne's march."

Whereupon Mr. Walker said, "My hearers, those of you who are willing to go had better leave at once." At which all the men in the meeting house rose and went out.

Phineas Eastman said "I can't go for I have no shoes," to which Samuel Thompson, a shoe-maker, replied "Don't be troubled about that, for you shall have a pair before morning," which was done.

Such was the reputation of John Stark that within four days 1492 men were enlisted for a period of 60 days. The different companies rendezvoused at the "Fort at Number 4" (Charlestown, N. H.) on the Connecticut River. While collecting supplies and men there, Stark received a request for assistance from Colonel Seth Warner of the Vermont continentals. Warner had received what turned out to be false rumors that Riedesel was marching eastward from Castleton. Stark sent several hundred men to Warner and promised to bring the others along as soon as possible. And, as instructed, he kept the New Hampshire Committee of Safety informed of his progress:

> Charlestown, No. 4, July 30th, 1777. We are detained a good deal for want of bullet molds, as there is but one pair in town. I am afraid we shall meet with difficulty in procuring kettles or utensils to cook our victuals, as the troops has not brought any. There is but very little rum in the store here; if some could be forwarded to us it would oblige us very much, as there is none of that article in them parts where we are agoing.

On August 2, Stark sent most of his army thirty miles west to Manchester, Vermont. He remained to finish collecting supplies and other necessities for the army, including a surgeon and a chaplain. Meanwhile, at Stillwater on the Hudson, Philip Schuyler had learned that New Hampshire was calling out the militia. He ordered General Benjamin Lincoln to ride to Vermont and take charge of all actions against Burgoyne's rear.

Lincoln arrived in Manchester a few hours before Stark on August 7, and ordered Stark's brigade to prepare to march to Bennington. The tall, wiry, hawk-nosed Stark put a quick stop to that as soon as he arrived, and he had a heated council with the fat general from Massachusetts. It did not help Lincoln's cause that he happened to be one of the junior colonels Congress had promoted over Stark's head. Lincoln was informed by Stark that he "considered himself adequate to the command of his own men." As for Schuyler's orders giving Lincoln command of all Vermont and New Hampshire troops, Stark appeared "exceedingly soured" and waved his independent New Hampshire commission under Lincoln's nose, telling him that he was "determined not to join the Continental Army till the Congress give him his rank therein."

Lincoln returned to Stillwater to report Stark's insubordination. He also wrote to Congress about Stark and the New Hampshire legislature. Schuyler, though, was wise enough to write a very diplomatic letter to Stark, acknowledging his independent command and even offering to send Lincoln with 600 continentals to work alongside him against Burgoyne's rear and his supply lines. Schuyler asked him to put aside any personal resentment and to cooperate by sacrificing "his feelings to the good of the country" in this emergency.

Stark softened and wrote to Schuyler, telling him he would work with Lincoln. So Lincoln made plans to join forces with Stark and Warner "in the northern district of Cambridge," west of Bennington. However, Lincoln was slow in starting his 600 continentals toward the intended August 18 rendezvous. If he had started sooner, Lincoln, instead of Stark, would have crossed paths with Baum, perhaps with much different results.

Meanwhile, back in Manchester, Stark had heard false rumors that Riedesel's division had left Castleton with the intention of invading New England via the Bennington road. Stark therefore left for Bennington with his militia on August 8, after writing a hasty note to his wife back in Derryfield:

> Dear Molly:
>   In less than one week the British forces here will be ours. Send every man from the farm that will come, and let the haying go to hell.

Stark's army probably traveled light. Having enlisted for only two months in the warmest part of the year, very few of the recruits brought along tents. A New Ipswich man describes the appearance of his company:

> To a man they wore small-clothes, coming down and fastening just below the knee, and long stockings with cowhide shoes ornamented by large buckles, while not a pair of boots graced the company. The coats and waist-coats were loose, with colours as various as the barks of oak, sumach and other trees, and their shirts were all made of flax and, like every other part of the dress, were homespun. On their heads was worn a large round-top and broad-brimmed hat.
>
> Their arms were as various as their costume ... Instead of a cartridge box, a large powder horn was slung under the arm, and occasionally a bayonet might be seen. Some of the swords of the officers had been made by our province blacksmiths, perhaps from some farming utensil; they looked serviceable, but heavy and uncouth.

After reaching Bennington on August 9th, General Stark spent much of his time meeting with the Vermont Committee of Safety "at the sign of the wolf" (Catamount Tavern). On August 13th, a lone female rider arrived on a much lathered horse to inform them that she had just come from Cambridge, where a party of about fifty Indians had been seen approaching the town. Stark dispatched 200 men under Lieutenant-Colonel Gregg to investigate. This is the party Baum encountered at San Coick's Mill.

Several hours later, another woman arrived ("for it was not safe for men to travel at that time"), saying that the Indians were in fact the vanguard of "a large body of the enemy." Stark promptly dispatched riders to rouse the countryside, including western Massachusetts, "to come in with all speed to our assistance." Word was also sent to Seth

Warner back in Manchester to bring on his Vermont regiment. Stark's army quickly broke camp and set off down the road to rescue Gregg's party. He later described his progress in his report to the New Hampshire Committee of Safety:

> [August 14]   About five miles from [Bennington] I met Colonel Greg on his retreat and the enemy in close pursuit after him. I drew up my little army in order of battle. But when the enemy hove in sight they halted [and began intrenching] on a very advantageous hill. I sent out small parties in their front to skirmish with them, which scheme had a good effect, but the ground that I was upon did not suit for a general action. I marched back about one mile and encamped, called a council. The 15th it rained all day; therefore, could do nothing but skirmish with them. On the 16th, in the morning, was joined by some militia from Berkshire County.

Leading a company from Pittsfield, Massachusetts, was the Congregational minister Thomas Allen. The "fighting parson" had been disgusted when his company was ordered to evacuate Ti, back on July sixth. Now, after a two day march, much of it in "a perfect torrent" of rain and high winds, they arrived at Stark's camp at 1 a.m. on the sixteenth.   Seeking out Stark's headquarters, a crude settler's cabin, Parson Allen loudly roused the general from bed and addressed him strongly:

> "The people of Berkshire have often turned out to fight the enemy, but have not been permitted to do so. We have resolved that if you do not let us fight now, never to come again."
> "Would you go [fight] now," observed the general, "in this dark and rainy night? No, go to your people; tell

them to take rest if they can; and if the Lord sends us sunshine tomorrow, and I do not give you fighting enough, I will never call upon you to come again."

Meanwhile, a mile west and two hours earlier, Colonel Friedrich Baum had received some encouraging news. A messenger had arrived on horseback, stating that the column of German infantry sent out by Burgoyne would arrive the next day. Before dawn, Baum ordered Skene to go back with the messenger, taking horses and a few empty carts to speed the arrival of the reinforcements. Baum was in good spirits that morning. It was still raining, which meant the rebels, without bayonets, would have to again put off the attack. Perhaps the attack could be delayed long enough for the German reinforcements to arrive.

More small parties of militia arrived during the morning and early afternoon, further swelling the American ranks. In addition, a group of friendly Stockbridge Indians who had served two years before, during the blockade of Boston, were now in the American camp. On the other side, Baum also benefitted from some late arrivals, thanks to a retired British officer named DePeyster, who brought in ninety hastily recruited Tories. All told, by the start of the battle, around 3:20 p.m., Stark's forces would outnumber Baum's by about 2050 to 850.

Colonel Baum was still supremely confident. He harangued his troops, telling them that the rebels owned the soil and would therefore fight hard to preserve it, but they could not possibly succeed against superior discipline, position, breastworks, and artillery. However, not all his men were so calm and confident. With no shelter from the rain, many of Baum's troops had slept little the night before. One sleepless German soldier spent the night "filled with an impending sense of danger." Of course, as the day progressed and battle became imminent, most of the men on both sides probably experienced that pre-battle apprehension universal to soldiers all the world over - a conflicting mixture of eagerness and fear.

Given Stark's reputation, everyone in the American camp knew that he would order an attack, as soon as the rains ceased. They did, around noon. Although Warner's Vermonters still had not arrived from Manchester, Stark raised his sword, pointed it, and declared: "There are your enemies, Hessians and Tories! We'll beat them today, or Molly Stark's a widow!"

Stark's troops knew, from the scouts, that the enemy was intrenched and had artillery. And they knew this meant that they would be the ones in the open, being fired at by a protected enemy. To encourage them, Stark had instructed his officers to tell the men that "all plunder taken in the enemy camp" would be divided equally.

Some of the men steeled themselves for the coming danger, while others developed cold feet. The son of Captain Stafford, of Berkshire County, Mass., many years later related the following reminiscence of his father:

> He was soon assigned a place in the line, and the tory fort was pointed out as his particular object of attack. When making arrangements to march out his men, my father turned to a tall, athletic man, one of the most vigorous of the band, and remarkable for size and strength among his neighbors. "I am glad," said he, "to see you among us. You did not march with the company; but, I suppose, you are anxious for the business of the day to begin." This was said in the hearing of the rest, and attracted their attention. My father was surprised and mortified, on observing the man's face turn pale, and his limbs tremble. With a faltering voice, he replied: "Oh no, sir, I didn't come to fight, I only came to drive back the horses!" "I am glad," said my father, "to find out we have a coward among us, before we go into battle. Stand back, and do not show yourself here any longer.
>
> This occurrence gave my father great regret, and he repented having spoken to the man in the presence of his company. However, an occurrence happened, fortu-

nately, to take place immediately after, which made amends. There was an aged and excellent old man present, of a slender frame, stooping a little with advanced age and hard work, with a wrinkled face, and well known as one of the oldest persons in our town, and the oldest on the ground. My father was struck with regard for his aged frame, and much as he felt numbers to be desirable in the impending struggle, he felt a great reluctance at the thought of leading him into it. He therefore turned to him, and said: "The labors of the day threaten to be severe; it is therefore my particular request, that you will take your post as sentinel yonder, and keep charge of the baggage." The old man stepped forward with an unexpected spring, his face was lighted with a smile, and pulling off his hat, he briskly replied: "Not till I've had a shot at them first, captain, if you please." All thoughts were now directed towards the enemy's line; and the company, partaking in the enthusiasm of the old man, gave three cheers.

Baum spread out his forces on a small cone-shaped hill on the west side of the Walloomsac River, and along the river at the base of the hill. About 250 yards east of a bridge across that river was the "Tory Redoubt," held by 150 men. There were three other smaller breastworks along the west side of the river: one close by the bridge; and one each to the north and south, to prevent the rebels from fording up or downstream and getting in their rear. These outposts were manned by the Canadians, the jagers, and one half of the British light infantry company.

Baum himself, with the other half of the light infantry and all his dragoons, was in the "Dragoon Redoubt" near the top of a hill, on its eastern slope, half a mile northwest of the bridge. Here he had dragged up one of the two field pieces, while the other one was placed at the small breastwork just west of the bridge. The 50 Indians were camped behind Baum, on the west slope of the hill, to guard his rear. The women who had accompanied their German husbands on this march were placed for safekeeping in a log cabin between the bridge and the Tory Redoubt.

Because of the hill's stony, root-laced soil, the Dragoon Redoubt was constructed of felled trees, their branches pointing outward. The outposts below the hill were built of boards from two nearby sheds, with flax stuffed between the boards.

On balance, for defense against an enemy known to be more than twice one's strength in numbers, Baum's dispositions were thoroughly bad. His five posts were so spread out that they could not support each other. In fact, because of the hill's steep, convex slope, from his Dragoon Redoubt Baum could not even see the bridge directly below him.

Seth Warner had ridden on ahead of his troops and arrived in Stark's camp the night before the battle. An expert on the local terrain, he was very helpful to the general in planning the attack. Colonel Nichols would lead 200 New Hampshire men on a wide and circuitous course, first to the north and then west. After this four mile march through the woods, they would approach the Dragoon Redoubt by climbing the north and northwest slopes of Baum's hill. Another detachment of 300 Vermonters under Colonel Herrick would mirror Nichols' route, to approach from the south. On the way, Herrick would overrun the small enemy outpost south of the bridge. Once in place, Nichols and Herrick would initiate the action against the Dragoon Redoubt, but wait to close in until more support arrived.

Meanwhile, two other New Hampshire parties, led by Colonels Stickney and Hobart (pronounced "Hubbard") and supplemented by the Berkshire militia, would advance on either side of the road and assault the Tory Redoubt. A fifth party of 100 men would demonstrate in front of the bridge in order to draw Baum's attention away from those climbing the north and south slopes of his hill. Stark, with the one thousand man, would wait until all units were engaged. He would then lead the reserve across the bridge, past the small post on the river's west bank, and finally up the hill's steep east slope to join the attack against the Dragoon Redoubt.

About noon, Pastor Allen went forward alone toward the Tory pickets. Recognizing some of them as former residents of Pittsfield, he mounted a fallen log and lectured them as if from a pulpit, calling "upon them to surrender, promising them good treatment." In response, one of them yelled out, "There's Parson Allen, let's pop him!" A flurry of bullets whizzed through the air, riddling the log, but missing Allen.

General Stark was busy all morning planning every detail needed for his well thought out assault. A man named Thomas Mellen relates some of the preparations for battle:

> Stark and ------ rode up near the enemy to reconnoitre; were fired at by the cannon, and came galloping back. Stark rode with shoulders bent forward, and cried out to his men: "Those rascals know that I am an officer; don't you see they honor me with a big gun as a salute."
>
> We were marched round and round a circular hill till we were tired. Stark said it was to amuse the Germans. All the while a cannonade was kept up upon us from their breastworks; it hurt no body, and it lessened our fear of the great guns.
>
> After a while I was sent, with twelve others, to lie in ambush, on a knoll a little north, and watch for Tories on their way to join Baum. Presently we saw six coming toward us who, mistrusting us for Tories, came too near us to escape. We disarmed and sent them, under a guard of three, to Stark.
>
> While I sat on the hillock, I espied one Indian whom I thought I could kill, and more than once cocked my gun, but the orders were not to fire. He was cooking his dinner, and now and then shot at some of our people.

To confuse the enemy, Stark directed the north and southbound detachments to slowly drift off into the woods, two or three men at a time. Baum clearly saw them through his spy-glass, but (according to his servant) he "supposed they were running away." Lieutenant Glich later recalled the prevailing mood inside the Dragoon Redoubt:

> We stood about half an hour under arms, watching the proceedings of a column of four or five hundred men [Stickney and Hobart] who, after dislodging the pickets, had halted just at the edge of the open country, when a sudden trampling of feet in the forest on our right, followed by the report of several muskets, attracted our attention. A patrol was instantly sent in the direction of the sound, but before it had proceeded many yards from the lines, a loud shout followed by a rapid though straggling fire of musketry warned us to prepare for a meeting the reverse of friendly. Instantly the Indians came pouring in, carrying dismay and confusion in their countenances and gestures. We were surrounded on all sides: columns were advancing everywhere against us. It was at this moment that the Indians lost all confidence and fled.

Colonel Herrick had been instructed to wait until Nichols' party, having the longer approach from the north, arrived and started the action. Jesse Field, a Bennington man with Herrick's party on the south slope, describes the opening moments of the battle:

> When we came in sight of the works we halted. We stood but a short time when the firing commenced from the party on the north. I recollect hearing Lieutenant --- ------ exclaim, "My God, what are we doing? They are killing our brothers. Why are we not ordered to

attack?"

In a moment our Adjutant ordered us to advance. We pressed forward and as the Hessians rose above their works to fire we discharged our pieces at them.

One of Herrick's Vermonters remembered that his group "came within ten or twelve rods of the redoubt and began firing from behind logs, trees, &c. and continued occasionally advancing." Despite being fired upon from more than one side, the dragoons stood up "by platoon" to return fire. In doing so, they exposed themselves above their breastworks. Their strict European training thus resulted in needless casualties.

Lieutenant Glich, inside the Dragoon Redoubt, observed the behavior of some of the "loyalists" who had joined Baum on the march, and were inside the redoubt when the attack began:

> During the last day's march our little corps was joined by many of the country people, most of whom demanded and obtained arms, as persons friendly to the royal cause. How Colonel Baum became so completely duped as to place reliance on these men I know not, but he was persuaded that the armed bands were loyalists.
>
> The very persons in whom he had trusted, and to whom he had given arms, lost no time in turning them against him. These followers no sooner heard their [American] comrades' cry than they deliberately discharged their muskets among the dragoons and, dispersing before any steps could be taken to seize them, escaped, excepting one or two, to their friends.

Before the struggle for the Dragoon Redoubt began, General Stark, down on the flats east of the river, had been slowly bringing on the reserve while under fire from the enemy artillery. Several times he had looked at his watch and muttered, "It is time they were there." Finally,

American musket fire was heard coming from Baum's hill, and he ordered Hobart and Stickney to advance against the Tory Redoubt. The fifty Canadians, who had been posted behind two log cabins between the Tory Redoubt and the bridge, fled at the first sounds of battle.

During their approach, the Americans passed through a cornfield, where they were ordered to each take a husk and "put it under the hat band." This would distinguish them from the Tories who were also "dressed in their working clothes." The action at the Tory Redoubt was fierce but short-lived. Many years later, one of the men who had been inside the Tory Redoubt related the following account of that assault to the son of the rebel Captain Stafford:

> We were all ready when we saw the rebels coming to attack us ... [we] felt perfectly safe and thought we could kill any body of troops they would send against us before they could reach the place we stood upon. We had not expected, however, that they would approach us underunder cover, but supposed we should see them on the way. We did not know that a little gully which lay below us was long and deep enough to conceal them; but they knew the ground, and the first we saw of the party coming to attack us [was when] they made their appearance right under our guns.
>
> Your father was at the head of them. I was standing at the wall, with my gun loaded in my hand. Several of us leveled our pieces at once. I took as fair aim at them as I ever did at a bird in my life, and thought I was sure of them; though we had to point so much downwards, that it made a man but a small mark. We fired together, and he fell. I thought he was dead to a certainty; but to our surprise he was on his feet in an instant, and they all came jumping into the midst of us.

Captain Stafford's account of how he was shot is told by his son:

On emerging [from the gully] and looking about to see where he was, he found the tory fort just above him, and the heads of the tories peeping over, with their guns leveled at him. Turning to call on his men, he was surprised to find himself flat on the ground without knowing why; for the enemy had fired and a ball had gone through his foot into the ground, cutting some of the sinews just as he was stepping on it, so as to bring him down. He was glad to find he was not seriously hurt, and was able to stand. He feared that his fall might check his followers; and, as he caught a glimpse of a man in a red coat running across a distant field, he cried out, "Come on, my boys! They run! They run!" So saying, he sprang up, and clambering to the top of the fort, while the enemy were hurrying their powder into the pans and the muzzles of their pieces, his men rushed on, shouting and firing, and jumping over the breastworks, and pushing upon the defenders so closely that they threw themselves over the opposite wall, and ran down the hill as fast as their legs could carry them.

The Tories had failed to "nourish" their fire - that is, space it out. Instead, they had all fired at once and then seen the enemy reach their walls before they could reload. Lt.-Colonel John Peters, who helped lead the brief Tory Redoubt defense, describes the struggle:

As they were coming up, I observed a man fire at me, which I returned. He loaded again as he came up, and discharged again at me, crying out, "Peters, you damn Tory, I have got you." He rushed on me with his bayonet, which entered just below my left breast but was turned by my bones. By this time I was loaded and saw it was a rebel Captain, Jeremiah Post by name, an old

267

school-mate and playfellow, and a cousin of my wife. Though his bayonet was in my body I felt regret at being obliged to destroy him.

As the Tory Redoubt fell, Stark was pushing the reserve toward the river. He had little trouble overwhelming the small post on the west bank despite its cannon (some American sharpshooters were probably assigned the task of eliminating the German gunners). One of the German women, in the log house on the east side of the river, fled from it. She was accidentally killed by a stray bullet while crossing the bridge.

Soon Stark was across the bridge and leading his troops up the hill to join in the assault on the Dragoon Redoubt. Stark dismounted to lead the attack on foot, and soon lost sight of his horse. He would never see his favorite mount again, despite repeated attempts to locate it, including an advertisement in the Connecticut Courant and other papers offering a $20 reward for its return.

The German Lieutenant Glich thought the assault on the Dragoon Redoubt had lasted about 45 minutes, when "an accident occurred." An American named Butler explains:

> A solitary wagon, containing all the Germans' spare ammunition, exploded in the midst of the redoubt. You would have thought that explosion to have been an order given for every American to charge, for the redoubt was instantly stormed and carried on every side.

Now it was hand-to-hand combat. Those heavy swords were finally put to use. Baum led a brave last defense where "the bayonet, the butt of the rifle, the saber, the pike were in full play," but his forces were hopelessly outnumbered. Jesse Field recounts the enemy's retreat from the Dragoon Redoubt:

> They left their works and ran down the hill to the south and southeast. ... The day was very warm. They

were in full dress & very heavy armed and we in our
shirts and trousers and thus had much the advantage in
the pursuit. Some were killed in their works. Many
were killed and taken in going down the hill and others
on the flat upon the river.

Led by Colonel Baum, who told them to shoulder their carbines and
trust to their broadswords, the dragoons twice broke through their
swarming enemies as they slowly retreated down the road toward San
Coick's Mill. But, overpowered by numbers, and soon left without
their leader (Baum had fallen with a bullet in his stomach) they surrendered, shortly after 5 o'clock. The veteran Stark considered this two
hour fight "the hottest I ever saw in my life."

Not all of Baum's forces surrendered. Some tried to avoid capture.
The Tory who shot Captain Stafford relates his own flight:

We had open fields before us, and scattered in all directions, some followed by our enemies. I ran some
distance with another man, and looking around saw
several of your father's soldiers who were coming after
us level their muskets to fire. We had just reached a rail
fence, and both of us gave a jump at the same instant to
go over it. While I was in the air I heard the guns go
off. We reached the ground together, but my companion fell and lay dead by the fence, while I ran on with all
my might, finding I was not hurt.

I looked back, hoping to see no one following, but I
was frightened on discovering a tall rawboned fellow,
running like a deer, only a short distance behind, and
gaining on me every step he took. I immediately reflected that my gun was only a useless burden, for it was
discharged, and had no bayonet; and although a valuable
one, I gave my gun a throw off to one side, so that if my
pursuer should choose to pick it up he should lose some

distance by it. And then without slackening my speed I turned my head to see how he took the maneuver; and found he had not only taken advantage of my hint, and thrown away his own gun, but was also just kicking off his shoes. I tried to throw off my own in the same way, but they were fastened on with a pair of old fashioned buckles.

I strained myself to the utmost to reach a wood which lay a little way before me, with the desperate hope of finding some way of losing myself in it. I ventured one look more; and was frightened almost out of my senses at finding the bare-legged fellow almost upon me. I ran on, though but an instant more; for I had hardly turned my head again before I found a frightful precipice, the edge of which I had reached. I felt as if it were almost certain death to go farther; but I had such a dread of my pursuer, that I ran right off without waiting to see where I was going.

I fell like a stone, and the next instant struck on my feet in soft mud, with a loud spatting noise, which I heard repeated close by me. I had sunk into the mud up to my knees, and was entirely unarmed. It was some relief to see that he had no pistol to shoot me, and was not quite near enough to reach me. He, however, was beginning to struggle to get his legs out. I struggled too, but found it was no easy work. I could not perceive, for some time, that either of us made any advances, although we had wasted almost all our remaining strength.

My enemy was standing much deeper in the mud than myself. Oh, thought I, the fellow was barefooted; that is the reason: the soles of my shoes had prevented me from sinking quite so deep; there is a good chance of my getting out before him. Still neither of us spoke a word.

So I struggled again most violently; but the straps of my shoes were bound tight across my ancles, and held them to my feet, while I felt that I had not strength enough to draw them out. This made me desperate; and I made another effort, when the straps gave way, and I easily drew out one bare foot, and placed it on top of the ground. With the greatest satisfaction I found the other slipping smoothly up through the clay; and, without waiting to regret my shoe buckles (which were of solid silver), or to exchange a blow or a word with my enemy, I ran down the shore of the brook as fast as my legs could carry me.

About an hour after the enemy surrendered, Stark's men "heard the report of cannon" toward San Coick's Mill. "The Hessians were marching up the road, their cannon in front clearing the way." It had taken these German reinforcements two full days of marching to cover the 24 miles from the Hudson. Lt.-Colonel Heinrich Christoph von Breymann led the regiment of grenadiers, supplemented by a company of jagers and a pair of 6-pounders. Breymann blamed the delay on muddy roads and a treacherous local guide who had "lost the way" the day before, when the column made only eight miles in eight hours. They had had to make "a long search" for another inhabitant "who was able to put us again on the right road." Partial blame for their late arrival must also go to Burgoyne for choosing the German grenadiers who, with the exception of Baum's horseless dragoons, were the slowest troops in his army. And Breymann should have foregone the needless formality of halting his column every fifteen minutes to reform and dress the ranks. One soldier mentioned another source of delay that morning: the troops' "grumbling induced Lt. Col. Brymen to wait unnecessarily for them to cook their kettles."

On the other hand, Breymann had not been told there was any urgency. He only knew he had received orders to march, "in consequence of the good news received from Baum." It was not until

Skene reached him at 2 p.m. on the day of the battle that Breymann had learned Baum was in trouble. However, back in the British camp in the days after the battle, Breymann's late arrival would be cited as the primary reason for Baum's defeat. One rumor claimed that "a pique" had existed between Baum and Breymann. Consequently, when Breymann first heard the sounds of battle in the distance, he allegedly said to a subordinate officer, "We will let them get warm before we reach them."

When Breymann's force first made contact with Stark's, the victorious Americans were spread out over several miles. They were variously engaged in chasing fugitives, herding prisoners toward Bennington, "resting, some refreshing themselves, some looking up the dead and wounded, and others in pursuit of plunder." Parson Allen had discovered several bottles of wine in the saddlebags of a German doctor, and was busy dispensing these spirits to the wounded (having set aside two of the curious square bottles for himself as a souvenir).

Thus, Stark's army was in no position to oppose a determined counterattack from tired but well equipped Regulars. Philip Skene, in the lead with Breymann and a half dozen jagers, saw a party of "Rebells at the end of a worms fence" - a split rail fence in a zigzag pattern.

> I galloped up to them, at the distance of 100 yards and desired them to halt; some did. I then asked them if they were for King George; they immediately presented and fired confusedly, hit my horse but missed me. The chesseurs [jagers] advanced near enough to return their fire and begin the action. Major Berner immediately took to the side of the hill on our left flank and rushed the enemy so close that they retreated before him. Lt. Col. Breymen always advanced in front to show his men an example. Unluckily the grenadiers did not close with the enemy but continued flinging away their ammunition at too great a distance; the cannon, two six pounders, advanced within point blank [range, firing] grape shot &

continued firing for an hour and a half and the enemy continually retreated about two miles.

Now it was, that the American reinforcements arrived. These were Colonel Seth Warner's decimated Vermont continental regiment (only 130 remained after Hubbardton) and 200 rangers under Lt.-Colonel Samuel Safford of Bennington. They had set out from Manchester the day before, after waiting for a party to return from searching the battlefield at Hubbardton for muskets. They now had an opportunity to put them to use. After stopping in Bennington for flints and ammunition, they halted again at Stark's camp. There they dropped their coats and knapsacks, drew a gill of rum per man, and filled their canteens with water. They marched on, and paused at the recently contested bridge "while the men drank at the river." An anonymous member of Colonel Warner's regiment describes what happened next:

> We continued our march until we came to the top of an eminence. The regiment had halted. On inquiring the cause, I was told that a reinforcement of the enemy was near. I mounted a fence and saw the enemy's flank guard beyond the next hill, say half a mile distant. We were then ordered to form a line for battle by filing to the right, but owing to the order not being understood in the rear of the line, was formed by filing to the left, which brought many of our men into a sort of swamp instead of on the hill above, where we should have been.
>
> We however waited the approach of the enemy and commenced firing as they came up, but owing, as I think, to the unfavorable nature of the ground, we soon began a retreat, which was continued slowly and in good order, firing constantly for about three-fourths of a mile until we reached the high ground west of the run of water, where we made a stand. The enemy had two pieces of cannon in the road and their line extended a

considerable distance both below and above the road. A party of Hessians undertook to outflank us on the right and partly succeeded but were finally repulsed and driven back. The action was warm and close for nearly two hours, when, it being near dark, the enemy were forced to retreat.

Warner had stopped Breymann's flanking movement by sending half of his own men to the right. At the same time, he extended his front further to the left toward the river to threaten Breymann's right. Warner's firm stand encouraged Stark's men to halt their own retreat, and the opposing forces remained fairly stationary after that, as "the battle continued obstinate on both sides till sunset." During this final phase of the fighting, which "lasted from 15 to 30 minutes," Jesse Field recalled that "Our men kept collecting in front and on their right, generally behind trees, and kept up a constant fire. The road appeared full of men and it was like firing into a flock of sheep."

Thomas Mellen, of Stickney's regiment, had been one of the men surprised by Breymann's first appearance:

> I and many others chased straggling Hessians in the woods; we pursued until we met Breymann with 800 fresh troops and larger cannon, which opened a fire of grape shot; some of the grape shot riddled a Virginia fence near me; one shot struck a small white oak behind which I stood; though it hit higher than my head I fled from the tree, thinking it might be aimed at again. We skirmishers ran back till we met a large body of Stark's men and then faced about. I soon started for a brook I saw a few rods behind, for I had drank nothing all day, and should have died of thirst if I had not chewed a bullet all the time. I had not gone a rod when I was stopped by an officer, sword in hand, ready to cut me down as a runaway, who, on my complaining of thirst,

handed me his canteen which was full of rum; I drank and forgot my thirst.

But the enemy outflanked us, and I said to a comrade, "we must run, or they will have us." He said, "I will have one fire first." At that moment, a major, on a black horse rode along behind us, shouting "fight on boys, re-inforcements close by." While he was yet speaking, a grape shot went through his horse's head; it bled a good deal, but the major kept his seat, and rode to encourage others.

In a few minutes we saw Warner's men hurrying to help us; they opened right and left of us, and one half of them attacked each flank of the enemy, and beat back those who were just closing round us. Stark's men now took heart and stood their ground. My gun barrel was at this time too hot to hold, so I seized the musket of a dead Hessian, in which my bullets went down easier than in my own. Right in front were the cannon, and seeing an officer on horse-back waving his sword to the artil-lery, I fired at him twice; his horse fell; he cut the traces of an artillery horse, mounted him and rode off. I afterward heard that the officer was Major Skene.

Soon the Germans ran, and we followed; many of them threw down their guns on the ground, or offered them to us, or kneeled, some in puddles of water. One said to me, *"Wir sind ein bruder!"* [We surrender brother!] I pushed him behind me and rushed on. The enemy beat a parley, minded to give up, but our men did not understand it [and kept firing]. I came to one wounded man flat on the ground, crying water or quar-ter. I snatched the sword out of his scabbard, and while I ran on and fired, carried it in my mouth, thinking I might need it. The Germans fled by the road and in a wood each side of it; many of their scabbards caught in the brush and held the fugitives till we seized them. We chased them till dark.

Defeat was inevitable once the Germans used up their ammunition. Skene attributed this to their having "wasted [it] at too great a distance" when they first arrived. And panic set in after Breymann fell with a bullet in his leg. As usual, the American marksmen had concentrated their fire on the unlucky Germans manning the artillery. Breymann received his wound when he "hastened with a number of men toward the cannon in order to bring them off. On this occasion the men received the most dangerous wounds." By now "the horses were all killed," forcing Breymann to abandon the two six-pounders. He told Riedesel and Burgoyne that he "gladly would have given his life to bring off one of the guns." At one point, Stark ordered his men to turn one of the captured field pieces about, for use against its former owners. However, he found that he had to load it himself, since no one could be found who knew how to work a cannon.

Because their attempt to parley for surrender terms had not been recognized by the Americans, more than half of Breymann's Germans managed to escape and eventually reach the army on the Hudson late the next night. Over the objections of at least one of his colonels, General Stark called off the pursuit when it became too dark to distinguish friend from foe, saying, "let us not ruin a good day's work." "Had day lasted an hour longer," he would write in his report, "we should have taken the whole body of them."

Colonel Baum was carried to a nearby house, where he died a few hours later. The next day, he was buried with military honors. The two detachments from Burgoyne's army, together, lost about nine hundred men in this raid - 207 killed, and nearly 700 taken prisoner. In contrast, Stark and Warner suffered less than 100 casualties.

Thomas Mellen concludes his account of the day's events, by describing the scene after the second battle was over:

I was coming back, when I was ordered by Stark himself, who knew me, as I had been one of his body guards in Canada, to help draw off a field-piece. I told him "I was worn out." His answer was, "don't seem to disobey; take hold, and if you can't hold out, slip away in the dark."

Before we had dragged the gun far, Warner rode near us. Some one pointing to a dead man by the road-side said, "Your brother is killed," "Is it Jesse?" asked Warner. And when the answer was "yes," he jumped off his horse, stooped and gazed in the dead man's face, and then rode away without saying a word.

On my way back I got the belt of the Hessian sword I had taken in the pursuit. I also found a barber's pack, but was obliged to give up all my findings till the booty was divided. To the best of my remembrance, my share was four dollars and some odd cents.

My company lay down and slept in a corn-field, near where we had fought - each man having a hill of corn for a pillow. When I waked next morning, I was so beaten out that I could not get up till I had rolled about a good while.

When the smoke cleared away, those who had vanquished the tories beheld their neighbors, and in some cases their kinsmen.

The German and British "were treated as prisoners of war and marched from the field in ranks," eventually ending up in eastern Massachusetts, where they were confined until exchanged or released. On the march through Berkshire and Hampshire counties, many of them were detached from their comrades and hired out to farmers and others left shorthanded because of the war. Quite a few eventually became settlers in Pittsfield, Massachusetts, in Londonderry, New Hampshire, and elsewhere. Henry Archelaus, Baum's servant, settled in Weare, New Hampshire, married a distant cousin of General Stark's wife, and later in the war enlisted in the Continental Army.

The Tories, however, were not used so kindly. Caleb Stark, the general's son, remembered the captured Tories entering Bennington:

> [They were] tied in pairs; to each pair a horse was attached by traces, with, in some cases, a negro for his rider. They were led away amid the jeers and scoffs of the victors - the good housewives of Bennington taking down beds to furnish cords for the occasion. Many of [them were] their neighbors [who] had gone over to the enemy the day before the battle.

Thomas Mellen years later recalled that "One tory, with his left eye shot out, was led in, mounted on a horse who had also lost his left eye. It seems to me cruel now - it did not then." Some of the Tories, probably the more prominent ones, were sent to Connecticut's infamous underground prison, the Symsbury Mines. Others were confined locally. The following January, the Council of Bennington passed a resolution putting some of them to work:

> Let the overseer of the tories detach ten of them, with proper officers to take the charge, and march them in two distinct files from this place through the Green Mountains, for breaking a path through the snow. Let each man be provided with three days provisions; let them march and tread the snow in said road of suitable width for a sleigh and span of horses ... at 6 o'clock tomorrow morning.

The two field pieces that Baum had brought on his march had quite a history of their own. Originally cast in France, they had been captured in Canada by the British during the late French War. After they were taken from the Germans at Bennington, the cannon went into the continental service and were inscribed "Taken at Bennington on August 16, 1777." Thirty-five years later, they were taken back by the British when Detroit fell into their hands, during the War of 1812. The British commander had the inscription on the shiny brass metal appended with "Retaken at Detroit on August 16, 1812." A year after that, they changed hands once more, when Fort George at the mouth of the Niagara River was captured by the Americans. One of the guns can be seen today at the State House in Montpelier, Vermont.

Bennington, more than any other battle, resembles the mythical image of the Revolutionary War that has come down to us today: raw militia, farmers inexperienced in war, fighting and defeating seasoned professional European soldiers. However, as such, it serves as the exception rather than the rule, for most of the battles were fought not by militia, but chiefly by the American "regulars" - the continentals.

Five days after the battle, Congress acted upon Benjamin Lincoln's letter and passed a resolution censuring John Stark for disobedience in not submitting to Lincoln's command at Manchester. However, the very next day, a letter arrived from Philip Schuyler, informing Congress of the glorious victory. They promptly passed a new resolution, praising John Stark and commissioning him as a brigadier-general in the Continental Army.

The New Hampshire legislature received Stark's official report and mementoes of the victory: two German swords, a cartridge box, a carbine, and a brass drum. He ended his report with a postscript, "I think we have returned the enemy a proper compliment in the above action for the Hubbartown engagement." For himself, Stark kept only the standard his brigade had carried into battle that day - the now famous "Bennington flag" of thirteen white stars painted on a blue field, with a green floater attached.

To honor their general, the New Hampshire legislature, or provincial congress, voted unanimously to present him with "a compleat suit of clothes becoming his rank, together with a piece of linnen." This resolution, along with Stark's official report to that body, was published in "a rebel newspaper." A copy of the paper reached the British camp and made for interesting conversation at the officers' mess one day: "It was remarked upon the reward that either the General was Stark naked or Congress stark mad."

CHAPTER ELEVEN
THE AMERICANS STAND THEIR GROUND
AUGUST - SEPTEMBER 1777

"We had high hopes of victory ... and when we crossed the Hudson and General Burgoyne said Britons never retreat, we were all in high spirits."

> - Baroness Friedericke Riedesel,
>   wife of General Riedesel.

"Let us get them into the woods."

> - A popular saying among the Americans after the Battle of Bennington.

For General Burgoyne, July, which had seen the stunning capture of Ticonderoga and the retreat of its panic-stricken defenders, had been a time of exultation. His prospects appeared so promising that he wrote to his superior in London, Lord George Germain, asking permission, once Albany and the lower Hudson were secured, to lead part of his army eastward, where he had "little doubt of subduing before winter the provinces where the rebellion originated."

But, oh! How quickly the fortunes of war can change, dashing the hopes of a cocksure general. The month of August saw Burgoyne's army lose nearly one thousand men to the rebels at Bennington. Another thousand were siphoned off to garrison duty at Ti and the lesser posts along what was becoming a dangerously long line of communication with Canada. The remaining force, barely 6000 strong, had seen its progress stalled on the upper Hudson for lack of carts and horses to transport provisions.

Burgoyne also learned that he could no longer expect to join forces at Albany with other British forces, from either the west or the south. In the west, St. Leger had "inexplicably" lifted his siege of Fort Stanwix and returned to Montreal. And in the south, Sir William Howe had set sail from New York, not up the Hudson, but out to sea. Howe informed Burgoyne that his "intentions are for Pennsylvania," and he expected Washington to follow by land with his main army to protect Philadelphia.

By late August, the dashing "Gentleman Johnny" Burgoyne had other reasons, too, for writing an uncharacteristically gloomy report to Colonial Secretary Germain. The rebel army in his front had been reinforced by 3000 continentals from the lower Hudson forts. And Bennington had shown him that "the most active and rebellious race of the continent hangs like a gathering storm on my left." The proud general even briefly considered retreating, but rejected the idea. However, he was starting to realize that pushing on might mean risking total defeat, and he might have to play the martyr. He concluded his letter to Germain:

> But my orders being positive to "force a junction with Sir William Howe," I apprehend I am not at liberty to remain inactive longer than shall be necessary to collect twenty-five days provisions.
>
> I yet do not despond. Should I succeed in forcing my way to Albany, I shall think no more of a retreat, but at worst fortify there and await Sir W. Howe's operations. Whatever my fate, I rest in the confidence that, whatever decision may be passed upon my conduct, my good intent will not be questioned.

As Burgoyne waited for his army's provisions to arrive, hundreds of men were marching west and north to go "agin Burgine." Their coming forth now was in contrast to their earlier behavior, when they had "taken the field as tardily as if they were going to be hanged." As word spread that the Mohawk and Bennington expeditions had been stopped, people began taking a less fatalistic view of the campaign. Perhaps Burgoyne could be stopped after all. Nothing breeds courage like a few victories, no matter how small. One British soldier had predicted this in his diary a few days after Bennington: "it no doubt will be a matter of great exultation to the Americans, and divest them of those fears they had entertained of the German troops, especially as they have been defeated by a set of raw militia."

The New Englanders were also encouraged by a recent change in command. Philip Schuyler, the aristocratic New York patroon they hated and "considered a traitor" had been replaced as commander of the Northern Department. On August 4, Congress appointed Virginia's Horatio Gates to the command. New York's John Jay noted that Congress had become convinced that unless a general favored by the Yankees presided in the Northern Department "the militia of New England would not be brought into the field."

Gates had worked hard to become "the darling of the New Englanders." He had repeatedly and publicly praised their militia and the democratic spirit of New England, and declared that New York's land speculating patroons were entirely wrong in the matter of the New Hampshire Grants.

As for Philip Schuyler, the fall of Ticonderoga and the army's continual retreat provided new fuel for his detractors. And Schuyler had hastened his own removal by writing frantic letters to Washington, who relayed the substance of them, in his own reports, to Congress. Sam Adams labeled Ti's evacuation "no more than I expected when he was appointed to the command there."

> Schuyler has written a series of weak and contemptible things in a style of despondency which alone, I think, is sufficient for the removal of him. For if his pen expresses the true feelings of his heart, it cannot be expected that the bravest veterans would fight under such a general. He writes in a tone of perfect despair.

283

The same week that it appointed Gates, Congress requested New Jersey, Pennsylvania and all states further north to draft one-sixth of each of their militia regiments for three months, and send them to aid the northern army. Later, Gates followed this up by writing his own letters to the governors. The recent victories at Fort Stanwix and Bennington, plus appointment of a new commander and the end of the harvest season all figured in the militia's new willingness to leave their homes and march to the Hudson.

* * * * *

To these factors was added the tragic story of the beautiful young Jane McCrea. Although General Burgoyne had earlier cautioned his Indian allies not to kill and scalp innocent inhabitants, they had paid no heed to his warnings, and he had not pressed the point. General Simon Fraser had dismissed one officer's objections to the barbaric practice by saying, "It is a conquered country and we must wink at such things." Perhaps that was also Burgoyne's private opinion, judging from a verse he had written on the cover of his journal during the voyage from England that spring:

> I will let loose the dogs of hell,
> Ten thousand Indians, who shall yell
> And foam and tear and grin and roar,
> And drench their moccasins in gore.

Jane McCrea, an unusually beautiful woman of about twenty, lived with her brother a few miles south of Fort Edward. About the middle of July, her brother urged her to join him in moving to Albany to be safe from Burgoyne's marauding Indians. She refused to go, and secretly made plans to head in the opposite direction, toward the advancing British Army. For Jane's fiance, David Jones, was serving as a lieutenant in a Tory regiment. He had written to her on July 11th from Skenesborough:

> In a few days we will march to Ft. Edward, for which
> I am anxious, where I shall have the happiness to meet
> you, after long absence. I hope if your brother John
> goes you will not go with him, but stay at Mrs. McNeil's.
> There I will join you.

So Jane went to stay with the corpulent old widow Mrs. McNeil, who had a home north of Fort Edward. Mrs. McNeil, too, looked forward to the arrival of the British Army, because her cousin was General Simon Fraser. Alone in the house, except for a Negro servant and her child, they heard musket fire on the evening of July 26th and went down into the cellar to hide.

Though the Americans had evacuated and burned Fort Edward three days before, they sent back patrols to watch for the enemy's approach. A member of one of these patrols, Samuel Standish, was captured by three Indians that evening on a hill just north of Mrs. McNeil's house. They stripped him of his coat and handkerchief and "pinioned him to a tree." Standish goes on to say that, "after a short time I saw a party of Indians coming with two women. They came up the hill to a spring and seemed to be in a quarrel. They shot one of the women and scalped her. This woman I knew to be Jennie McCrea."

According to the British accounts, Jane's fiance, anxious for her safety, had sent out a small party of Indians to fetch Jane to him, promising a keg of rum for bringing her safely into camp. When they arrived at the house, they searched it and discovered the occupants in the cellar. They did not harm the Negro woman and child, but drew Jane and Mrs. McNeil out by the hair and proceeded toward Sandy Hill, on the way to the British camp. Jane was placed on a horse and led swiftly away. Jane's nephew describes what a soldier claiming to be a witness told him happened next:

> They had gone but a short distance when they met an-

other party of Indians returning from Argyle where they had killed the family of Mr. Bains. This party disapproved of taking Miss McCrea to the British camp, and one of them struck her with a tomahawk and tore off her scalp.

The victim was stripped and then rolled down the hill, where she was later found and buried. The fat Mrs. McNeil was also stripped, though not harmed. Upon reaching the British camp, she immediately called for her cousin, General Fraser. He meekly listened to her berate him for the behavior of his allies, while he covered her with his own greatcoat - there being no one among the 327 females in camp large enough to provide a suitable garment.

The Indian Chief LeLoup, also known as the Wyandot Panther, soon returned to the British camp with numerous grisly trophies, among them one that was readily recognized by Mrs. McNeil - "a fresh scalp-lock which I could not mistake because the hair was unusually fine, luxuriant, lustrous, and dark as the wing of a raven." The young Lieutenant Jones, her fiance, also recognized her scalp, and for a while went mad with rage and anguish. Years later, his grandniece told his sad story:

> He was so crushed by the terrible blow and disgusted with Burgoyne in refusing to punish the miscreant, that he and his brother asked for a discharge, and were refused. They deserted - having first rescued the precious relic of his beloved from the savages. He retired to this Canadian wilderness.

The outraged General Burgoyne proposed that the murderer be hung. But his Indian agent, St. Luc de La Corne, interceded. He insisted that if Burgoyne did so his Indian allies, already resentful over the restrictions placed on them, would promptly desert, and massacre all in their path on their return to their homelands. Thomas Anburey explains:

> The chief of the tribe to which the Indian belonged said to the General it was the rules of their war, that if two of them at the same instant seized a prisoner and seemed to have equal claim, in case any dispute arose between them they soon decided the contest and the unhappy cause was sure to become a victim to their contention.

A few weeks later, General Burgoyne sent a letter to the new American commander, asking if a British surgeon could be sent to Bennington to care for the wounded German and Tory prisoners being held there. In the letter, Burgoyne chided General Gates regarding reports he had received that some Tories had been killed when they were trying to surrender during that recent battle. In his response, Horatio Gates denied the charge and, as proof, enclosed "letters from your wounded officers, prisoners in my hands" by which Burgoyne would "be informed of the generosity of their conquerors." Before closing the letter, Gates took full advantage of the opportunity to give the proud Briton "a tickler upon scalping."

> That the savages of America should in their warfare mangle and scalp the unhappy prisoners who fall into their hands, is neither new nor extraordinary; but that the famous Lieutenant General Burgoyne, in whom the fine gentleman is united with the soldier and the scholar, should hire the savages of America to scalp Europeans and descendents of Europeans, that he should pay a price for each scalp so barbarously taken, is more than will be believed in Europe untill authenticated facts shall, in every gazette, convince mankind of the truth of the horrid fate.

Gates went on to recount the tragedy of Jane McCrea, one of "upwards of one hundred" innocent non-combatants who had suffered the same fate. As a crafty way of providing emphasis, Gates crossed out - but still left clearly legible - a warning that "The law of retaliation is a just law, and you must expect to feel its force."

There was propaganda value in the tragic story of the young Tory maiden, brutally murdered while waiting "in bridal array" for her betrothed. Gates dispatched couriers to spread the story across New York and New England, and provided copies of his masterful rebuke of Burgoyne to the newspapers. George Washington even enclosed copies of it when writing to the governors, again urging them to call out the militia to stop the invaders. The more ardent patriots came out, of course. But with them also came men who until then had felt they could remain neutral and not become involved in the war. As the nineteenth century historian George Trevelyan put it, the men of New England

> were determined that the story of Jane McCrea should not be repeated in their own villages. In order to protect their families from the Wyandot Panther and his brother warriors, the shooting must be done not from the windows of farmhouses, but in the line of battle outside the borders of New England.

* * * * *

Horatio Gates, one of the very few American generals with any experience in a regular army, had served in the British Army during the late French war. Injured during his first action, he had spent the rest of his British career in staff positions and rose to the rank of major. However, possessing neither wealth nor a noble birth, he found further advancement impossible and decided, in 1772, to sell his commission and emigrate to Virginia.

When the war broke out in 1775, Congress chose Gates as Washington's adjutant general, with the rank of brigadier. His considerable skills in administration were invaluable to the commander of the fledgling army. However, Congress needed him in the field, and with a promotion to major-general he was transferred to the army's Northern Department in May of 1776. He served in the northern army periodically thereafter, either as the commander, or as a subordinate to Philip Schuyler, depending on which one was currently in favor with Congress.

When Gates arrived in camp to take command on August 19th, 1777, the northern army's main force was at the mouth of the Mohawk River, only nine miles north of Albany. One part of the army was detached and seeking a rendezvous with Stark near Bennington, while another part was on the relief expedition to Fort Stanwix. In recent weeks, Schuyler had continued to fall back toward Albany with his remaining forces, rather than attempt a stand against Burgoyne. The troops, according to Jonathan Trumbull, Jr., were tired of retreating, and "will fight if officers will lead them."

Gates received a warm welcome, and promptly pledged to "not wait to be attacked, but to endeavour to turn the tables on the antagonist." The dramatic effect that the change of command had on the soldiers' morale can be seen in their diaries and letters. One man wrote, "Gladness appeared in every countenance. Joy circulated through the camp." Another: "General Gates takes command of the Northern army this day, which I think will put a new face upon our affairs." A third declared, "from this miserable state of despondency and terror, Gates' arrival raised us, as if by magic. We began to hope, and then to act."

Gates inherited the army at a very opportune time. The day after he arrived, news reached camp of Stark's one-sided victory near Bennington. A few days later, word came from the west that St. Leger had returned to Canada. On August 28, Benedict Arnold returned with his Fort Stanwix relief column, now swelled by New York militia to 1200. And that same day, an equally significant force also marched into camp: 367 long-shirted riflemen, led by the Viginian, Daniel Morgan.

Morgan had led Arnold's attack on Quebec, and was taken prisoner there on January 1, 1776. After Morgan was exchanged, Washington asked him to recruit an entire regiment of riflemen. Morgan was promoted to full colonel. Though Washington needed them in his own fight with Howe for Philadelphia, he knew that Morgan's new rifle corps would be perfectly suited for action in the forests of upstate New York. "I expect," he wrote to Gates, "the most eminent services from them, and I shall be mistaken if their presence does not go far towards producing a general destruction among the savages." Washington suggested that news of the riflemen's coming be made known, "with proper embellishments, to the enemy. It would not be amiss, among other things, to magnify numbers."

Knowing Morgan's abilities, Gates had been overjoyed when he received Washington's letter. Upon their arrival, he asked Morgan and his men to serve as "the advance of the army." To strengthen this force, Gates attached a newly formed battalion of light infantry under Major Henry Dearborn, of New Hampshire, another veteran of the Kennebec expedition. Dearborn selected 250 "vigorous young men," each equipped with musket, bayonet, tomahawk and knife.

The first few hundred militia, two contingents from Connecticut, arrived on September 6. Two days later, with his army's strength up to about 6300 men, Gates felt he was ready to advance and meet the enemy. He sent his Polish engineer, Tadeusz Kosciuszko, ahead with orders "to select a position on the western bank of the Hudson, which from its hilly tree covered surface would be best suited for defence." He found one, halfway between Fort Edward and Albany. It was Bemis Heights, a hill that rose from the Hudson's west bank. It was named after the keeper of a tavern on the riverbank road at the base of the hill. "A fatigue of 1000 men were put to work under Colonel Kosciuszko." Full of confidence now, the Americans dug in and waited for the invaders.

* * * * *

Burgoyne's army spent four weeks (August 14 to September 11) at Fort Miller collecting the provisions it would need to complete the march to Albany. This was a monumental undertaking, since the army consumed ten tons of food and drink each day. A German soldier wrote home, describing the ordeal:

> All our regiments were now engaged in the difficult task of bringing up the necessaries for the remainder of the campaign, very laborious work, on account of the scarcity of carts and horses. My dear sirs, only think of it! It was August, the hottest time of the year, when, although sitting quietly in our tents, we could hardly draw a breath. The dysentery was also causing fearful havoc among us; and notwithstanding it all, we were obliged to work like beavers, since the very life of our army depended on our doing so.

Another German soldier also noted the inhospitable North American weather:

> The heat in this vicinity is uncommonly severe, and exceeds that of the warmest summer day in our own country. Almost daily we are visited by thunderstorms which, while being terrific, pass away very quickly and do not last as long as with us at home. They do not, however, cool the atmosphere after they are over; and in the night - more especially toward morning - there is such a heavy fall of due and mist that it penetrates through our tents, into our blankets even, causing them to become soaking wet.

John Burgoyne realized how the odds had changed, and what a great risk he was taking by continuing on toward Albany. But he also had an idea of the rewards that would be his if he succeeded, unsupported by St. Leger or Howe. Furthermore, he had seen how General Carleton had been censured for retreating to Canada the previous fall. As the Earl of Harrington remarked in Parliament in 1778, Burgoyne's reputation "would not have stood very high if he had halted at Fort Edward."

Burgoyne's army was now advancing without its "eyes," as all but fifty of its Indian allies had gone home on August 19th. The Indians had been persuaded to desert by their French Canadian interpreter and Indian agent, Louis St. Luc de La Corne. He had been angered by Burgoyne's attempts (more concerted since the Jane McCrea affair) at "controlling the use of the hatchet and scalping-knife."

On September 13, the army reached the settlement of Saratoga (present day Schuylerville). There they found

> a handsome and commodious dwelling-house, an exceedingly fine saw- and grist-mill, and at a small distance a very neat church, with several houses round it, all of which are the property of General Schuyler. This beautiful spot was quite deserted, not a living creature on it. On the grounds were great quantities of fine wheat, as also Indian corn. The former was instantly cut down, threshed, carried to the mill to be ground, and delivered to the men to save our provisions; the latter was cut for forage for the horses.

Evidently, the scorched earth policy that Philip Schuyler had had his army enforce upon the settlers in the region had not been applied to his own fields. Burgoyne moved right into Schuyler's summer home. Inviting his favorite gambling partners to join him, he spent the next few evenings like many earlier ones during this campaign: "singing, drinking, and amusing himself in the company of the wife of a commissary, who was his mistress and, like him, loved champaign."

That quote is from the journal of a brave little woman who was above such scandalous behavior, the Baroness Friedericke von Riedesel. When her husband, the major-general, had left Europe for Canada the previous year, she had just given birth. She therefore stayed in Germany until the child was old enough to travel. Then, with her servants and three young daughters, she set out to find her husband in the wilds of North America.

Traveling first to London, she was dismayed to learn she would have to wait several months for passage to Canada, where she planned to join her husband. She was also shocked to find that the latest fashions from Paris so popular on the continent were definitely not in style on the streets of London (where she had to ask her chauffeur what the English word "whore" meant that people were shouting at her). The family's passage over the Atlantic also brought other irritations, including unsolicited advances from a British rogue passing himself off as a gentleman.

After several weeks boarding with some nuns in Canada, she received word from her husband, who was by then at Fort Edward. She set out again, to find him. The first leg of that part of her journey almost proved to be her last. She was crossing a river in a canoe, when a sudden hailstorm burst from the sky, making her young children scream hysterically and try to jump out of the canoe. This was followed by a night on a tiny, rattlesnake infested island. Finally, in mid-August, she was joyously reunited with her worried husband. There she and her children and servants squeezed into a calash and "followed the army right in the midst of the soldiers, who sang and were jolly, burning with the desire for victory." Her journal, published in Germany after the war, provides a different perspective on the campaign.

The German baroness was not the only woman of quality traveling with the army. Lady Acland, wife of Lord Acland, major of the British grenadiers, was sleeping with her husband in his tent on the night of September 15 when an unfortunate incident occurred. One of Acland's men explains:

Being the advanced post of the army, we seldom slept

out of our clothes. In one of these situations a tent, in which Major Acland and Lady Harriet were asleep, suddenly caught fire; the Major's orderly sergeant, with great danger of suffocation, dragged out the first person he got hold of, which was the Major. Lady Harriet made her escape by creeping under the walls in the back part of the tent. The Major ... [returned] in the midst of the flames, in search of her! The sergeant again saved him, but the Major's face and body was burnt in a very severe manner. Everything they had with them in the tent was consumed. This accident was occasioned by a favourite Newfoundland dog, who being very restless, overset a table on which a candle was burning, and it rolling to the walls of the tent, instantly set them on fire.

Shortly before reaching Saratoga, our "gentleman volunteer" diarist, Thomas Anburey, was asked to fill a vacancy in the 24th Foot. He was now a lieutenant. Anburey took time to visit the camp of a few dozen Mohawks who arrived on September 4th, led by Chief Joseph Brandt. These warriors had come with their families after local militia destroyed their village in the wake of St. Leger's failed expedition. The women and children were soon sent to join the other refugees at Fort Ticonderoga while the warriors joined Fraser's advance corps. Anburey recorded some of his observations to satisfy the curiosity of his European readers.

The mode of confining their infants is by binding them flat on their backs to a board, and as they are swaddled up to their heads, it makes them resemble living mummies; this method of binding their young, I am led to imagine, is the cause of that perfect symmetry among the men.

When they arrive in hearing of the camp, they set up the war whoop, as many times as they have prisoners. It consists in the sound of <u>whoo</u>, <u>whoo</u>, <u>whoop</u>! which is continued till the breath is almost exhausted, and then broken off with a sudden elevation of voice; some of them modulate it into notes by placing the hand before the mouth, but both are heard at a great distance.

Whenever they scalp, they seize the head of the disabled or dead enemy, and placing one of their feet on the neck, twist their left hand in the hair, by which means they extend the skin that covers the top of the head, and with the other hand draw their scalping knife. A few dextrous strokes takes off the part that is termed the scalp; they are so exceedingly expeditious in doing this, that it scarcely exceeds a minute. If the hair is short, they stoop and with their teeth strip it off. They tie with bark or deer's sinews their trophy in a small hoop, to preserve it from putrefaction, painting part of the scalp and the hoop all round with red. These they preserve as monuments of their prowess.

I saw several scalps hanging upon poles in front of their wigwams; one of them had remarkably fine long hair hanging to it. An officer that was with me wanted to purchase it, at which the Indian seemed highly offended, nor would he part with this barbarous trophy, although he was offered so strong a temptation as a bottle of rum.

Should I at any time be unfortunate enough to get wounded, and the Indians come across me with an intention to scalp, it would be my wish to receive at once a <u>coup</u> <u>de</u> <u>grace</u> with their tomahawk, which in most instances they mercifully allow. This instrument they make great use of in war, for in pursuing an enemy, if they find it impossible to come up with them, they with the utmost dexterity throw and seldom fail striking it into the skull or back of those they pursue, by that means arresting them in flight. The tomahawks are mostly made to answer two purposes, that of a pipe and a hatchet. When they purchase them off the traders they take off the wooden handle, and substitute in its stead a hollow cane one.

On September 17th, Burgoyne moved his army a few miles south of Saratoga and halted two miles north of Bemis's tavern along the river-bank road. The army remained there the next day while supplies were brought forward by cart and bateau. The sick and wounded were also brought forward with the army. Burgoyne could not leave them in the comfort of the houses at Saratoga for fear of reprisals by the cowboys. "Cowboys" was the term for bands of civilians who preyed upon travellers, especially anyone driving wagons or cattle to supply either army.

But local cowboys were not the only ones harassing Burgoyne's army. General Riedesel indicated in his journal that, ever since the departure of most of the Indians, "the enemy began to molest the outposts and became very troublesome." With the arrival of Morgan's riflemen, moreover, Burgoyne's army began to suffer constant harassment by sniper fire from the woods. On September 18, work parties were fired upon, while repairing bridges over the many creeks that came down out of the steep hills. And, not far from camp, a party of unarmed British soldiers digging potatoes was surprised, and suffered thirty casualties in the attack. The firing by Americans on British soldiers poaching potatoes made a strong impression on the British. One of them commented on it in his journal:

> They might without difficulty have been surrounded and taken prisoners, but the Americans could not resist the opportunity of shedding blood. Such cruel and unjustifiable conduct can have no good tendency, while it serves greatly to increase hatred and thirst for revenge.

Burgoyne was likewise incensed, and immediately issued a general order against further unauthorized foraging:

> The General will no longer bear to lose men for the pitiful consideration of potatoes or forage - the life of the soldier is the property of the King and since neither friendly admonition, repeated injunctions, nor corporal punishment have effect, after what has happen'd, ye army is now to be informed that the first soldier caught beyond the advanced sentries of the army will be instantly hanged.

The country was heavily wooded and therefore extremely dangerous for the invading army marching through it. A German jager wrote home, describing the hazards of the march: "here there is nothing but thick forest, thus when we come into these woods we cannot neglect any suspicious tree, for on these the rascals sit and shoot our men dead." Another German, an officer named Du Roi, reflected in his journal upon the frustrations of chasing the snipers:

> Never are they so much to be feared as when retreating. Covered by the woods, the number of enemies with which we have to deal can never be defined. A hundred men approaching [us] are attacked, they retreat fighting. We think ourselves victors and follow them; they flee to an ambush, surround and attack us with a superior number of men.

Samuel Woodruff waited on Bemis Heights for the invading army to attack.

> The American army was daily augmenting by militia, volunteers and the "two months men" as they were then called. The boats which had served the British army for

a bridge, being considered by them as of no further use, had been cut loose and most of them floated down the river. During these few days of dreadful preparation, information daily arrived in our camp, by deserters and otherwise, that an attack would soon be made upon our entrenchments at Bemis's Heights.

The expected conflict awakened great anxiety. All considered that the expected conflict would be decisive of the campaign at least, if not the war.

On the morning of September 18th, the day before the battle, General John Stark finally arrived at headquarters with 1500 men, veterans of Bennington. General Gates and the army were "animated by the arrival of a band of citizen-soldiers who had conquered the Germans ... but the term of service, for which these men were engaged, expired with the day." Gates, "sensible that a battle must shortly take place, was desirous of adding these victorious troops to his camp; but all to no purpose. The troops were drawn up and harangued by Generals Gates and Stark; not more than three of the whole number were willing to tarry." A New Hampshire man explained their departure this way:

They had expressly stipulated that they should know no commander but Stark, as he had stipulated that he should not be placed under the Continental officers. He was now willing to waive this scruple, but they were not.

Despite Stark's departure, Gates still held a slight numerical superiority over Burgoyne, and a formidable defensive position on Bemis Heights. His lines, made of earth, logs and fence rails and fronted by an abatis, stretched nearly a mile, starting at the narrow riverbank near Bemis's tavern, then moving up the slope and across the plateau some 200 feet above.

The terrain separating the opposing armies was broken by several ravines and was, for the most part, thickly wooded. "A great part of the battle field," one observer noted, "was occupied by lofty trees, principally pine, with here and there a few cleared fields of which the most conspicuous was Freeman's Farm," one mile north of American headquarters on Bemis Heights. Burgoyne would be advancing with only vague reports of his adversary's location and strength, blocked by Morgan's men from "obtaining a view of the American position."

On September 19th, John Burgoyne wanted to set his army in motion at dawn, but a lingering fog delayed them until nearly ten o'clock. About 4000 troops then set out in three columns, with each column bringing forward several light field pieces, mostly six-pounders. Burgoyne counted on their effectiveness, for he knew that "artillery was extremely formidable against raw troops."

Most of the German division, under Riedesel, advanced along the river road, repairing bridges and clearing the road of felled trees as it slowly moved forward. Georg Pausch, the artillery captain, marching along the river road, noticed that each time the column either halted or resumed its march a glint of sunlight flashed on a hilltop across the river. The plan called for Riedesel to halt his column after about a mile, and wait there for Burgoyne's signal gun before proceeding along the road.

Meanwhile, the center column, led by General Hamilton and accompanied by Burgoyne, was to march west (uphill), turn south along the "Great Ravine," and then continue west to Freeman's farm. There they would await the arrival on their right of the third column, headed by General Fraser. This third column was to travel two miles west, then turn south and halt on high ground west of Freeman's farm.

Once Burgoyne received word that all columns were in position and roughly parallel with one another, he would fire three cannon as the signal for everyone to resume the advance. Fraser's objective was to first locate, then seize, whatever high ground was to the left of the American lines. Then, while Riedesel and Burgoyne assaulted the American right and center, respectively, Fraser would turn their left with a flank attack, forcing Gates to retreat. This was the grand plan, a very risky one. The distances and rough terrain separating the three columns would make it very difficult for them to support each other.

All morning, reports flowed into American headquarters. One tree climber from across the Hudson had observed the enemy breaking camp early and reported that "the crisis is near." A militia colonel returned from a scout late in the morning, saying the advancing enemy force was too large for his scouting party "to pick a wrangle with."

To complicate matters, Benedict Arnold fretted, fumed, and argued continuously, trying to persuade Gates to attack Burgoyne's army while it was divided. Horatio Gates was reluctant to send forth any troops from his strong fortifications, reminding Arnold that the enemy was better trained and equipped. But Arnold persisted in arguing that, if they did nothing, by nightfall the enemy's substantial artillery might well be in place on a hill less than a mile west of the American left on Bemis Heights. The American position was vulnerable after all.

By noon, Arnold persuaded Gates to "detach Colonel Morgan's corps to observe their direction and harass their advance." Gates also instructed Arnold to hold his infantry regiments in readiness, if needed to support Morgan.

While Arnold and Gates argued, Burgoyne's three columns were marching through the woods, "every man prepared with 60 rounds of cartridge and ready for instant action." About noon, the center column was halted when it approached a break in the woods. This was Freeman's farm, an oblong east-west clearing of about 350 yards which sloped downward to the east and south. Hamilton's forces waited there for an hour, to give Fraser enough time to make his more circuitous route to the west. Then, at one o'clock, the three signal cannon were fired, to resume the advance.

The first action of the day occurred about this time. The vanguard of the British right column (comprised of Fraser's Canadians, Tories and Indians) made contact with part of Morgan's corps which he had divided in search of the enemy. Captain Wakefield, of Dearborn's light infantry, later recalled how Benedict Arnold arrived on the scene at this opportune moment:

> Arnold rode up, with his sword pointing to the enemy emerging from the woods into an opening partially cleared, covered with stumps and fallen timber. Addressing Morgan, he said, "Colonel Morgan, you and I have seen too many redskins to be deceived by that garb of print and feathers; they are asses in lions' skins, Canadians and Tories; let your riflemen cure them of their borrowed plumes." And so they did; for in less than fifteen minutes the "Wagon Boy," with his Virginia riflemen, sent the painted devils with a howl back to the British lines.

A British soldier in Fraser's corps found the "desertion of the Indians, Canadians, and Provincials exceedingly mortifying." At "the very first fire, the Indians ran through the wood. As to the Canadians and Provincials, they withdrew on perceiving the resistance of the Americans would be more formidable than had been expected."

Half a mile to the east, General Hamilton sent forward Major Forbes of the 9th Foot with an infantry picket of 100 men to reconnoiter Freeman's cabin. By now a handful of Morgan's men had reached the farm and were posted around the "house and behind split rail fences." They offered token resistance before falling back to the woods and brush on the southern edge of the clearing where they joined others from Morgan's corps.

Each rifleman then took careful aim at one of the approaching redcoats. Their white crossbelts made perfect targets. At a signal, the woods belched fire, lead and smoke. Major Forbes was "obliged to fall back, every officer being either killed or wounded except one." Their retreat was "secured by the battalion of Light Infantry sent from the column on the right commanded by Brig'r General Frazer."

As the wounded Forbes and his decimated picket ran through the smoke, they were mistaken for Americans by some of their comrades who "commenced a fire without orders, by which many were killed in retreating." Seeing this, someone "proposed the firing of a gun [cannon], which had the desired effect" of grabbing the attention of those firing. Only then did they hear their officers telling them they were firing on their comrades.

For the American riflemen, the thrill of the chase overcame caution, as they streamed across the clearing after the fleeing redcoats. Entering the woods bordering Freeman's fields to the north, they ran right into the main body of Hamilton's column, who repulsed them with a heavy volley of musket fire.

When Gates's deputy adjutant-general, Colonel James Wilkinson, heard the distant firing he "asked leave to repair to the scene of action." But General Gates replied, "It is your duty, sir, to wait my orders." Not to be denied, Wilkinson soon "made an excuse to visit the picket on the left for intelligence, put spurs to my horse and, directed by the sound, entered the wood." However, as he neared the Freeman farm the firing ceased. He soon met Major Morris, who had led the riflemen's hasty charge:

> To shew me where the action commenced, he leaped a fence into the abandoned field of Freeman, choked up with weeds, and led me to the cabin, almost encircled with dead. I crossed the field, leapt the fence, and just before me on a ridge discovered Lieutenant Colonel Butler with three men, all tree'd. From him I learnt that they had "caught a Scotch prize" - having forced the picket, they had closed with the British line, had been instantly routed, and from the suddenness of the shock scattered in all directions.
>
> ... [Butler] informed me that he had seen a heavy column moving towards our left. I then turned about, to regain the camp and report to the General, when my ears were saluted by an uncommon noise. I approached and perceived Colonel Morgan attended by two men only,

who with a turkey call was collecting his dispersed troops. The moment I came up to him, he exclaimed, "I am ruined, by God! Major Morris ran on so rapidly with the front that they were beaten before I could come up with the rear, and my men are scattered God knows where."

While Morgan blew on his turkey call to regroup his men on the southern edge of Freeman's farm, Lieutenant Thomas Anburey, at the northern end, was making the acquaintance of one of them. Anburey was in a company of light infantry that Fraser had detached from his right column to aid Hamilton's embattled center column. Anburey explains:

> In this skirmish, a batman of General Fraser's rescued from the Indians an officer of the Americans, one Captain Van Swearingham. They were on the point of stripping him, which the man prevented, and recovered his pocket-book from them, containing all his papers of consequence and his commission. He offered the soldier all his _paper_ dollars, and lamented he had no _hard_ ones to reward him with.
>
> The batman brought him up to General Fraser (who now had come up to the two companies he had detached) when he interrogated him concerning the enemy, but could obtain no other answer than that their army was commanded by Generals Gates and Arnold. General Fraser, exceedingly provoked that he could gain no intelligence, told him if he did not immediately inform him as to the exact situation of the enemy he would hang him up directly; the other officer, with the most undaunted firmness, replied, "You may, if you please." The General, perceiving he could make nothing of him, rode off, leaving him in the custody of Lieutenant Dun-

bar of the artillery.

My servant, just at this period, arrived with my canteen, which was rather fortunate, as we stood in need of some refreshment after our march through the woods and this little skirmish. I requested Dunbar, with his prisoner, to partake of it, and sitting down upon a tree, we asked this Captain a variety of questions, to which he always gave evasive answers, and we both observed he was in great spirits. At last I said to him, "Captain, do you think we shall have any more work upon our hands today?" to which he replied, "Yes, yes, you'll have business enough, for there are many hundreds all round you now." He had hardly spoken the words, than from a wood a little way in our front there came an excessive heavy fire.

The "excessive heavy fire" was caused by two New Hampshire regiments under Benedict Arnold attacking Fraser's left flank. However, they soon found themselves outflanked by Fraser's "grenadiers and light infantry, who gave them a tremendous fire," forcing Arnold to fall back after contesting the ground for an hour. Arnold then changed tactics, realizing that his force had driven a wedge between two British columns. If he could keep them separated, they would be susceptible to "defeat in detail." So he ordered Morgan to use some of his riflemen and Dearborn's light infantry to keep Fraser at bay while he led the infantry regiments against Hamilton's smaller force at Freeman's farm. The open ground there promised good shooting for his relatively accurate musketmen (at least they took aim, unlike the British), as long as they avoided the British bayonets. Arnold quickly rode back to Bemis Heights to bring forward reinforcements for his planned assault. Wilkinson describes the attack on the British center, which resumed close to 3 o'clock:

The British line was formed on an eminence in a thin

pine wood having before it Freeman's farm, which was bordered on the opposite side by a wood. The fire of our marksmen from this wood was too deadly to be withstood by the enemy. They gave way and broke, our men rushing from their cover pursued them to the eminence, where they rallied; and, charging in turn, drove us back into the wood - from whence a dreadful fire would again force them to fall back. And in this manner did the battle fluctuate for four hours without one moment's intermission.

Fortunately for the Americans, the more numerous British right division, under General Fraser, did not come to the aid of Hamilton and Burgoyne, whose center division was under the heaviest attack and outnumbered. Fraser only had to contend with Morgan, who was holding him in place on the high ground above Freeman's farm. Lt. Anburey thought it was because Fraser deemed it "unadvisable to evacuate the heights where [he was] advantageously posted." More likely, Fraser was waiting for the center column to make some forward progress, so he could attack the American lines' left flank, as planned.

Benedict Arnold soon had most of his division at Freeman's farm: General Enoch Poor's brigade of New Hampshire and New York continentals, plus two attached regiments of Connecticut militia. Encouraged by the experienced and steady continentals, and led by the inspirational Arnold (a Connecticut native), the militia stood their ground as well as anyone. Recalling the action, one soldier remarked that, "Both armies seemed determined to conquer or die." Another called it a "truly gallant affair, in which death, by familiarity, lost its terrors." Lieutenant William Digby could not believe the "explosion of fire" his ears were subjected to that afternoon. The British "artillery joining in concert like great peals of thunder, assisted by the echoes of the woods, almost deafened us with the noise." Another man wrote that "the noise from the artillery and small arms sounded like the roll of drums."

305

Sergeant Roger Lamb, serving as surgeon's mate in a British regiment, noted that "several of the Americans placed themselves in high trees and, as often as they could distinguish a British officer's uniform, took him off by deliberately aiming at his person." At one point, it was falsely reported to Gates that Burgoyne himself had been killed. One of the riflemen had knocked another officer from a horse he mistook for the British commander's because of its richly embroidered saddlecloth. Burgoyne described such tactics in his official report of the battle:

> The enemy had with their army great numbers of marksmen, armed with rifle-barrel pieces; these hovered upon the flanks in small detachments and were very expert in securing themselves and shifting their ground. In this action many placed themselves in high trees. There was seldom a minute's interval in any part of our line without officers being taken off by a single shot.

General Hamilton lost the services of Fraser's light infantry when Fraser called them back to help fight off Morgan. This left Hamilton with only his original four infantry regiments to oppose Arnold. He held in reserve the 9th regiment (which had already suffered at the hands of the riflemen) and formed the other three regiments into a V, or salient, with the 62nd at the point, the 20th on their left, and the 21st on their right. The 62nd was subjected to an arc of withering fire for three hours and lost 212 of its 280 men to death, wounds, or capture. The fate of one officer was recorded by Thomas Anburey:

> Lieutenant Hervey, of the 62nd, a youth of sixteen and nephew of the Adjutant-General of the same name, received several wounds, and was repeatedly ordered off the field by Colonel Anstruther; but his heroic ardor would not allow him to quit the battle while he could stand and see his brave lads fighting beside him. A ball

striking one of his legs, his removal became absolutely necessary, and while they were conveying him away, another wounded him mortally.

In this situation the surgeon recommended him to take a powerful dose of opium, to avoid a seven or eight hours' life of most exquisite torture; this he immediately consented to, and when the Colonel entered the tent he asked whether he had any affairs they could settle for him? His reply was that, "being a minor, every thing was already adjusted;" but he had one request, which he had just life enough to utter, "Tell my uncle I died like a soldier."

The north branch of Mill Creek cut through the most hotly contested part of Freeman's farm. As the tide of battle swept back and forth across it, many soldiers were hit and fell into the tiny stream, coloring and thickening its waters with American and British blood. The fire "raged most furiously," the air filled with flying lead. Near Anburey, "Lieutenant Don of the 21st Regiment received a ball through his heart. I am sure it will never be erased from my memory; for when he was wounded he sprang from the ground nearly as high as a man."

The four six-pounders of Hamilton's center column had been brought onto the field early, the gun crews doubling up on the drag ropes to pull the pieces one at a time across the ditch of the creek's north fork. One battery of two guns was placed on a slight rise to the left of the V, the other battery to the right. Lieutenant James Hadden worked the left pair, firing round shot into the trees in his front where rebels were forming for the charge. From time to time, he also sprayed grapeshot into a cornfield on his left where others were trying to get behind the 62nd. American sharpshooters sitting in the trees concentrated their fire on Hadden's crew, as his journal explains:

Having lost in killed and wounded nineteen out [of]

twenty-two [men] attached to my two guns, I applied to Brig'r Gen'l Hamilton for a supply of infantry. While speaking to him my cap was shot thro in the front.

Capt. Jones was order'd to let me have all the men from one of Lt. Reids [right flank] guns. Capt. Jones was order'd to accompany me himself.

The enemy being reinforced and advancing closer since the fire of the flank guns were silenced, I found on my return that the 62nd Regiment had made an unsuccessful effort to force them.

This vigorous bayonet charge by the 62nd, chasing the Americans into the woods, resulted in the capture of 25 Regulars when other Americans hidden in the woods closed in on both sides. The rest of the 62nd managed to retreat back to their original position. Lt. Hadden continues his account, as he arrives with the gun crew borrowed from the right flank's battery:

[The 62nd] being worn down had begun to get into confusion, in which situation I found them. Capt. Jones immediately began firing, but being himself very soon wounded as were also the whole of the men we brought up, I was desired to endeavour to effect the retreat of my guns. But before I could accomplish it, the 62nd Regt. were forced to abandon the hill & on it my guns.

New Hampshire's Thomas Blake was among those who alternated possession of the open ground with the 62nd Regiment. He recalled that "the enemy had two field pieces which we took three or four times." But they could not use the captured guns against their former owners, because each time Hadden or someone else would carry off the linstocks (slow matches). And there was never enough time to drag the guns away before the next British bayonet charge took them back.

It was at this point that General Phillips stepped forward. Earlier, traveling with Riedesel's column along the river road, he had ridden up the hill to see if Burgoyne needed any assistance. He immediately sent for four of his own field pieces. When they arrived, he had them begin firing grapeshot at the woods where the Americans were again forming for the charge. Burgoyne helped by repositioning the 20th further to the left to counter American flankers who were threatening the British rear. Under cover of the four new guns, Phillips then led the 9th, which had been held in reserve, in a charge that cleared the Americans from the British left. Lt. Hadden watched this action from one of Freeman's outbuildings:

> Having supported Capt. Jones in my arms for some time, I carried him into one of the huts which was filled with wounded. The whole of the troops had quitted the height. It was with difficulty I got within our own line which was advancing under Gen'l Phillips, and at that time not more than a hundred yards from the enemy, who were following the retreating troops.
>
> During this attack the 20th Regt. was thrown into the wood on the left of the corn field and repulsed the enemy, which saved the rear of the 62nd Regt. from being galled by them. Gen'l Phillips advanced at the head of the British line (with two German Regiments on their left), repossessed the height and my two guns.

As Hadden mentions, Phillips was not the only help that arrived just in time. General Riedesel had halted his left column along the river road about 1 o'clock, upon hearing the action on the hill above him. After a while, he sent a messenger to inform Burgoyne that he "stood here in readiness, and was only waiting for orders to reinforce him." At 5 o'clock the messenger finally returned with word that Riedesel should secure the ordnance and baggage trains, then quickly march to the aid of the center column, where he should "attack the enemy or their right flank and, if possible, follow them up."

Anticipating this, Riedesel had already positioned his own regiment Riedesel and two companies from the Rhetz regiment to the right of his main column, and thus lost no time in setting out. Burgoyne's repositioning of the 20th regiment further to the left (east) had cleared those woods of Americans and resulted in Riedesel's approach going unnoticed. The German baron provides us with the following account:

> He [Riedesel] hastened, with two companies of the regiment Rhetz as an advanced guard [followed by the regiment Riedesel] as quickly as possible on a road one and half English miles long through the woods till he arrived on an eminence, from the top of which he could see the engagement. The enemy were posted on a corner of the woods, having on his right flank for a defence a deep muddy ditch.
>
> When General Riedesel arrived on the eminence, the battle was raging the fiercest. The Americans, far superior in numbers, had for the sixth time hurled fresh troops against the three English regiments - the 20th, 21st and 62nd. The guns on this wing were already silenced, the artillery men having been either killed or wounded. The three brave English regiments had been, by the steady fire of fresh relays of the enemy, thinned down to one-half, and now formed a small band surrounded by heaps of dead and wounded.
>
> Quickly, without waiting for the rest of his troops - with drums beating and his men shouting "hurrah!" - he attacked the enemy on the double. Posting his troops at the edge of the ditch, he sent such a well-directed volley among the Americans, that those troops who were coming out of the woods and about to fall upon the English were startled and turned back. The British, animated with fresh courage, pressed forward at the point of the

bayonet.

Meanwhile, Captain Pausch arrived with his guns at the right moment, and forming into line with the English, opened fire with grapeshot. The regiment Riedesel also arrived at the nick of time, and, joining the two companies on the ditch, considerably extended the line of fire.

Captain Georg Pausch was instructed to take his two guns "to the right wing of the 21st English regiment," thus replacing the battery that had been lent to Hadden on the left. Pausch provides his own account:

> My wagon-master, who was well mounted, was sent ahead to find a way through a cornfield, that we might avoid the ditches and swamps and not get stuck in them. Under a shower of the enemy's bullets, I safely reached the hill just as the 21st and 9th Regiments were about to abandon it. Nevertheless, I continued to drag my two cannon up the hill, while Gen. Phillips exhorted the English Regiments to face the enemy. English captains and other officers and privates, and also the Brunswick Chasseurs [jagers] which happened to be detailed here, grasped the ropes. The entire line of these regiments faced about, and by this faithful assistance, my cannon were soon on top of the hill. I had shells brought up and placed by the side of the cannon; and as soon as I got the range, I fired twelve or fourteen shots in quick succession into the foe, who were within good pistol shot distance. The firing from muskets was at once renewed and assumed lively proportions, particularly the platoon fire from the left wing of Riedesel.

Having by now conferred with Burgoyne and Phillips, Riedesel quickly ordered his own regiment to "do their best to cross the ditch and unite with the English." They succeeded and "immediately poured another volley of musketry into the enemy's flank, accompanying it with a 'hurrah!' This was the turning point; for the English and Germans, throwing themselves upon the enemy in the woods, repulsed them." The German baron concludes his immodest account by stating, "Thus had General Riedesel, with his German troops, once more [as at Hubbardton] saved the English from a great misfortune. ... [But] Burgoyne and a few other English commanders regarded the German general with secret envy. British pride did not acknowledge bravery other than their own."

Benedict Arnold was not on hand to orchestrate the American part in this final phase of the day's fighting, for Gates had recalled him to headquarters. Gates was furious with Arnold for having sent forward yet another brigade (Ebenezer Learned's Massachusetts and New York continentals), thus leaving the works atop Bemis Heights almost undefended.

Without Arnold on site to direct the action, Learned's brigade was wasted, as they went too far to the west and engaged Fraser's larger column instead of assisting Poor against the British center. Learned ran into some stiff opposition from Breymann's grenadier regiment, who "received them with a vigorous fire, and compelled them to retreat after a few discharges."

However, by then, daylight was fast disappearing. So Burgoyne declared it enough fighting for one day. Pausch mentions that darkness set in about fifteen minutes after the battle ceased. Another soldier states that some of Fraser's British troops actually fired on Breymann's blue-coated grenadiers, mistaking them in the twilight for Americans.

Possession of the disputed ground, Burgoyne wrote, "demonstrated our victory beyond the power of even an American news-writer to explain away." But, in fact, he had achieved very little at a very high cost - 600 casualties, nearly twice the American figure. Gates was still blocking Burgoyne's path to Albany. One of the German soldiers thought that all the bloodshed had accomplished "nothing more than make a previously unknown farmer famous." Thomas Anburey provides a realistic assessment of the battle, usually called by historians the Battle of Freeman's Farm, or the First Battle of Saratoga:

> Notwithstanding the glory of the day remains on our side, I am fearful the real advantages resulting from this battle will rest on that of the Americans, our army being so much weakened by this engagement as not to be of sufficient strength to venture forth and improve the victory, which may, in the end, put a stop to our intended expedition. The only apparent benefit gained is that we keep possession of the ground where the engagement began.
>
> The courage and obstinacy with which the Americans fought were the astonishment of everyone, and we now become fully convinced they are not that contemptible enemy we had hitherto imagined them, incapable of standing a regular engagement, and that they would only fight behind strong and powerful works.

New Hampshire's Major Henry Dearborn exulted, writing home to his family, "We who had something more at stake than six pence per day kept our ground til night. I trust we have convinced the British butchers that the 'cowardly' Yankees can, and where there is a call for it, will fight." Among the dead Yankees were two women who evidently had accompanied their husbands to load spare muskets, for one of them was found with a cartridge in her hand.

Lt. Thomas Anburey later recalled his feelings before and after the battle:

> During the action, every apprehension and idea of danger forsakes the mind, which becomes more animated and determined the nearer the time of attack approaches. Every soldier feels inspired with an

impatient ardor, as if he conceived the fate of the battle will be decided by the level of his musket or the point of his bayonet. But the conflict once over, the eye glances over the field of slaughter where so many brave fellows are laid low in the dust, and the ear continually pierced with the groans of the wounded and the dying. Even the joy at the sight of surviving friends and brother officers is saddened by the reflection of those who fell.

Burgoyne's soldiers spent an uneasy night on the battlefield. Lt. William Digby:

> During the night we remained in our ranks, and tho we heard the groans of our wounded and dying at a small distance, yet could not assist them till morning, not knowing the position of the enemy, and expecting the action would be renewed at day break. Sleep was a stranger to us.
>
> 20th. At day break we sent out parties to bring in our wounded, and lit fires, as we were almost froze with cold, and our wounded who lived till the morning must have severely felt it.

The ghastly wagons, transporting the dead and wounded, passed by Captain Pausch's company, prompting him to note in his journal his wish that "they had been taken by some other route; for it is an unpleasant sight for all soldiers, causing, as it does, reflection and awakening in them fear of the future."

Fortunately, not all of the wounded had to lie, unattended, all night on the battlefield. Shortly after the battle ceased, some of the officers were taken to the house in which the Baroness Riedesel and a few other officers' wives were staying. During the battle, the baroness had been "full of care and anguish for her husband, and shivered at every shot." She recalls the scene in the house, after the battle ended:

[The ladies] sat together bewailing our fate, when one [party] came in, upon which they cast silent glances toward me. This awakened in my mind the dreadful thought that my husband had been killed. I shrieked aloud, but they assured me that this was not so, at the same time intimating to me by signs, that it was the lieutenant - the husband of our companion - who had met with misfortune. A moment after, she was called out. Her husband was not yet dead, but a cannon ball had taken off his arm close to the shoulder. During the whole night we heard his moans, which resounded fearfully through the vaulted cellars. The poor man died toward morning.

During the next few days, the baroness nursed and comforted as best she could a young English officer who finally died when the surgeons belatedly amputated his gangrenous leg. He was, she wrote, "the only son of his parents. It was for this reason that he grieved; on account of his own sufferings he uttered no complaint."

"Order on Morgan to begin the game."

> *- General Horatio Gates, at the start
> of the Second Battle of Saratoga.*

At 7 a.m. on September 20th, the day after the battle, a British de-serter reached the American lines, having "left the ranks not 15 minutes before, pretending an occasion of nature." He informed the American commander "that the whole army was under arms, and or-ders had been given for the attack, that the mutiny act had been read at the head of each corps, and that they expected to march in ten minutes ... that we should have the grenadiers at our lines on the left in fifteen minutes." Instantly the "lines were manned." The Americans, peering into a dense fog that "obscured every object at twenty yards, passed an hour of awful expectation and suspense, during which hope, fear and anxiety played on the imagination." However, no attack came. The British General Phillips explains why:

> The army was formed early on the morning of the 20th, and we waited only for the dispersion of the fog. When General Fraser observed to General Burgoyne that the grenadiers and light infantry who were to lead the attack appeared fatigued by the duty of the previous day, and that if he would suspend the operation until the next morning they would carry the attack with more vi-vacity. Burgoyne yielded to the proposition and the

corps returned to camp.

In the course of the night, a spy reached Burgoyne with a letter from General Sir Henry Clinton, advising him of his intended expedition against the [Hudson River] highlands, which determined Burgoyne to postpone the meditated attack and wait events; the golden, glorious opportunity was lost.

Wilkinson felt that "if General Burgoyne had attacked us on the 20th or 21st, it is highly probable he would have gained a decisive victory," forced Gates to retreat, "and taken our artillery and baggage." Little of the defending army's artillery was posted with the left wing on Bemis Heights, while the defenders there had not yet drawn new ammunition and "could not boast a bayonet for every three muskets."

Clinton's message, written in code on September 12th, informed Burgoyne:

> You know my poverty, but if with 2000 men, which is all I can spare from this important post, I can do anything to facilitate your operations, I will make an attack upon Fort Montgomery [south of Albany] in about ten days if you will let me know your wishes.

From Burgoyne's standpoint, Clinton's proposed attack on the lower Hudson would provide a useful diversion, perhaps scaring Gates into dividing his forces to protect his supply base at Albany. Thus weakened, he would be more vulnerable to attack. So Burgoyne immediately dispatched a messenger, and two more the following night by different routes, urging Clinton to hurry. "An attack," Burgoyne suggested, "or menace of an attack upon Montgomery must be of great use, as it will draw away part of this force. Do it, dear friend, directly." However, none of the messengers succeeded in reaching Clinton. One, when captured, was found to have concealed the letter "in a double wooden canteen."

A week later Burgoyne sent another message, this time asking Clinton "whether I should attack or retreat to the lakes." Now that his chances of success appeared dim, he wanted someone to share the blame. This letter reached Sir Henry Clinton on October 8, only hours after he had captured Fort Montgomery and Fort Clinton. Early that morning a force of 2000 British, German and Tory troops had climbed rugged Bear Mountain and assaulted these well positioned forts. Sir Henry described it as "a desperate attempt on a desperate occasion." They were fiercely resisted by brave but hopelessly outnumbered garrisons led by Governor George Clinton and his brother, General James Clinton. After suffering 200 casualties, Sir Henry's forces prevailed, and the victorious general immediately responded to Burgoyne's letter. He took the precaution of writing on a tiny piece of paper which he then folded and placed inside a hollow silver bullet. The American Dr. Thacher explains what happened to the bullet and its carrier:

> A messenger to Burgoyne was taken on his way as a spy, and finding himself in danger, he was seen to turn aside and take something from his pocket and swallow it. Governor Clinton, into whose hands he had fallen, ordered a severe dose of emetic tartar be administered. This produced the happiest effect as respects the prescriber; but it proved fatal to the patient. He discharged a small silver bullet, which being unscrewed, was found to enclose a letter from Sir Henry Clinton to Burgoyne. "Out of thine own mouth thou shalt be condemned." The spy was tried, convicted and executed. The following is an exact copy of the letter inclosed:
> "Fort Montgomery, October 8th, 1777. *Nous y voici* [We are here] - and nothing between us but Gates. I sincerely hope this little success of ours may facilitate your operations. In answer to your letter of the 28th, I cannot presume to order, or even advise, for reasons obvious. I heartily wish you success."

Such was Clinton's reply, which Burgoyne would never receive. He would also be disappointed in his expectation of St. Leger bringing reinforcements from Canada, via Lake Champlain. Captain Georg Pausch's journal informs us that, on September 24, the "unpleasant news" that St. Leger had abandoned his siege of Fort Stanwix a month before was just then spreading through camp (Burgoyne had managed to keep it secret until then). "We look for him now, with great interest," Pausch wrote, "by way of Lake Champlain. This news is only whispered, not spoken."

Burgoyne had taken "secret means" to enable St. Leger to join him. His orders, back on September 10th:

> I desire to have batteaux, with their oars, buried as quietly as possible. Shovel earth upon them and give them the appearance of graves, a cross might be placed upon each hillock. All this must be done in the night, and only by trustworthy soldiers. ... I have told him [St. Leger] where to find the batteaux.

However, St. Leger's relief column, in fact, would never progress much further south than Ticonderoga, and it was actually General Stark's New Hampshire brigade who soon happened upon the site. A Doctor Gordon explains:

> The Americans made a discovery. ... close with the river, they found the appearance of a grave, with an inscription on a board. "Here lies the body of Lieutenant -------." They were at a loss what it should mean. On searching, they discovered three batteaux instead of a body. Having none of their own, they sent scouting parties over the river.

More disconcerting news was reaching the British camp. The rebels had made an attempt to recapture Ticonderoga, on September 20. General Benjamin Lincoln had directed Colonels John Brown and Seth Warner to make a surprise night attack against the fort's outposts, including Mount Defiance and Fort Independence. These were taken, along with over three hundred captives, and one hundred American prisoners were freed. After a two day siege of the main fortress, Lincoln withdrew his forces when German reinforcements from Montreal (part of St. Leger's relief corps) arrived. Fort Ticonderoga would remain in British hands.

A British officer named John Clunes wrote home, describing how he had been surprised at one o'clock in the morning by Seth Warner's Green Mountain Boys regiment:

> I [was] on the top of a high hill [Mount Defiance] close to Tyconderoga where with 72 artificers I was riseing a fortification on purpose to secure Gen. Burgoyne's retreat if he was oblig'd to retreat. A detachment of 1500 of the rebellious crew came back to Tyconderoga to take it. Accordingly, their first attack was upon me on top of the mount, of which they took and killed every man of us but 9 ... a retreat almost incredible to believe without you was to see the precipice.
>
> When we came to the water side our difficulty was to get over to Tyconderoga. But fortunately I saw an old battoux which we all got into. [It] was so leaky that she was like to sink with us, but we kept bailing her out with hats and caps the best ways that we could. We had no oars. In this condition did I make Tyconderoga all tore almost to pieces. I lost all my clothes & 40 guineas I had in my purse which I lost in the retreat by a stump that tore my breeches and thy.

An incorrect early report, claiming Ticonderoga had been retaken from the British, reached the American camp at Bemis Heights on

September 21st. Jeduthan Baldwin noted in his journal that day, "Recd the news of Col. Browns being at Ty, fired 13 cannon & gave a genl whooray throo all the camp." This puzzled their enemies just a mile away, who had not yet received the news.

When Burgoyne's troops learned what had actually happened, they realized their rear was no longer secure. Some must surely have begun pondering what might await them if the army was forced to retreat. To judge from Lt. Digby's journal, much time was spent debating what the army should do:

> [Sept.] 23rd. It was said we were to strengthen our camp and wait [for] some favourable accounts from Gen Clinton, and began to fell trees for that purpose. I visited our hospitals, which were much crowded, and attended the auctions of our deceased officers, which for the time caused a few melancholy ideas. All kinds of supplies and stores from Canada were entirely cut off, as the communication was dropped, and the variety of reports and opinions circulating were curious and entertaining.
>
> [A] few thought we should be ordered to retreat suddenly under cover of some dark night, but that was not thought probable, as it would be cruel to leave the great numbers of sick and wounded. We also were certain our general would try another action before a retreat was thought on. Others said we waited either to receive a reinforcement from Ticonderoga or Gen Clinton, which last might have some weight, but as to the former we knew there were too few troops there to be able to spare us any. Others again thought when the enemy saw us determined to keep our ground and heard of Gen. Clinton's movements, they would draw off part of their great force to oppose him; but that was not thought very probable by their receiving so large reinforcements daily

to their camp.

Our few remaining Indians appeared very shy at going out on any scouting parties.

We got some [Albany] news papers of the enemy taken from [a] deserter, in which there was an account of the 19th by a Mr. Wilkinson, adjutant genl. to their army. Very partially given, saying we retreated the 19th from the field of battle, which was absolutely false as we lay that night on the same ground we fought on, as a proof of which we buried their dead the morning of the 20th - they not venturing near. He concludes with a poor, low expression, saying, "On the 20th the enemy lay very quietly licking their wounds."

The standoff continued, and a week later Digby was again commenting in his journal:

About day break our picquet was fired on from the wood in front, but the damage was trifling. I suppose seldom two armies remained looking at each other so long without coming to action. A man of theirs in a mistake came into our camp in place of his own, and being challenged by our sentry, after recollecting himself, "I believe," says he, "I am wrong and may as well stay where I am." That he might be pretty certain of.

Despite the clamorings of Benedict Arnold for offensive action, General Gates used the weeks following the September 19th battle to soldify his defenses. He wrote to his wife that the enemy would either attempt a retreat to Canada or "by one violent push, endeavour to recover the almost ruin'd state of their affairs." To New York's governor, Gates predicted that, being "an old gamester," Gentleman Johnny would "risque all upon one throw."

Gates refused to panick over the threat of Clinton advancing in his

323

rear. Rather than divide his forces, he ordered most of the Fort Stanwix garrison to Albany. During this period, he stockpiled the plentiful
supplies that Schuyler diligently sent forward from Albany. And Gates
had the knoll west of his Bemis Heights lines fortified, to prevent British artillery from being placed there. Detachments also chopped down
many trees over the roads west of Burgoyne's position, to prevent a
wide flanking movement like the one that had led to the American defeat on Long Island the year before.

Swarms of militia arrived from New York and New England now
that the tide had turned. Gates assigned most of them to existing continental regiments, so the green troops would benefit from fighting
alongside veterans. Thus, with each passing day, Gates's numerical
superiority grew while Burgoyne waited in vain for help. Deserters
also steadily trickled into the American camp. A British sergeant credited the Tories' "accelerated estrangement from our cause and army"
to the riflemen's "sedulous" efforts to place them in their gunsights.

The Tories were not the only turncoats. "The Germans," Gates
wrote, "desert to us in shoals." According to General Riedesel, the
Americans sent "agents" into his camp, and they often "found a willing
ear." They "endeavoured to induce the soldiers to desert" with propaganda like this letter, written by a German-American from Albany:

> I am a free tradesman, a shoemaker by profession, yet
> I live better than most of your nobles in Germany. I am
> amazed at your believing us to be barbarians. But my
> dear countrymen, believe not the English that tells you
> so. Come and see us here as friends - even blood rela-
> tions you will find here. You'll not repent it, for we
> want all sorts of tradesmen who can get employment
> immediately, and even if they have no trade, they may
> get employment and live better with half the labor in this
> country than in Germany. They call us Rebels but be-
> lieve them not, we call God and the world to witness
> that we are not. We do not pretend to anything but

what God has allowed to all men - freedom.

I hope as soon as you receive this you will come over to us, and if not, leave the ugly name Rebel out of your thoughts.

Burgoyne's men now had to stay within their earthworks or risk being ambushed, a demoralizing state of affairs for an army on an offensive campaign. The riflemen shot at anyone who exposed himself above or outside the walls. At the evening meal, meat had to be eaten raw because cooking fires called attention to the men around them and provided easy targets. The Regulars were "harassed and fatigued with continually sitting and lying on the ground, all huddled in a small compass." Even their horses were restricted to a grassless ravine. "So sure as a poor horse was allured by the temptation of some refreshing grass which grew in the meadows in great abundance, it met with instant death by a rifle shot." And the parties assigned the unenviable task of hauling in the next day's provisions from the main depot near the river sometimes suffered heavy casualties for their efforts. On October first, several British soldiers were captured only 500 paces from headquarters "in the very face of their comrades."

Gates also used psychological warfare against his enemy. A small cannon was brought forward each day "to fire the morning gun, so near to the [British pickets] that the wadding rebounded against the works." And recently arrived Oneida and Tuscarora Indians were put to work "scouting." Within hearing of the British pickets, they pretended to roast their captives alive.

There was also another unsettling nighttime disturbance, as Thomas Anburey explains:

> We have within these few evenings, exclusive of other alarms, been under arms most of the night, as there has been a great noise, like the howling of dogs, upon the right of our encampment; it was imagined the enemy set it up to deceive us, while they were meditating some at-

tack. The two first nights this noise was heard General Fraser thought it to have been the dogs belonging to the officers, and an order was given for the dogs to be confined within the tents.

The next night the noise was much greater, when a detachment of Canadians and Provincials were sent out to reconnoitre, and it proved to have arisen from large droves of wolves that came after the dead bodies. They were similar to a pack of hounds, for one setting up a cry, they all joined, and when they approached a corpse their noise was hideous till they had scratched it up.

Time was running out for the proud John Burgoyne, who before leaving England the previous March had bet fifty guineas in a London club that he would return victorious within the year. A German soldier later recalled these trying days:

> At no time did the Jews await the coming of their Messiah with greater expectancy than we awaited the coming of General Clinton. Rumors from time to time reached our camp in regard to his army; and although they continually filled us with renewed hope, they proved, alas! to be nothing but rumors.
>
> Our provisions continued to decrease; the soldiers were reduced [to] half a pound of bread and the same quantity of meat per day, which they endured with patience.

Having received no word from Clinton, Burgoyne finally called Generals Riedesel, Fraser and Phillips into council on October 4. He proposed a full attack, leaving only 800 men behind to guard the supplies and headquarters. His proposal was deemed too risky. Riedesel reminded them that because of the screen provided by Morgan's riflemen "nothing as yet [was] known respecting the position of the enemy." Besides, their supplies and artillery park would be virtually defenseless if Gates sent out a strong force along the river road while they were away. Riedesel suggested a retreat to the Fort Edward area, there to re-establish communications with Canada and await word from Clinton. The council adjourned without a decision.

The next day, they met again and Burgoyne informed his generals of his decision: 1500 British and German Regulars, with artillery, would advance from Freeman's Farm along the high ground. Small work parties, protected by this "reconnaisance in force," would go along to harvest grain for the army's starving horses. As the troops advanced, they would force the American pickets to fall back to their lines on Bemis Heights, so Burgoyne would at last get a clear view of their works. He would then decide whether to retreat in the night, or attack the next morning.

Burgoyne's earlier proposal of attacking with nearly his entire army (an assault force of perhaps 5000 men) had been risky due to the lack of intelligence about the American defenses. However, it had at least offered the chance for great rewards if it worked. By contrast, the new "reconnoitering expedition" would put 1500 men at considerable risk if Gates decided to venture out of his works to attack them. According to Lt. Digby, Burgoyne did not think Gates would do that:

> [The] intended design was to take post [on the 7th] on
> a rising ground on the left of their camp with the detach-
> ment, thinking [the Americans] would not have acted on
> the offensive, but stood to their works, and on that night
> our main body was to move, so as to be prepared to
> storm their lines by day break of the 8th.

Burgoyne's objective - the American left wing atop Bemis Heights - was no longer under the leadership of the popular and fiery Benedict Arnold. Horatio Gates had taken personal command of it, shifting command of the right wing near the river to Benjamin Lincoln. The uneasy truce between Gates and Arnold had utterly disintegrated following the September 19th engagement. In Gates's report to Congress he gave Morgan's corps total credit for the victory. All forces engaged were labeled "detachments from the army." No mention was made of Arnold, or of Poor or Learned, whose brigades, like Morgan's corps, had been part of Arnold's division.

Gates took further steps to humiliate Arnold. He transferred the rifle corps and a militia regiment out of Arnold's division without informing him beforehand, so that he was publicly embarassed when he tried to give them orders. Gates also refused to honor bills for provisions signed by Arnold, and even demanded that Arnold dismiss his two aides (holdovers from Schuyler's command), whom Gates accused of "poisoning" Arnold's mind against him. Arnold wrote a scathing letter of protest to Gates, which he ended by asking to be relieved of command and allowed to join Washington's main army.

To Arnold's surprise, Gates called his bluff and granted his request. News of Arnold's imminent departure swept through the camp and caused much consternation among the troops. Arnold was considered by many to be "the heart and soul of the army," a leader who they, "to a man, would follow to conquer or die." Many generals and colonels signed a petition to Arnold which thanked him for his services and asked him to stay. Probably less for that reason than for the adverse effect which his departure at such a critical time would have on his career, Arnold decided to stay. However, he was now a volunteer without any command, and banned from headquarters.

Ready to commence the second battle, Burgoyne made one last attempt to communicate with Clinton, who he hoped was nearby (actually, he was still forty miles away). From Lieutenant Digby's journal:

> [Oct.] 6th. At night we fired a rocket from one of our cannon at 12 o'clock, the reason I could never hear for doing so. In general it is a signal between armies.
>
> 7th. A detachment of 1500 regular troops with two 12 pounders, two howitzers and six 6 pounders were or-

dered to move on a secret expedition and to be paraded at 10 o'clock, though I am told Major Williams (Artillery) objected much to the removal of the heavy guns; saying, once a 12 pounder is removed from the park of artillery in America (meaning in the woods) it was gone.

At 1:30 p.m., General Burgoyne halted his forces after they had marched southwest from their Freeman's farm camp for three quarters of a mile. They were now in some clearings owned by farmers Joseph Munger and Asa Chatfield, about a half mile north of the most westerly point of the American works. While the troops "sat down in double ranks with their arms between their legs," Burgoyne, Phillips and Riedesel climbed atop the roof of Munger's abandoned log cabin. Using its ridgepole to steady their spyglasses, they sought in vain for the American works, which remained "concealed from their view by intervening woods." In the foreground, the generals could see their own foragers harvesting Chatfield's wheat and corn.

After a while, the foragers near the far end of the clearing suddenly stopped their work, turned, and ran back as fast as they could. Puffs of smoke appeared from the woods behind them, and the distant pop of muskets became audible. The Regulars quickly stood up, straining their necks to see the action, while their officers barked out commands preparing them for battle.

One of the foragers under fire was "an old soldier of the 20th Regiment." He had "thought himself invulnerable" ever since the previous war, when he had survived first being shot down, and then trampled by a horse. According to Lt. Thomas Anburey, the man "held the Americans in great contempt."

When they attacked the foraging party, the hardy old veteran, sitting upon the forage which he had got on the horse, kept loading and firing his piece at the enemy, and in this manner he brought his forage into camp. Upon

329

his arrival, his master reprimanded him for the danger he had exposed both himself and his horse to; when he said, "May it please your honour, I could not throw away my forage; I'd sooner lose my life, than my poor horses should starve."

Soon American headquarters was busy making preparations for what would be known as the Battle of Bemis Heights, or the Second Battle of Saratoga. Ebenezer Mattoon, a young American lieutenant, provides the following account:

> About one o'clock of this day, two signal guns were fired on the left of the British army, which indicated a movement. Our troops were immediately put under arms, and the lines manned. At this juncture Gens Lincoln and Arnold rode with great speed towards the enemy's lines. While they were absent, the picket guards on both sides engaged near the river. In about half an hour, Generals Lincoln and Arnold returned to headquarters, where many of the officers collected to hear the report, General Gates standing at the door.
>
> Gen. Lincoln says, "Gen. Gates, the firing at the river is merely a feint; their object is your left. A strong force of 1500 men are marching circuitously, to plant themselves on yonder height. That point must be defended, or your camp is in danger." Gates replied, "I will send Morgan with his riflemen, and Dearborn's infantry."
>
> Arnold says, "That is nothing; you must send a strong force." Gates replied, "Gen. Arnold, I have nothing for you to do; you have no business here." Arnold's reply was reproachful and severe. Gen. Lincoln says, "You must send a strong force to support Morgan and Dearborn, at least three regiments."
>
> Capt. Furnival's company of artillery, in which I was

lieutenant, was ordered to march towards the fire, which had now opened upon our picket in front, the picket consisting of about 300 men. We advanced to a height of ground which brought the enemy in view, and opened our fire. But the enemy's guns, eight in number, and much heavier than ours, rendered our position untenable.

Burgoyne appeared in no hurry to make the American pickets fall back to their works. His forces were positioned as follows. On the right, or west, under General Simon Fraser, was the 24th Regiment, as well as the light infantry, under Major the Earl of Balcarres. In the center, General Riedesel had several companies of grenadiers and one of jagers. The left wing was composed of Major Acland's grenadiers. Captain Georg Pausch was supporting the German troops in the center with 6-pounders, and Major Griffith Williams the British left with his beloved 12-pounders. Meanwhile, in the woods far west of everyone else, upwards of 500 Tories, Canadians and Indians were trying to infiltrate the American rear and make a diversion.

Burgoyne had chosen his elite troops for this "reconnaisance in force." But these 1500 would not be nearly enough to effectively oppose the forces thrown against them this day. General Gates, profiting from the September 19th experience and having thousands more men to work with now, would eventually commit more than 6000 men before the end of the day. However, the brunt of the fighting would fall to the initial 2100 troops sent out under Morgan, Learned and Poor.

Gates sent out those three detachments about 2:30 p.m. Colonel Morgan's rifle corps, including Dearborn's light infantry battalion, was to make a wide circuit through the woods to the west, and then fall upon the British right as soon as action started in the center. (Wilkinson attributes Gates with the dramatic quote, "Order on Morgan to begin the game.") General Ebenezer Learned would assault the enemy's center with five regiments from Massachusetts and New York. And General Enoch Poor was to oppose the British left with his brigade, chiefly three New Hampshire regiments. Several militia regiments were also readied to support Learned and Poor.

About 3 o'clock, the leading units of Learned's brigade, having the shortest distance to march, fell in with the enemy's center. However, Learned did not engage the Germans vigorously until about 3:30, when firing started on his right as Poor's brigade advanced against Acland's grenadiers. Crossing a shallow ravine, the three New Hampshire regiments marched steadily up a sloping wheatfield in the face of "a tremendous discharge of cannon and musquetry." However, as is generally the case when fired downhill, most of the British lead flew over their heads and struck the trees behind them. The Americans withheld their fire, but kept advancing.

Now Major Acland was shouting to his grenadiers, "Fix bayonets and charge the damn rebels!" But the New Hampshire men, most of them veterans of the September 19th action, did not turn and run from the awful 14-inch steel blades. Instead, they obeyed Colonel Cilley, who yelled to his men, "It takes two to play at that game; charge and we'll try it." Before the Americans reached the charging grenadiers, though, their officers had them make ready, take aim, and fire. The resulting close-range fire of "ball and buck" stopped the grenadiers' charge and decimated their ranks.

General Burgoyne was impressed by the discipline of the rebels. "I was very much astonished," he wrote, "to hear the shot from the enemy fly so thick, after our cannonade had lasted a quarter of an hour." Samuel Woodruff, of Connecticut, noticed that now the British fire

> was returned with equal spirit by the Americans. For thirty or forty minutes the struggle was maintained with great obstinacy. Several charges with fixed bayonets were made by the English grenadiers with but little effect. Great numbers fell on both sides.

Possession of the British artillery changed hands several times. Lt. Digby took command of his company of grenadiers upon the death of its captain. By the end of the day, Digby's company, fifty strong when it left Canada, was down to four men. "Our cannon," Digby later wrote, "were surrounded. They rushed on with loud shouts, when we drove them back a little with a great loss to ourselves. They still advanced under a storm of grape-shot."

Finally, Colonel Joseph Cilley's New Hampshire men secured them. Cilley leaped upon one brass 12-pounder, waved his sword, and dedicated it "to the American cause." Then he jumped off and had it turned so it could be fired upon its former owners. These had been the guns of the British Major Williams. He had "kept the battery in action until the artillery horses were all destroyed, and his men either killed or wounded." One of his colleagues described this sad day for the artillery officer:

> Old Major Williams, who can only be likened to an old 12-pounder himself, and who adores no creature on earth more than a 12-pounder and none, by the way, can handle one better than him, was captured along with his beloved 12-pounders. The old warrior is said to have shed tears upon the occasion.

According to one account, Colonel Cilley was not the only soldier to straddle one of the brass guns during the pitched battle in the wheatfield. Thomas Haines, of the First New Hampshire Regiment,

> was severely wounded in the encounter for this piece of cannon. He was selected by Col Cilley among others to man and keep the piece. At the time the British rallied and retook it, he was seated astride the muzzle. In this position Haines fought with desperation, killing two soldiers with his gun; one he thrust through the thigh with his bayonet. He had attempted to run him through the body, but the British soldier struck the gun down and the bayonet struck him in what is called the pope's eye,

and he fell dead.

A second soldier came to the assistance of his comrade before Haines had fully recovered his piece, and made a thrust at him with his bayonet, but Haines struck the gun out of his hands with his own, and as the soldier stooped to pick it up, Haines thrust his bayonet through his head.

While in the act of withdrawing the bayonet from the discomfited soldier, Haines was struck in the side of his face with a large musket ball and fell from the cannon to the ground. The ball struck on the right cheek bone, passed through his mouth, carrying away eleven teeth, and about a third of his tongue and came out near the left ear. From such a frightful wound he at once became insensible, and lay as one dead on the field for two nights.

When the detachment went round to collect and bury the dead, Haines was carried and deposited with the dead to be buried with his comrades. Lieut Robert B. Wilkins was present, who knew Haines well, and seeing that his body was not stiff insisted that he was still alive.

Between life and death he lingered. At length he recovered so as to rejoin his regiment, and served out his full term of three months.

In the center, Riedesel's 300 German grenadiers and handful of jager sharpshooters were now being pressed hard by Learned's brigade, who "marched out at a 'double quick' in squares." Though badly outnumbered, the Germans stood firm, exhibiting their famous discipline. At the beginning, they had tried surprising their attackers by firing from "a field of corn" where they "were secreted." But their officers soon had them form "a curve supporting the artillery." There Captain Pausch's gun crews were loading and firing grapeshot as fast as possible. At one point, his guns "became so heated that it was impossible for any man to lay his hands on them."

When most of the gunners supporting Acland on the left had been shot down, a British sergeant rode over to request a loan of some men to work the 12-pounders. Pausch refused, firmly telling his British ally that his men would remain at their own guns. Pausch later recalled telling the British officer, "a six-pounder, on account of its rapidity in firing, was more effectual than a twelve-pounder, with which only one-third the number of shots could be fired; and furthermore, I had no desire to silence my own cannon to raise the honors of another corps."

Meanwhile, on the British right, Fraser's column had turned to the right to oppose a flank attack by Morgan's corps, who "poured down the hill like a torrent." They had been delayed on the way, dispersing Tories, Canadians and Indians they met in the woods to the west. Morgan and Dearborn ordered their men to concentrate their fire on the "epaulet men" rather than "the poor fellows who fought for six pence a day." Wilkinson describes the action:

> Dearborn, at the moment when the enemy's light in-
> fantry were attempting to change front, pressed forward
> with ardour and delivered a close fire, then leapt the
> fence, shouted, charged and gallantly forced them to re-
> tire in disorder. Yet, headed by that intrepid soldier, the
> Earl of Balcarres, they were immediately rallied and
> reformed behind a fence in the rear of their postion.

By now even Burgoyne had felt the effects of American lead, as his horse had been shot, and his coat and hat had bullet holes in them. Observing all the actions on three fronts, he reluctantly ordered a retreat. His messenger, Sir Francis Clerke, soon reached Fraser and gave him the order; and the right wing started to withdraw. The left wing, Acland's grenadiers, were already retreating as best they could. Their formations had disintegrated into pockets of men, forcing them to fight in an unfamiliar style, as individuals.

However, the order to retreat never reached the Germans in the center, because Clerke was shot from his horse before he could reach Riedesel. He was carried to American headquarters, where Gates entertained him with tea and a discourse on why it was inevitable that the forces of liberty would win the war. Captain Georg Pausch, supporting the center with his battery, was angered that the left wing - Acland's grenadiers - had "left their position without informing me. Each man for himself, they made for the bushes." Another German soldier recalled this stage of the battle:

> The centre, whose flanks were no longer covered, stood its ground for a long time; but as the enemy's regiments kept pouring in from all sides, nothing was left to it but to retreat. A more galling discharge of musketry could not be imagined.

Captain Georg Pausch explains how he tried to save a pair of his six-pounders:

> Finally, our right wing was repulsed in our rear; its infantry fortunately retreating in better order than our left wing had done. I still could see, as far as the clearing reached, the road open, and a chance, therefore, to retreat. Accordingly, myself, the artillery-man Hausemann and two other artillery-men, hoping to save one of the cannon, dragged it towards this road.
>
> [We] marched briskly along the road, hoping to meet a body of our infantry and with them make a stand. But this hope proved delusive and was totally dispelled; for some ran in one, and others in another direction; and by the time that I came within gunshot of the woods, I found the road occupied by the enemy. They came towards us on it; the bushes were full of them; they were hidden behind the trees; and bullets in plenty received us.

Seeing that all was irretrievably lost, and that it was impossible to save anything, I called to the few remaining men to save themselves. I myself took refuge through a fence, in a piece of dense underbrush on the right of the road, with the last ammunition wagon, which, with the help of a gunner, I saved with the horses. Here I met all the different nationalities of our division running pell-mell.

Connecticut's Samuel Woodruff relates the incident that had ensured the collapse of the British left:

The British grenadiers, under the command of the brave Major Acland, made a stand. This little field soon became literally "the field of blood." These grenadiers, the flower of the royal army, unaccustomed to yield ... fought with that obstinate spirit which borders on madness. Acland received a ball through both legs, which rendered him unable to walk or stand. This occurrence hastened the retreat of the grenadiers, leaving the ground thickly strewed with dead and wounded.

The British Sergeant Roger Lamb describes Acland's capture:

Major Acland when wounded observed the British troops were retreating. He requested Capt. Simpson of the 31st regiment, who was an intimate friend, to help him into camp. Upon which, being a stout man, he conveyed the major on his back a considerable way; when the enemy pursuing so rapidly, he was obliged to leave him behind to save himself. As the major lay on the ground, he cried out to the men who were running by him, that he would give fifty guineas to any soldier who would convey him to camp. A stout grenadier instantly took him on his back, and was hastening into camp, when they were overtaken and both made prisoners.

Baroness Riedesel relates Major Acland's subsequent fate and his wife's role in it:

> Lady Acland had a tent not far from our house. A messenger came to tell her that her husband had been mortally wounded and taken prisoner. She was deeply saddened. We urged her to go to him, as she would surely be permitted to do, in order that he be better nursed. She loved him dearly, although he was a rough fellow who was drunk almost every day, but, nevertheless, a brave officer.

Overcoming her apprehension, Lady Acland went through the lines and was escorted to Albany, where she nursed her husband back to health, just as she had after the battle of Hubbardton. Afterwards, while in New York on parole, Major Acland was very active in trying to improve the treatment of American officers held prisoner there. Years later in England, he was killed in a duel after taking exception to someone's remarks which impugned the courage of Americans.

Colonel Wilkinson rode onto the wheatfield just after the British grenadiers left it, "fifty-two minutes after the first shot was fired."

> A surgeon, who was dressing one of the officers, raising his blood-besmeared hands in a frenzy of patriotism, exclaimed, "Wilkinson, I have dipt my hands in British blood!" He received a sharp rebuke for his brutality.
>
> With the troops, I pursued the hard-pressed flying enemy, passing over killed and wounded until I heard one exclaim, "Protect me, sir, against this boy!"
>
> Turning my eyes, it was my fortune to arrest the purpose of a lad, thirteen or fourteen years old, in the act of

taking aim at a wounded officer who lay in the angle of a worm fence. Inquiring his rank, he answered, "I had the honour to command the grenadiers." Of course, I knew him to be Major Acland. I dismounted, took him by the hand and expressed hopes that he was not badly wounded.

"Not badly," replied the gallant officer and accomplished gentleman, "but very inconveniently. I am shot through both legs. Will you, sir, have the goodness to have me conveyed to your camp?" I directed my servant to alight, we lifted Acland into his seat, and ordered him conducted to head-quarters.

Up to this point in the conflict, Benedict Arnold had been restlessly roaming about the American camp, "betraying great agitation and wrath." Finally he could stand it no longer and left camp, "not by the order or permission of General Gates." Gates quickly dispatched an aide to chase after Arnold and recall him to headquarters, for "the battle was going well." He feared Arnold would "by some rash act do mischief" and lose what had been gained.

Arnold soon galloped onto the battlefield astride a short, dark "Spanish" horse. This was when the Germans were still stubbornly holding their ground. When Riedesel had seen that his flanks were no longer protected by the British, he had consolidated his courageous Germans into a semi-circular line. However, they soon found that "balls struck their lines from three different sides" as Arnold now led the American attack.

When Arnold arrived on the battlefield, he recognized militia companies from his home state of Connecticut which had been sent out to support Learned in the center. They cheered him and asked for orders. He replied lustily, "Victory or death!" and rode on to the front, where General Learned welcomed him. Taking command, Arnold personally led a charge against the Germans, ignoring the grapeshot and bullets flying about him. The Germans repulsed the charge, but Arnold reformed the men and led them again, acting "more like a madman than a discreet general." This time they were successful and the Germans finally began to retire from the field.

Now it was time for General Simon Fraser, "the idol of the British Army," to spring into action. First, he detached the 24th Regiment from his slowly withdrawing right wing. He combined this nucleus with pockets of Acland's retreating grenadiers, and made a stand to cover the German retreat. The men rallied around him, and this threatened the Americans' prospect of total victory. Benedict Arnold, "knowing the military character and efficiency" of General Fraser, quickly rode over to Daniel Morgan and said, "That officer upon a gray horse is of himself a host and must be disposed of. Direct the attention of some of the sharpshooters among your riflemen to him." Morgan selected a few of his best shots and pointed at Fraser, saying, "That gallant officer is General Fraser. I admire and respect him, but it is necessary that he should die; take your stations and do your duty." Samuel Woodruff personally observed this scene, and later learned its results from a British prisoner:

> Immediately upon this, the crupper of the grey horse was cut off by a rifle bullet, and within the next minute another passed through the horse's mane a little back of his ears. An aide of Frazer, noticing this, observed to him, "Sir, it is evident that you are marked out for particular aim; would it not be prudent for you to retire from this place?" Frazer replied, "My duty forbids me to fly from danger," and immediately received a bullet through his body. A few grenadiers were detached to carry him.

Lieutenant Digby witnessed both Fraser's demise and Burgoyne's reaction, "When General Burgoyne saw him fall, he seemed then to feel in the highest degree our disagreeable situation." Lieutenant Anburey, bored and irritable at having been assigned to guard the camp on Freeman's farm, was on hand when Fraser was carried into camp. The officers there were

> all anxious and eagerly enquiring as to his wound. All the answer he could make to the many enquiries was a shake of his head, expressive that it was all over with him. When he had reached his tent and was recovered a little from the faintness occasioned by loss of blood, he told those around him that he saw the man who shot him; he was a rifleman, and up in a tree.
>
> After the surgeon dressed his wound, he said to him, very composedly, "Tell me, son, to the best of your skill and judgment, if you think my wound is mortal." He replied, "I am sorry, sir, to inform you that it is, and that you cannot possibly live four and twenty hours." He then called for pen and ink, and after making his will, and distributing a few little tokens of regard to the officers of his suite, desired that he might be removed to the general hospital.

According to Lt. Digby, General Fraser's fall helped "to turn the fate of the day" in favor of the Americans. The British and Germans now made such haste to reach their intrenchments that Fraser was the only wounded man "we were able to carry off." The Americans pursued their fleeing enemy as "the battle was continued by a brisk running fire [through] a thin growth of pine wood. Colonel Morgan with his riflemen hung upon the wing of the retreating enemy and galled them by a destructive fire." Thomas Anburey was observing the troops "pouring back to camp" when Burgoyne rode up and declared, "you must defend this post to the very last man."

Many of the survivors took refuge within the largest redoubt there, named for the Earl of Balcarres. North of it, on slightly higher ground, was another redoubt, about 200 yards long and defended by Colonel Breymann with 200 German infantrymen. Both redoubts were made of logs, stood about six feet high, and were surrounded by a ditch and abatis. The trees had been felled all around for 100 yards to give free play to the artillery inside the works. Between the two redoubts were two log cabins manned by a depleted force of Canadians.

"With true military instinct," a British officer wrote, Arnold "seized the opportunity for a general attack upon the British entrenchments." He led an impetuous assault against the Balcarres Redoubt. After reaching as far as the abatis, they were turned back by a "severe fire of grapeshot and small arms" at point-blank range. As soon as that attack was repulsed, General Learned arrived with his brigade. "Raging like a madman," Arnold raced across the line of fire, took command of them, and overran the Canadians at the log cabins.

This left the Breymann Redoubt's left side unprotected. Arnold then directed several regiments, including Morgan's riflemen and Colonel Brooks's Massachusetts militia, in an attack against the Breymann Redoubt "in front and on both flanks." One soldier claimed that Arnold's "energy gave spirit to the whole action." Another, years later, remembered him as "our fighting general, and a bloody fellow he was. He didn't care for nothing; he'd ride right in. It was 'Come on, boys!' twasn't 'Go, boys!'" Ebenezer Mattoon recalls the charge:

> We all wheeled to the right and advanced. No fire was received, except from the cannon, until we got within eight rods, when we received a tremendous fire from the whole line. But a few of our men, however, fell. Still advancing, we received a second fire, in which a few men fell, and Gen Arnold's horse fell under him, and he himself was wounded. He cried out, "Rush on, my brave boys!" After receiving the third fire, Brooks mounted their works, swung his sword, and the men rushed into their works. When we entered we found Col Bremen dead.

Some accounts claim that the brave but brutal Colonel Breymann was shot by one of his own men after he slashed several soldiers with his sword as they tried to leave the redoubt. Arnold's horse was shot in the chest as he entered the redoubt through a sally port. The dying horse landed on Arnold's leg and broke it - the same leg that had taken a bullet during the assault on Quebec. (Later in the war, after his defection to the British, a popular saying arose: If Arnold should be captured, this leg must be cut off and buried with honors, and the rest of him hung as a traitor.)

The German who had shot Benedict Arnold's horse was wounded and lying on the ground when he fired. An enraged American started toward the German to run him through with a bayonet, but Arnold intervened, shouting, "Don't hurt him. He's a fine fellow. He only did his duty." Moments later, Gates's aide finally caught up with Arnold in the captured redoubt and conveyed the commander's orders: Don't do anything rash, and come back to camp.

The fall of Breymann's Redoubt ended the battle. It also forced Burgoyne to abandon the Balcarres Redoubt and concentrate his army behind his other earthworks near the Hudson River. Lieutenant Digby explains:

> During the night, we were employed in moving our cannon, baggage, etc., nearer to the river. It was done with silence, and fires were kept lighted to cause them not to suspect we had retired from our works where it was impossible for us to remain, as the German lines [Breymann's Redoubt] commanded them, and were then in possession of the enemy, who were bringing up cannon to bear on ours at day break.

In this Second Battle of Saratoga, Burgoyne's forces had suffered six hundred men killed, wounded and taken prisoner, four times the American losses. Charles Neilson, who was raised in the house which formed the midpoint of the Bemis Heights fortications, recorded the following anecdote concerning some of the women camp followers:

Accompanying the American army were a great number of women, principally foreigners, many of whom had husbands or brothers in the action, and many who followed merely for the sake of plunder, as was manifested during the night after the action of the 7th October. The next morning after the battle, every man that was left dead on the field, and even those who were supposed to be mortally wounded, and not yet dead, but helpless, were found stripped of their clothing, which rendered it almost impossible to distinguish between American and British.

But during the action, a heart-rending, and yet to some a laughable, scene took place in the American camp. While the cannon were constantly roaring like peals of thunder, some of those women, wringing their hands, apparently in the utmost distress, and frantically tearing their hair in the agony of their feelings, were heard to cry out, in the most lamentable exclamations, "Och, my husband! My poor husband! Lord Jesus, spare my poor husband!" which would be often repeated, sometimes by fifteen or twenty voices at once; while the more hardened ones, and those rejoicing in the prospects of plunder, would break out in blasphemous imprecations, exclaiming, "D--n your poor husband, you can get another!"

At the close of the battle, the dying General Fraser had been taken, along with a few other high-ranking wounded officers, to the house where Baroness Riedesel was staying. She describes his arrival:

In the afternoon, instead of my dinner guests arriving as expected, poor General Fraser, who was to be one of them, was brought to me on a stretcher, mortally wounded. The table, which had already been set for dinner, was removed and a bed for the General was put in its place. The bullet had gone through his abdomen precisely as in Major Harnage's case; unfortunately the General had eaten a heavy breakfast, so that the intestines were expanded, and, as the doctor explained, the bullet had gone through them, not between them, as in Major Harnage's case.

I heard him often exclaim, between moans, "Oh, fatal ambition! Poor General Burgoyne! Poor Mrs. Fraser!" Prayers were said, then he asked that General Burgoyne have him buried the next day at six o'clock in the evening on a hill which was a sort of redoubt.

We had been told that we had gained an advantage over the enemy, but the sad, disheartened faces I saw indicated quite the contrary. My husband took me aside and told me that things were going badly and that I must be ready to leave at any moment, but not to let anyone know this.

I could not sleep, as I had General Fraser and all the other gentlemen in my room, and I was constantly afraid that my children might wake up and cry, thus disturbing the poor dying man, who kept apologizing to me for causing me so much trouble. Toward three o'clock in the morning I was told that the end was near.

... [After Fraser died] I wrapped the children in blankets and went into the hall with them. His body was washed, wrapped in a sheet and put back into the bed. Then we returned to the room and had to see this sad sight throughout the day.

There was talk of making a retreat but no steps were taken in this direction.

That evening, October 8th, Fraser was buried on a knoll above the

Hudson, as he had requested. The baroness describes the scene:

> This caused an unnecessary delay and served to increase the army's misfortune. At precisely six o'clock the body was actually carried away, and we saw all the generals and their staffs take part in the funeral services on the hilltop. The English chaplain, Mr. Brudenel, held the services. Cannon balls constantly flew around and over the heads of the mourners. The American General Gates said later on that, had he known that a funeral was being held, he would have allowed no firing in that direction. A number of cannon balls also flew about where I stood, but I had no thought for my own safety, my eyes being constantly directed toward the hill, where I could see my husband distinctly, standing amidst the enemy's fire.

Immediately after the burial, Burgoyne ordered a retreat northward up the river road, "leaving the sick and wounded in large hospital tents with several surgeons to attend them." After a night march of several hours in the rain, the army halted so the provision bateaux could catch up, and the men could rest and be given rations.

According to Lieutenant Thomas Blake, of New Hampshire, the next day the Americans marched in pursuit and "came up with them at Saratoga; where we formed a line almost around them on the west side of the river, and a party of militia on the opposite or east side." Baroness Riedesel explains:

> About two o'clock in the afternoon, the firing of cannon and small arms was again heard, and all was alarm and confusion. My husband sent me a message telling me to betake myself forthwith into a house not far from there. I seated myself in the calash with my children, and had scarcely driven up to the house when I saw on

the opposite side of the Hudson River five or six men with guns, which were aimed at us. Almost involuntarily I threw the children on the bottom of the calash and myself over them. At the same instant the churls fired, and shattered the arm of a poor English soldier behind us.

Immediately after our arrival a frightful cannonade began, principally directed against the house in which we had sought shelter, probably because the enemy believed, from seeing so many people flocking around it, that all the generals made it their headquarters. Alas! it harbored none but wounded soldiers, or women!

We were finally obliged to take refuge in a cellar, in which I laid myself down in a corner not far from the door. My children lay down on the earth with their heads upon my lap, and in this manner we passed the entire night. A horrible stench, the cries of the children, and yet more than all this, my own anguish, prevented me from closing my eyes. On the following morning the cannonade again began, but from a different side. I advised all to go out of the cellar for a little while, during which time I would have it cleaned, for the women and children, being afraid to venture forth, had soiled the whole cellar. I fumigated them by sprinkling vinegar on burning coals.

A fresh and terrible cannonade threw us all once more into alarm. Eleven cannon balls went through the house, and we could plainly hear them rolling over our heads. One poor soldier, whose leg they were about to amputate, having been laid upon a table for this purpose, had the other leg taken off by another cannon ball, in the very middle of the operation. His comrades all ran off, and when they again came back they found him in one corner of the room, where he had rolled in his anguish, scarcely breathing.

The defeated army spent much of their time building earthworks to prepare against an assault, and provide protection from the Americans who "swarmed around the little army like birds of prey." With the only water source safely accessible being "a very muddy spring," some soldiers "got water out of the holes the cattle made with their feet." For a while, the baroness quenched her young children's thirst with wine.

> As the great scarcity of water continued, we at last found a soldier's wife who had the courage to bring water from the river, for no one else would undertake it, as the enemy shot at the head of every man who approached the river. This woman, however, they never molested.

Burgoyne considered leaving the artillery and baggage behind, and, under cover of darkness, breaking through the lines. But everywhere he looked, large forces were blocking his path. So Burgoyne resigned himself to staying put and waiting for Clinton's arrival. With provisions down to three days' short rations, he called a council of war on October 13th. His generals unanimously agreed that he should "treat with the enemy." At last, despairing of help from Clinton, the proud General John Burgoyne sent a messenger under a flag of truce to suggest a meeting of staff officers "to negotiate matters of high importance to both armies."

Horatio Gates opened the negotiations by demanding an unconditional surrender. But John Burgoyne's generals objected to such a "dishonorable" arrangement. They declared the army was "determined to die to a man rather than submit to terms repugnant to national and personal honour." They were also offended by Gates's improper etiquette; traditionally, in such negotiations, the defeated party was supposed to be be the first one to offer terms. Burgoyne sent a reply to Gates, telling him that more acceptable terms must be arranged or se "this army will rush on the enemy determined to take no quarter."

For his part, Gates did not feel he had time to negotiate, since he .d just received a report from the governor that twenty enemy sail ere moving upriver, south of Albany. Gates had no way of knowing at Clinton would turn around and return to New York within a few ıys. So he accepted virtually all of Burgoyne's proposals, including ıanging the title of the document from a "Treaty of Capitulation" to a reaty of Convention."

Under the terms, Burgoyne's Canadian allies were granted "leave to turn to Canada, according to their petition." And the "convention my" would march to Boston and return to England, "upon condition : not serving again in North America during the present contest."

During the two days of negotiations, a cease fire was in effect. The ritish Sergeant Roger Lamb provides the following account of an in- dent that occurred during this time:

> A soldier of the 9th regiment, named Maguire, came down to the bank of the river, with a number of his com- panions, who engaged in conversation with a party of Americans on the opposite shore.

> Maguire suddenly darted like lightning from his com- panions, and resolutely plunged into the stream. At the very same moment, one of the American soldiers, seized with a similar impulse, resolutely dashed into the water, from the opposite shore. The wondering soldiers on both sides beheld them eagerly swim towards the middle of the river, where they met; they hung on each others necks and wept; and the loud cries of "My brother! my dear brother!!!" which accompanied the transaction soon cleared up the mystery to the astonished spectators.

> They were both brothers, the first had migrated, and the other had entered the army; one was in the British and the other the American service, totally ignorant that they were engaged in hostile combat against each other.

At ten o'clock on the morning of October 17th, Burgoyne presented his sword to Gates, who "received it in his left hand, extending his right hand to take the right hand of General Burgoyne. After a few minutes conversation, Gates returned the sword. Then all repaired to the table [planks placed over barrels] and while dining, the prisoners were passing by." When the two commanders first met,

> General Burgoyne, raising his hat most gracefully, said, "The fortune of war, General Gates, has made me your prisoner," to which the conqueror, returning a courteous salute, promptly replied, "I shall always be ready to bear testimony, that it has not been through any fault of your excellency." Major General Phillips then advanced and he and General Gates saluted, and shook hands with the familiarity of old acquaintances. The Baron Riedesel and the other officers were introduced in their turn.

Upon being introduced to Colonel Daniel Morgan, Burgoyne declared, "Sir, you command the finest regiment of rangers in the world." After dinner, "General Gates called upon General Burgoyne for his toast, which embarassed General Burgoyne a good deal; at length, he gave General Washington; General Gates, in return, gave the King."

The American drummers and fifers, asked to play a lively tune for the prisoners' consolation, chose *Yankee Doodle*. A total of 5791 prisoners filed past the American regiments, standing quietly at attention. Ephraim Squier thought it "a very agreeable sight for some time, but was weary before they had all passed by, though they marched brisk. They were more than three hours in passing."

First came the British, then the Germans, some of whom carried or led pets they had acquired during the campaign: a bear, a deer, several young foxes, and a raccoon. Next came the wives and camp followers, and the wagon-drivers and sutlers. Alexander Milliner, an American drummer boy, recalled that "the British soldiers looked down-hearted. When the order came to 'ground arms,' one of them exclaimed with an oath, 'You are not going to have my gun!' and threw it violently on the ground and smashed it." But that was the exception, and the piling of small arms was carried out in an orderly and solemn fashion in a meadow beyond view of the American troops. A German soldier wrote of the Americans:

> Each one had on the clothes he was accustomed to wear in the field, the tavern, the church and in everyday life. The determination which caused them to grasp a musket and powderhorn can be seen in their faces. Not a man among them evinced the least sign of hate or malicious joy as we passed by. It seemed rather as if they wished to do us honor.

The Baroness Riedesel was watching as a group of British officers rode by the poor soldier's wife who had risked her life to fetch water from the Hudson. Someone yelled to her to hold out her apron, and "everyone threw a handful of money in it," amounting to twenty guineas.

Lieutenant William Digby, of the grenadiers, sadly later recorded his feelings on this historic occasion:

> About 10 o'clock we marched out, according to treaty, with drums beating & the honors of war, but the drums seemed to have lost their former inspiriting sounds, and though we beat the *Grenadiers March*, which not long before was so animating, yet then it seemed by its last feeble effort as if almost ashamed to be heard on such an occasion. As to my own feelings, I cannot express them. Tears, though unmanly, forced their way, and if alone, I could have burst to give myself vent.
>
> I never shall forget the appearance of their troops on

our marching past them; a dead silence universally reigned through their numerous columns, and even then, they seemed struck with our situation.

Thus ended all our hopes of victory, honour, glory, &c &c &c.

CHAPTER THIRTEEN
PRISONERS OF WAR

"The word 'rebel' was thought by the enemy sufficient to sanctify whatever cruelties they were pleased to inflict, death itself not excepted."

- Ethan Allen, prisoner of war.

This chapter will discuss the fate of prisoners of war on both sides. We'll start with Burgoyne's army, then consider British and German captives in general, before finishing with a discussion of American prisoners.

The six thousand captives taken at Saratoga were nearly all British and German regulars, since the Canadians were freed under the terms of surrender, and most of the Tories had fled the night before the surrender. Because of Burgoyne's insistence on the surrender document being titled a "Convention" rather than a capitulation, his army came to be known as the Convention Army. The Convention included one term which soon became extremely controversial: that all captured soldiers be allowed to return to England, on condition that they not serve in North America again "during the present contest."

Accordingly, on October 18, 1777, the day after the surrender, the Convention Army set off, under escort, for Cambridge, just outside Boston. There they were to await transports to England. The trip to Cambridge took three weeks, marching on primitive frontier roads and, at times, through early winter storms. With each new town they passed through, their reception varied, depending on the disposition of the inhabitants. One officer recorded his impressions of Americans in a letter home to a friend in Germany. First, he described the Dutch girls of Kinderhook, New York, then the trials of the tedious march.

Their teeth are very white, their lips pretty, and their eyes very animated and laughing. On their heads a sunhat, from beneath which they can peep out very roguishly with their mischievous eyes, now and then extending us an apple with a curtsy. On October 23 [they] cost us some good men, who would not have deserted their comrades but for the alluring voices of some pretty sirens.

I wish to acquaint you with one of the necessary evils of this world: the domination of the women over their husbands. This petticoat rule is spread throughout America, but in quite different type than in Canada where it aims at the welfare of the man, while here it seeks his ruin. The daughter simply must put on style, for that is the mother's will. If a mother dies, she orders her daughters on her deathbed to maintain the mastery in the house and to hold the father's purse strings.

We marched seventeen miles to a miserable village, Nobletown, near which we had to sleep in the open air for want of houses; we got so covered with frost during the night that we looked like great sugar dolls. ...

Great Barrington. I never saw ruder, more spiteful people, and never have I been more on my guard against blows. ...

West Springfield. They took us into their houses. The inhabitants damned curious. From the village and all the neighborhood whole families came marching in and went from house to house in order, as they said, to have a look at the prisoners. Every one from the general on down had to stand for this. The greater the rank, the longer and more attentively was one looked at, no matter how sour a face he made. I offered the pretty girls chairs, which they accepted. Thus I gained time to get revenge by looking at them. ...

Brookfield. The inhabitants would not receive us into their houses; they maintained that neither the Congress, nor General Gates could ask that of them.

The German general, Baron von Riedesel, traveled with the army to Cambridge, as did Burgoyne. Each was "gnawed with grief on account of all that had happened, and on account also of his captivity." However, Riedesel, like many a soldier, was comforted by having a wife along. The baroness, affectionately called "Mrs. General," recorded her own observations of the march.

> Some of their generals who accompanied us were shoemakers; and upon our halting-days they made boots for our officers and, also, mended nicely the shoes of our soldiers. They set a great value upon our money coinage, which with them was scarce. One of our officers had worn his boots entirely into shreds. He saw that an American general had on a good pair, and said to him jestingly, "I will gladly give you a guinea for them." Immediately the general alighted from his horse, took the guinea, gave up his boots, and put on the badly worn ones of the officer, and again mounted his horse.

The Convention Army prisoners found the inhabitants of Cambridge less than congenial. The citizens vividly recalled the British burning nearby Charlestown during the Battle of Bunker Hill. Most of them therefore adamantly refused to accomodate the enemy. The captive officers, expecting comfortable lodgings, were at first crowded "seven or eight together in rooms ten feet square." Even the Riedesel family and their servants had to share a single room in a small farmhouse out in the country. They ate together with the host family at mealtime in the only other room in the house. According to the baroness, "The man was kind, but the woman, in order to revenge herself for the trouble we brought upon her, every time we sat down to table [would] comb out her children's heads, which were full of vermin - which very often entirely took away our appetites."

The rank and file, as well as the lower ranking officers, were housed in barracks that had been hastily constructed by the New England army two years before, during the blockade of Boston. One of the Germans described his quarters as "made of boards, and the windows of paper, so that we have had no lack of fresh air this winter. Each one is occupied by four officers or twenty privates." Another officer found quarters in the attic of an American's house, where the walls were insufficient to keep out the wind. "Never," he wrote home, "have I been colder in any winter. I haven't been able to move a step from the fire, and the ink has frozen on my pen over a hundred times. In a snowstorm with high winds, I had a foot of snow in my room."

Burgoyne and Riedesel, used to the high life even in wartime, tried to make their own confinement bearable. But with little success, according to a German officer:

> General Burgoyne, as well as Major-General von Riedesel, has given a ball and invited ladies from Boston and the vicinity. However, the Committees have forbidden any one to dare to go. Hence those invited did not come; only the two daughters of General Schuyler have ventured to disobey both times. So we live here with no intercourse save what we have with each other. No great fetes are given and Generals Burgoyne and Phillips live very retired. Since we all live far apart, and the roads are bad in winter, we generally live in a sad loneliness. Our officers and the American officers do not associate either. The regiments here are militia and nearly all their officers are artisans. It cost a lot of pains to get the idea into the heads of the inhabitants here that our officers have no [civil] occupation.

For some of the prisoners, the tediousness of confinement was pleasantly broken by frequent visits from several French officers awaiting a return ship to France. The German officers welcomed the company of these European gentlemen, who shared their low opinion of American officers. The Frenchmen "declared often that the French and Americans do not like each other at all." They gladly carried the Germans' letters when they sailed for Europe.

In April of 1778, General Burgoyne sailed for home. He had been given his parole by Congress, so he could defend himself against his critics back in London. However, his subsequent requests for first a court martial, then a Parliamentary inquiry, were both refused. The Administration preferred to shed as little light as possible on its part in the disastrous campaign. They were particularly sensitive to the issue because, about this time, a letter from Governor Carleton of Canada received wide circulation. In it, he pointed out the absurdity of "ministers pretending to direct operations of war in a country at three thousands miles distance."

In a further effort to silence Burgoyne, the Administration ordered him to return to captivity in America. He resisted, claiming ill health. Because public opinion was by now in his favor and running against the Administration, the order was soon rescinded. So Burgoyne remained on parole in England, and busied himself writing a popular treatise on his expedition. He would never again have a military command, though he kept his seat in Parliament.

Meanwhile, back in America, the months passed slowly for the Convention prisoners. They were "unhappy middle things between free and unfree, in anxious expectation of the hour of deliverance." Unfortunately for them, that hour was years away, for Congress resolved on December 27, 1777, that their return to Europe be suspended "till a distinct and explicit ratification of the Convention shall be properly notified to these States by the Court of Great Britain." This, Thomas Anburey explained in his journal, was "an event which can never happen, as it would be allowing [recognizing] the authority of the Congress, and the independence of the Americans."

George Washington had lost no time in expressing to Congress his dim view of the Convention. "I do not think," he wrote, "it to our interest to expedite the passage of the prisoners to England; for you may depend upon it that [the government] will, immediately upon their arrival there, throw them into different garrisons [Ireland, Gibraltar, etc.] and bring out an equal number" from those garrisons to reinforce Howe. Congress's new President, Henry Laurens, suspected that the troops, if allowed to sail from Boston, would land in New York instead of England.

He was correct to suspect this, for among some correspondence of Howe's, discovered in 1932, was a letter marked "Secret" and addressed to Burgoyne. In it he directed Burgoyne to wait until the convoy of transports was at sea, then give the naval commander Howe's "secret directions" to sail the Germans to England but bring the English troops to New York. This, Howe explained, would "repair an injury in which Mr. Washington so obstinately persists." It seems that Washington had refused to hand over an agreed upon number of British prisoners in exchange for 2202 Americans who were released from New York prisons "in such a debilitated condition that many of them died before reaching home."

By November of 1778, it was clear that Great Britain was not going to ratify the year-old Convention. Therefore, the British command in New York gave notice that it would cease sending provision ships to Boston; if Congress wanted to consider the Convention Army true prisoners of war, it would have to feed them itself. With the British thus signaling the end of their patience, Washington suspected they would soon attempt a rescue, so he advised Congress to immediately relocate the Convention Army away from the coast. Thus, after a year in Massachusetts, the prisoners set out on a winter march of nearly 600 miles for Charlottesville, in western Virginia. There they would be safe from recapture, and in a warmer climate requiring less wood - and less food (military commanders believed that soldiers wintering in warmer climates required less food).

On the march, the Convention Army passed through some predominantly German areas of Pennsylvania. There the German prisoners were surprised to be received with "much meanness from our countrymen." But in one town, where they spent Christmas and gave a ball, the reception was quite warm, at least from the females. Officer Du Roi noticed that "all the German maidens came and danced with our officers [and] did their best to keep them for husbands." In fact, wherever British and German officers were located during the war they were extremely popular with American females, smitten by what one wit termed "Scarlet Fever." They especially loved the dances, including a new one called "Burgoyne's Surrender."

In Virginia, the prisoners "worked with great industry to build themselves better dwellings" than the hastily constructed barracks the militia provided. By now, they suspected their chances of being exchanged or released before the war's end were dim. So, in this "remote corner of Virginia, almost cut off from the rest of the world," the prisoners put their collective strength to work and made life as comfortable as "the nature of the country would allow." One British soldier even rigged up a cold bath, "to tense up the relaxed state of the body the intense heat of the climate occasions." A German officer wrote a letter home, describing the camps:

> The English soldiers have built covered walks in front of their barracks. The Germans, on the other hand, as lovers of vegetables, have laid out countless gardens, and in order to raise poultry have fixed up henyards which are surrounded by palisades. These German gardens attract visitors from sixty miles around. The 21st English Regiment has built itself a large church. Two enterprising Americans have erected taverns in which there are already two billiard tables.
>
> A group of English soldiers has put up a Comedy House, where plays are given twice a week and in which there are three sets of scenery. On the curtain is painted

a harlequin who points with his wooden sword to the words: "Who would have expected this here?" Very good pieces are performed, which, because of their satirical additions, do not always please the Americans, wherefore they are forbidden by their superiors to attend these comedies.

During the march to Virginia, several hundred of the Germans had disappeared while passing through the Dutch and German settlements of New York and Pennsylvania. German escapees sought "a chance to practice their trade." By contrast, when British soldiers escaped, they usually sought out their army. One example was Sergeant Roger Lamb, who managed to reach the main British Army, only to be taken prisoner again at the Yorktown surrender in 1781.

Escape was evidently easy, as several hundred men accomplished it during the army's stay in Virginia. One prisoner's letter home mentions that, because of the frequent escapes, "there is a threat to surround the barracks with a stockade." However, that threat apparently was never carried out. In fact, the commandant, Colonel Bland, even allowed the prisoners to write and mail uncensored letters. For this and other liberal practices, Bland's homestead was spared by British General Phillips when he later invaded Virginia, after being exchanged in 1780.

Occasional deaths further reduced the size of the Convention Army. Thomas Anburey noted that "numbers fell a sacrifice to spirits," literally drinking themselves to death. The moonshine sold by their frontier neighbors kept some of the prisoners "in a continual state of intoxication." And a Lieutenant Brown died when shot by a sentinel "for not stopping when repeatedly challenged as he was riding out of the lines with two women."

When release finally came in 1783, less than one fourth of the original Convention Army was exchanged. (Among those returning to Europe was the Riedesel family, which by then included a new baby girl, Amerika.) Many, about 1500 by one estimate, nearly all of them Germans, simply refused to be returned. Most of them had been farmers, craftsmen or laborers. Now, after several years in America, they knew that better wages were to be had here for skilled craftsmen, and virgin forests awaited anyone willing to start a farm on property he could claim as his own - something he could never dream of doing in Europe.

* * * * *

Members of the Convention Army were in some ways atypical of British and German prisoners. They were not, for example, eligible for parole or exchange, and in most cases were not eligible to be hired out by the inhabitants. These were the three methods which American authorities used to reduce the expenses of maintaining prisoners - parole, exchange, and hiring out.

Throughout the war, it was a struggle to find enough resources to house, feed and guard prisoners. A Congressional report to Washington explained that local authorities often had to hire out as many prisoners as possible, "to save public provisions and because we had not guards to keep them safely." When a prisoner was "hired out," a citizen would take him home. There the prisoner would be housed, fed, and in most cases, paid a wage in return for services rendered on the farm or in the shop. Skilled artisans were especially in demand. The employer usually had to post a substantial bond as security for the prisoner's appearance when called upon to return.

The Germans earned a reputation as "industrious." Thereafter, newly captured Germans "quickly found employment" wherever they were sent. The British, on the other hand, were considered more likely to either run off or be "troublesome." According to George Washington, British captives were haughty, contemptuous of their captors, and addicted to robbery and seducing patriots from their allegiance to the revolution.

The Convention Army prisoners could not be hired out, paroled or exchanged. One such German prisoner, taken at Saratoga, wrote jealously of some acquaintances - Germans who had been captured at

Bennington (and therefore not subject to the restrictive Convention):

> The inhabitants came [up to] one hundred English
> miles to pick out such men. Those with trades come out
> real well and even earn some money. Those who have
> no trade must thresh, cut wood, and do other menial
> services. They get good food, and the cider barrel is not
> locked from them. Whether the young ladies, in houses
> where these young fellows are working, will not keep
> many from returning, time alone will tell.

While privates, corporals and sergeants were commonly hired out as
laborers, officers were generally given parole. Parole was a written
contract between the prisoner and his captors. In return for release
from prison, he promised upon his honor as a gentleman to not take up
arms, engage in spying or propaganda, or travel beyond defined
boundaries. The prisoner also agreed to return to captivity when
called upon to do so. While on parole, he had to pay the owner of the
house in which he lodged and boarded a weekly or monthly sum of
money. If in arrears on these payments when his time came for exchange, he would not be exchanged until the debts were paid.

A British lieutenant named Thomas Hughes was granted parole and
sent, along with another officer and their servants, to live with a poor
farming family in Pepperell, Massachusetts. The parolees were restricted to a one mile radius of the house. To their chagrin, they found
the town was so sparsely settled that in most cases the houses were a
mile distant from each other. They consequently felt "almost as much
out of the world here as if we were in the deserts of Arabia."

> Oct. 22nd. Procured quarters in a house, in which I
> have agreed to pay two silver dollars pr week for board,
> &c. The family are very civil - it consists of Father (who
> is almost deaf), Mother (a talkative old woman), and
> two daughters, who are of the order of old maids, con-

founded ugly, with beards an inch long.

Oct. 26th. I find that the people here have not the least idea of a gentleman. Our servants are treated just like ourselves, and they are surprised to find our men won't eat at the same table with us, to which they are always invited.

November 1st. We have but one room to eat and sit in, which is in common with all the family. What to call it I know not, for it serves for parlour, kitchen and workroom. About 9 o'clock, Lt. Brown and myself breakfast, but they all wonder how we can sleep so long. Our breakfast is bread and milk, or boiled Indian corn with butter and treacle [molasses] spread over it. This is pretty substantial, and after it we generally walk in the woods, to gather chestnuts or throw stones at squirrels.

About 12 o'clock the whole family collects for dinner. Father shuts his eyes and mutters an unintelligible monstrous long grace, and down we all sit with no other distinction but Brown and me getting pewter plates - whereas the others have wooden platters. Our food is fat salt pork and sauce (the name they give to roots and greens). Neither gentleman or lady use any ceremony - all hands in the dish at once - which gives many pretty opportunities for laughter, as two or three of us often catch hold of the same piece.

The meal over, another grace is said, and we all disperse to our different employments. At nightfall a large fire is made on the hearth, and the kitchen (or whatever it is) receives the whole family. Mother, Brown and me round the fire, she knitting and asking us silly questions; our servants at the opposite corner ... [the daughters] spinning with large noisy wheels, and in the middle sits Father and the apprentice boy shelling Indian corn. We have no candles, but the room is lighted by splinters of pine. At 8 o'clock we get bread and milk for supper; a little after Father begins to yawn - upon which we stand up. He says prayers, and we depart to our beds.

Our apartment, or rather the place we lay in, extends over the whole house and is what is comonly called the garret. We have three beds in it - one of which contains Brown and me, in the second sleep our two young ladies, and close at their feet, in the third, rest the servant and apprentice. Our room is not the worse for being a repository of fruit and nuts, as we generally make an attack on the apples before we get up of a morn.

If this is the kind of life the poets say so much of and call Rural Happiness, I wish to my soul that they were here, and I in London.

While German prisoners were sometimes "given special treatment" and were much more likely to be hired out, British names always headed the lists of men to be exchanged for American prisoners. The British Commander-in-Chief naturally wanted his own troops back, but he also knew that the German "landgraves," or dukes and princes, who owned the services of these German troops preferred this arrangement. Thirty extra marks were paid to the landgrave for each man killed, wounded or taken prisoner, and this extra fee was forfeited if the prisoner was exchanged. The Duke of Brunswick, for example, made it clear that he "hoped the British government would not for one moment dream of having German prisoners exchanged." Some were exchanged, though, to appease the German generals, who wished to see their own regiments strengthened and their men freed.

Of course, not all British and German prisoners were hired out or granted parole. Many spent months or years in prisons. However, in general, they were treated humanely. Like Washington, Congress consistently called for all prisoners to be "securely confined, though in a manner most consistent with humanity." In winter, the responsible local committees were often reminded to "see that they are comfortable in this season," or to ensure that their "apartments are glazed and in other respects secured from the weather."

Captives most frequently complained about the quality and quantity of their food. Continental Army quartermasters and prison commissaries found that obtaining sufficient foodstuffs was difficult, and at times impossible. Unlike the British (who had their prisoners concentrated along the coast, where supplies could be transported by the navy), Americans kept their captives far inland. Overland transport by wagon was expensive and unreliable, so alternative measures were required. For example, Washington wrote to the officer in charge of the Convention Army on Virginia's frontier, advising him to procure Indian cornmeal from nearby settlements instead of ordering Pennsylvania flour which might never arrive. To avoid such problems, Congress frequently selected York, Lancaster, and other farming communities in Pennsylvania - the "bread colony" - as the destination for newly captured prisoners.

Judging from prisoners' correspondence and journals that survived the war, it appears that British and German prisoners were generally treated fairly. The Germans, in particular, benefitted from a remarkable change in the prevailing attitude toward them. During their first year in America, they had been objects of fear and hatred. This resulted from patriot propaganda, as well as from reports of their ferocity in the Battle of Long Island. However, after proving themselves less than invincible at Trenton and Bennington, they gradually came to be viewed as pitiable creatures, victims of an oppressive system that forced them into the army and brought them to America to fight and die against their will. For example, a Pennsylvanian named Captain Biddle noted in his diary that his chief motive for enlisting had been to have a shot at the Hessians. But, after he came to know some German prisoners, his opinion of them changed; thereafter, he saw them as "poor wretches, obliged to go wherever they were ordered by their prince."

* * * * *

While American treatment of British and German prisoners, in general, could be characterized as humane, and in many cases liberal, the same, unfortunately, could not be said for British treatment of American captives. (A notable exception is Canada's Governor Guy Carleton. His humane treatment of Americans captured in the Canadian campaign has already been discussed in earlier chapters, and will not be repeated here.)

From the beginning of the war until their final departure in 1783, the British Army and Navy high command consistently maintained this unwritten policy: 1) American independence must not be recognized in any way; 2) the colonies were in rebellion, and therefore Americans captured while bearing arms were rebels; and 3) because they were rebels - not true prisoners of war - they must not be given the consideration normally shown to soldiers and sailors of acknowledged belligerent nations.

However, putting such a policy into practice posed a problem for the British commanders. The customary penalty for men caught in armed rebellion was death by hanging. But to resort to mass executions would invite a reciprocal bloodbath. On the other hand, treating rebels humanely as true prisoners of war might be misconstrued as acknowledging American independence.

Faced with this dilemna, how did the British treat their prisoners? The answer - pure neglect - was a compromise between hanging and humane treatment. A minimum of resources would be expended on the administration of prisoners. For example, Americans wounded and captured in battle might have their wounds dressed by British doctors on the battlefield, but thereafter they could expect no medical attention. Clothing and blankets would have to come from rebel authorities or private citizens, not from British supplies. Likewise, little or no efforts would be made to ensure that prisoners were provided with adequate lodging, food, or wood for heat in the cold months.

The results were predictable. Prisons were almost always overcrowded and unsanitary, with very little circulation of air, and no segregation of well and sick prisoners. They weakened and became vulnerable to scurvy, dysentery, pneumonia, and frequent epidemics of influenza, smallpox, and yellow fever that ravaged the prisons.

Congress could disperse British and German prisoners throughout the states, and allow local authorities to hire them out to civilians who wouldwould house and feed them. By contrast, the British Army and Navy had little choice but to concentrate their prisoners at their bases. For most American sailors, that meant the infamous prison ships (which will be discussed shortly). And for the great majority of American soldiers, capture meant detention on Manhattan Island, which the British held from September of 1776 until the war ended and they went back to England in 1783.

The 1776 campaign for New York resulted in a great influx of prisoners, especially the Battles of Long Island and Fort Washington, which together put almost 5000 soldiers in British hands. Very few were exchanged because Washington at that time had almost no captives of his own to offer in return. Some of the officers were granted parole in New York and Brooklyn, but most of the 5000 were herded into makeshift prisons. These included three New York "sugar houses" (warehouses that had formerly stocked rum, sugar and molasses), seven churches, King's College, City Hall, the two small city jails, and four prison ships.

Ethan Allen survived a year in prison in England before being transferred to New York, where he found lodging while on parole. He often visited the prisoners.

> I have gone into the churches and seen sundry of the prisoners in the agonies of death, pleading, for God's sake, for something to eat, and at the same time shivering with the cold. Hollow groans saluted my ears, despair on every one of their countenances. The filth in these churches, in consequence of the fluxes, was almost beyond description. I have seen in one of the churches seven dead, at the same time, lying among the excre-

ments of their bodies.

It was a common practice with the enemy to convey the dead from these filthy places in carts, to be slightly buried, and I have seen whole gangs of Tories making derision, and exulting over the dead, saying "There goes another load of d----d rebels!"

I was persuaded that I might endanger myself by frequenting these places, the most nauseous and contagious that could be conceived of. I refrained going into the churches, but frequently conversed with such of the prisoners as were admitted to come into the yard. The guard would often drive me away with their fixed bayonets but sometimes I could obtain a little conversation.

The prisoners came with their usual complaints to me, and among the rest a large-boned, tall young man, as he said from Pennsylvania, who was reduced to a mere skeleton. He said he was glad to see me before he died, which he had expected to have done last night, but was a little revived. He further informed me that he and his brother had been urged to enlist into the British army, but had both resolved to die first; that his brother had died last night, in consequence of that resolve, and that he expected shortly to follow him.

I made the other prisoners stand a little off, and told him with a low voice to enlist. He then asked whether it was right in the sight of God? I assured him that it was, and that duty to himself obliged him to deceive the British by enlisting, and deserting the first opportunity; upon which he answered that he would enlist. I charged him not to mention my name as his adviser, lest it should get air and I should be closely confined.

The integrity of these suffering prisoners is incredible. Many hundreds of them, I am confident, submitted to death rather than enlist.

Nearly all personal narratives of prisoners who survived to write about their experiences mention the pressure to enlist in the British Army or Navy. Just how many were strong willed enough to resist such temptation and endure an almost certain agonizing death is hard to say. The records that the British jailers kept were destroyed at the end of the war. A number of American soldiers, though, kept track of what happened to the men of their own companies. For example, Private Henry Bedinger recorded that, of the 79 men captured from his Virginia rifle company, 7 enlisted in the British service, 52 died in prison, and the remaining 20 survived long enough to be exchanged.

The most populous and infamous of New York's sugar houses was located, ironically, on Liberty Street. It was a dark, five-story, stone building. Inside, the prisoners used a nail to scratch their names and dates on the walls. Outside, a small exercise yard was surrounded by a board fence nine feet high. During the day, captives were sent into this yard twenty at a time for half hour periods. A path, nearly broad enough for a cart, circled the building and yard. Night and day, two British or German guards walked their weary rounds along that path.

Levi Hanford, years later, recalled one particular day's yard time:

> One day, while I was standing in the yard, near the high fence which enclosed the prison, a man passed by, in the street, and coming close to the fence, without stopping or turning his head, said in a low voice, "General Burgoyne is taken with all his army. It is a truth. You may depend upon it."
>
> This news was grateful to us indeed, and cheered us greatly in our wretched abode. Kept in entire ignorance, we had the most gloomy fears as to the result of our cause. How sweet to our ears, how soothing to our hearts! It gave us hope of liberation.

The sugar house had a row of small, deep windows resembling portholes on each of its five floors. Many years later, New Yorker William Dunlap still vividly recalled the sight he had beheld one summer's day: "In the suffocating heat, I saw every narrow aperture of these stone walls filled with human heads, face above face, seeking a portion of the external air." According to one of the unfortunate men who dwelled within those walls, the prisoners "divided their numbers into squads of six each. No. 1 stood for ten minutes as close to the windows as they could, and then No. 2 took their places, and so on." Although most of the windows had no shutters, one did. Each morning during good weather, they would take the shutter down from its hinges to use as a checker board. There were no seats to sit on, just the straw that served as their bedding.

Thomas Stone, of Connecticut, was captured in December of 1776 and spent six weeks on a prison ship before being transferred to one of the sugar houses.

> We left the floating Hell with joy, but alas, our joy was of short duration. Cold and famine were now our destiny. Not a pane of glass, nor even a board to a single window in the house, and no fire but once in three days to cook our small allowance of provision. Old shoes were eaten. A bone of four or five ounces, after it was picked clean, was sold by the British guard for as many coppers.
>
> In the spring our misery increased; frozen feet began to mortify. By the first of May, out of sixty-nine taken with me only fifteen were alive. Death stared the living in the face.
>
> About the twentieth of June I made my escape from the prison-yard. Just before the lamps were lighted, I got safely out of the city, passed all the guards, was often fired at, but still safe as to any injury done me; arrived at Harlem River eastward of King's Bridge. Hope and fear were now in full exercise. The alarm was

struck by the sentinels firing at me. I arrived at the banks of the Harlem - five men met me with their bayonets at my heart; to resist was instant death, and to give up, little better.

I was conducted to the main guard, kept there until morning then started for New York with bayonets at my back, arrived at my old habitation about 1 o'clock, p.m.; was introduced to the prison keeper who threatened me with instant death, gave me two heavy blows with his cane; I caught his arm and the guard interfered. Was driven to the provost, thrust into a dungeon, a stone floor, not a blanket, not a board, not a straw to rest on. Next day was visited by a refugee [Tory] lieutenant, offered to enlist me, offered a bounty, I declined. Next day renewed the visit, made further offers, told me the general was determined I should starve to death where I was, unless I would enter the service. I told him his general dare not do it. (I shall here omit the imprecations I gave.)

The third day I was visited by two British officers, offered me a sergeant's post, threatened me with death as before, in case I refused. I replied, "Death if they dare!" In about ten minutes the door was opened, a guard took me to my old habitation the sugar house, it being about the time of day I left my cell that I entered it, being three days and nights without a morsel of food or a drop of water - all this for the crime of getting out of prison. When in the dungeon reflecting upon my situation I thought if ever a mortal could be justified in praying for the destruction of his enemies, I am the man.

The 16th of July was exchanged. Language would fail me to describe the joy of that hour; but it was transitory. On the morning of the 16th, some refugees cast into the prison yard a quantity of warm bread, and it was devoured with greediness. The prison gate was opened, we marched out about the number of 250. Those belonging to the Eastern States were conducted to the North [Hudson] River and landed at New Jersey while those of the South were sent in an opposite direction as far from home as possible. Those who ate of the bread soon sickened; there was death in the bread they had eaten. The cry was "Poison, poison!" About half our number did not eat of the bread, as a report had been brought into the prison that the prisoners taken at Fort Washington had been poisoned in the same way.

The Commissary of Prisoners was responsible for the administration of all prisoners taken by the army. General Howe appointed Joshua Loring, a loyalist from Boston, to that powerful post. In return for being given this lucrative position, Loring allowed his wife, "a flashing blonde," to become Howe's mistress. The loyalist New Yorker, Judge Thomas Jones, commented on this arrangement in his history of the war. He wrote, that while Loring "fingered the cash, the General enjoyed Madam." Since Howe rarely interfered or showed much interest in prisoner administration, Loring took full advantage of his influential position. Rations for each prisoner were officially set at two-thirds that of a British soldier (a ration so meager the British soldiers had to supplement their rations by "foraging"). But even the two-thirds ration was rarely received by the prisoners, because Loring profited by having his Provost Marshal, William Cunningham, sell most rations on New York's flourishing black market.

Cunningham earned an even more notorious reputation than Loring, since he dealt with the prisoners on a day-to-day basis. A former soldier in the British Army, Cunningham came to New York in 1774 with a boatload of immigrants. He had promised them bright futures, but then secretly sold them into indentured servitude as payment for their passage. When war broke out, his blatant Toryism soon made him obnoxious to the New York Whigs and he was mobbed. Soon after, he fled to a British man-of-war which sailed to Boston, where Howe appointed him Provost Marshal, or chief jailer, in 1775. He was eventually hung in London, in 1791, as a convicted forger. Shortly before his death, he admitted having murdered over 250 American prisoners in New York by secret midnight hangings, and hundreds more by selling their rations. It was said he often boasted that "he had killed more rebels with his own hand than had been slain by all the King's forces in America."

Cunningham took sadistic pleasure in abusing the prisoners. For example, he would parade them in front of his guests while reciting, "This is a d----d rebel colonel, this one a rebel judge, &c." Some he had "play the fool by making them ride with a rope around their necks, seated on coffins, to the gallows," only to be released. His hangman, a large mulatto named Richmond, would parade around the jail with coils of ropes about his shoulders, requesting the prisoners to choose their own halters. Adrian Onderdonk saw Cunningham kick over vessels of soup, brought by local women who pitied the prisoners. Many captives wrote of Cunningham and others robbing them of their clothes, money, pocket watches and silver shoe buckles, declaring such things "too good for rebels."

Not all the captives were kept in the city's makeshift prisons. Many officers were paroled and lodged with inhabitants of New York or, more frequently, Long Island. The British assumed that, without their officers, the other prisoners would be more easily disciplined and less likely to plan escapes. Besides, since Howe wanted rebel authorities to grant parole to captured British and German officers, he had to reciprocate.

At times, Howe showed some humanity. This usually came after a large number of British soldiers were taken by the rebel army. For instance, after Trenton and Princeton, he released 2000 prisoners, "all that could walk, after taking their oath not to take up arms against His Majesty." Many released prisoners died before they arrived home. And many who did manage to struggle back to their loved ones unwittingly brought virulent companions. Diaries of the inhabitants often mention the outbreak of epidemics soon after the return of released soldiers, who had contracted fatal diseases while in prison.

Prison ships, known as "floating Hells," were an even worse stain on Britain's reputation than their land-based prison facilities. The most notorious prison ship was the former man-of-war *Jersey*. Most historians estimate that several thousand men died on this one ship alone. A woman who lived on the Long Island shore, and observed the almost daily burials there for years, claimed to have counted more than 11,000 corpses taken from the ships.

A profound feeling of dread could overwhelm anyone newly assigned to one of these infamous prison ships. Thomas Dring, of Rhode Island, describes his arrival on the *Jersey*:

> The prisoners were ordered into the [row]boats and told to apply themselves to the oars, but declined to exert themselves, whereupon Sproat scowled at them and remarked, "I'll soon fix you, my lads!"
>
> My station in the boat as we hauled alongside was exactly opposite one of the air-ports in the side of the ship. From this aperture proceeded a strong current of foul vapor which produced a sensation of nausea far beyond my powers of description. Here, while waiting for orders to ascend on board, we were addressed by some of the prisoners from the air-ports. After some questions whence we came, and the manner of our capture, one of the prisoners said that it was a lamentable thing to see so many young men in the prime of health and vigor condemned to a living grave.

In 1778, the Connectiuct Gazette published an account of Robert Sheffield's first descent to his new residence below decks.

> On opening these hatches, the steam of the hold was enough to scald the skin and take away the breath, the

stench enough to poison the air all around. On descending, and beholding the numerous spectacles of wretchedness and despair, his soul fainted within him.

Thomas Dring describes the terrors of the night:

> Silence was a stranger to our dark abode. The groans of the sick and dying, the curses poured out upon our inhuman keepers, the restlessness caused by the suffocating heat and the confined and poisonous air, mingled with the wild and incoherent ravings of delirium, were the sounds which every night were raised around us. On the upper deck the sentinels paced through the night with the ringing cry, "All's well!"

That first night on the *Jersey*, Dring recalled, "Thoughts of sleep did not enter my mind." He continues his account:

> During the night, I had been tormented with what I supposed to be vermin, and on coming upon deck [in the morning] I found that a black silk handkerchief, which I wore around my neck, was completely spotted with them. Although this had often been mentioned as one of the nuisances of the place, yet as I had never before been in a situation to witness anything of the kind, the sight made me shudder. I knew at once that, as long as I should remain on board, these loathsome creatures would be my constant companions and unceasing tormentors.
>
> The next disgusting object which met my sight was a man suffering from small-pox, and in a few minutes I found myself surrounded by many others laboring under the same disease in every stage of its progress.
>
> The first of the crew of the *Chance* to die was a lad

named Palmer, about twelve years of age, a waiter to our officers. The night he died was a truly wretched one for me. I spent most of it in total darkness, holding him during his convulsions. I assisted to sew a blanket around his body, which was, with others who had died during the night, conveyed upon deck in the morning.

Each day, the jailors selected a "working party" from among the prisoners. Their duties included hoisting aboard supplies, hauling up the latrine tubs and dumping them overboard, and rowing the night's dead ashore for a quick burial without benefit of clergy. The resulting shallow graves often proved to be temporary, since storms would expose the decaying bodies and eventually wash them out to sea.

Despite the physical labor required of the working party members, the keepers had no trouble rounding up volunteers. They received an extra ration of food, the work gave them something to do, and they were able to temporarily leave the hated ship. Dring recalls one trip to the Long Island shore:

> It was a high gratification for us to bury our feet in the sand and to shove them through it as we passed on our way. We went by a small patch of turf, some pieces of which we tore up from the earth, and obtained permission to carry them on board for our comrades to smell ... [on board] every fragment was passed from hand to hand, and its smell inhaled, as if it had been a fragrant rose.

Thomas Philbrook was a frequent member of a working party assigned the tasks of scrubbing the decks, attending the sick, and bringing up the dead.

> As the morning dawned, there would be heard the loud, unfeeling and horrid cry, "Rebels! Bring up your

dead!" Staggering under the weight of some stark still form, I would at length gain the upper deck, when I would be met with the salutation "What! you alive yet? Well, you are a tough one!"

Prison ship guards were rotated weekly and came from the different regiments stationed on Long Island. According to one prisoner:

> We always preferred the Hessians, from whom we received better treatment. The English merely obeyed their orders, but the [Tory] Refugees were viewed by us with scorn and hatred. Their presence occasioned much tumult and confusion; for the prisoners could not endure the sight of these men, and assailed them with abusive language, while they, in turn, treated us with all the severity in their power.

Poor food added to the utter wretchedness of life aboard a prison ship. Ebenezer Fox explains:

> All our food appeared to be damaged. The bread was mostly mouldy, and filled with worms. It required considerable rapping upon the deck before these worms could be dislodged from their lurking places in a biscuit. The cooking was done in a great copper vessel. The *Jersey*, from her size and lying near the shore, was embedded in the mud, and I don't recollect seeing her afloat the whole time I was a prisoner. All the filth that accumulated among upward of a thousand men was daily thrown overboard and would remain there until carried away by the tide. The impurity of the water may be easily conceived, and in that water our meat was boiled.

George Washington felt for all prisoners deeply, and perhaps especially for the prison ship inmates. However, he could not justify exchanging American sailors on the verge of death for healthy captive British soldiers. He therefore insisted that army prisoners be exchanged for army prisoners, and navy for navy. Furthermore, he absolutely refused to give up British soldiers for captive American civilians, since that would have encouraged unscrupulous British commanders to tap the unending supply of rebel suspects in occupied territories.

Because of this policy, soldiers had a better chance of being exchanged than sailors. Thus, most of the men on the prison ships (chiefly American privateersmen and some French sailors) stayed there until they either died or were released. Also hindering the exchange of American sailors was a shortage of captive British seamen to offer in return. The reason for this shortage was explained by Washington to a Congressional committee looking into the matter:

> It was a common practice for them [British seamen captured by privateers] to enter [enlist] as seamen. When this was not the case, they were usually set at liberty as soon as the privateers arrived in port; as neither the owners, nor the town or state where they were landed, would be at the expense of their confinement and maintenance.

For many prison ship captives, "the long endurance of their privations rendered them almost indifferent to their fate, and they appeared to look forward to death as the termination of their captivity." Yet others "lived on hope." For Thomas Dring, that hope was realized when he and the other members of his crew were exchanged. Dring was given a ride home to Providence by an American sea captain. He describes his arrival:

> It was a beautiful moonlit evening, and the intelligence

378

of our arrival having spread through the town, the nearest wharf was in a short time crowded with people drawn together by curiosity, and a desire for information relative to the fate of their friends and connections.

Continual inquiries were made from the anxious crowd on the land respecting the condition of several different individuals on board. At length, the information was given that some of our number were below, sick with the yellow fever. No sooner was this fact announced than the wharf was totally deserted, and in a few moments not a human being remained in sight. The Old Jersey fever, as it was called, was well known throughout the whole country. All were acquainted with its terrible effects.

Even when a former prisoner didn't have a contagious disease, his wasted appearance often shocked his loved ones. Andrew Sherburne was finally released and went home to Rhode Island in 1783, when the British finally abandoned the *Jersey* and left America for good.

My brother Sam took me into another room to divest me of my filthy garments and to wash and dress me. He having taken off my clothes and seen my bones projecting here and there, was so astonished that his strength left him. He sat down on the point of fainting, and could render me no further service. I was able to wash myself and put on my clothes.

Though broken in health, Andrew Sherburne was one of the lucky ones, for he survived.

SELECTED BIBLIOGRAPHY

Author's Note: Many of the sources, both primary and secondary, listed here were first published in the nineteenth or late eighteenth century, and later reprinted in the twentieth century. I have listed here not necessarily the original edition, nor the most recent reprint, but rather the edition that I consulted.

Primary Sources

Ainslie, Thomas, *Canada Preserved, The Journal of Captain Thomas Ainslie.* Edited by Sheldon S. Cohen. New York: New York University Press, 1968.

Allen, Ethan, *The Narrative of Colonel Ethan Allen.* Bedford, Mass.: Applewood Books, 1989.

Anburey, Thomas, *Travels Through the Interior Parts of North America.* Boston: Houghton Mifflin, 1923.

Anonymous, *Blockade of Quebec in 1775-1776 by the American Revolutionists (Les Bastonnais).* Edited by Fred C. Wurtele. Port Washington, N.Y.: Kennikat Press, 1970.

Anonymous, *Letters From America 1776-1779, Being Letters of Brunswick, Hessian and Waldeck Officers with the British Armies During the Revolution.* Translated and edited by Ray W. Pettengill. Boston: Houghton Mifflin, 1924.

Baldwin, Jeduthan, *The Revolutionary Journal of Colonel Jeduthan Baldwin 1775-1778.* Edited by Thomas Williams Baldwin. Bangor, Maine: The DeBurians, 1906.

Baxter, James Phinney, *The British Invasion from the North, Digby's Journal of the Campaigns of Generals Carleton and Burgoyne from Canada, 1776-1777.* New York: Da Capo Press, 1970.

Beebe, Lewis, *Journal of Lewis Beebe, A Physician on the Campaign Against Canada, 1776.* Edited by Frederic R. Kirkland. Philadelphia: Historical Society of Pennsylvania, 1935.

Bushnell, Charles I., *A Narrative of the Life and Adventures of Levi Hanford, a Soldier of the Revolution.* New York: Privately printed, 1863.

Commanger, Henry Steele, and Richard B. Morris, ed., *The Spirit of 'Seventy-Six, The Story of the American Revolution as told by the Participants.* New York: Harper & Row, 1975.

Crary, Catherine S., ed., *The Price of Loyalty, Tory Writings from the Revolutionary Era.* New York: McGraw-Hill, 1973.

Dearborn, Henry, *Revolutionary War Journals of Henry Dearborn 1775-1783.* Edited by Lloyd A. Brown and Howard H. Peckham. Chicago: The Caxton Club, 1939.

Dorson, Richard M., ed., *America Rebels, Personal Narratives of the American Revolution.* New York: Pantheon, 1953.

DuRoi, *Journal of DuRoi the Elder, Lieutenant and Adjutant in the Service of the Duke of Brunswick 1776-1778.* Edited by Charles S. J. Epping. New York: D. Appleton & Co., 1911.

Emerson, William, *Diaries and Letters of William Emerson 1743-1776.* Edited by Amelia Forbes Emerson. Boston: Thomas Todd, 1972.

Fellows, Rozzle, "Letter" from Crown Point, September 2, 1775, to his father in Canaan, Conn. Hartford: Unpublished manuscript in the Connecticut State Archives collection, Conn. State Library.

Greenwood, John, *The Revolutionary Services of John Greenwood of Boston and New York 1775-1783.* Edited by Isaac Greenwood. New York: DeVinne Press, 1922.

Hadden, James M., *A Journal kept in Canada and upon Burgoyne's Campaign in 1776 and 1777. Also Orders kept by him and Issued by Sir Guy Carleton, Lieut. General John Burgoyne and Major General William Phillips.* Albany: Joel Munsell's Sons, 1884.

Hart, Albert Bushnell, ed., *American History Told By Contemporaries, v. 2.* New York: MacMillan, 1898.

Herbert, Charles, *The Prisoners of 1776 ... compiled from the journal of Charles Herbert.* Edited by Reverend R. Livesey. Boston: George C. Rand, 1854.

Hughes, Thomas, *A Journal by Thos. Hughes, for his Amusement, & Designed only for his Perusal by the Time he Attains the Age of 50 if he Lives so Long.* Edited by E. A. Benians. Cambridge, England: The University Press, 1947.

Lamb, Roger, *An Original and Authentic Journal of Occurrences during the late American War, from its commencement to the year 1783.* Dublin, Ireland: Wilkinson & Courtney, 1809.

Lowenthal, Larry, ed., *Days of Siege, A Journal of the Siege of Fort Stanwix in 1777.* Eastern Acorn Press, 1983.

Moore, Frank, ed., *Diary of the Revolution, from Newspapers and Original Documents.* New York: Scribner, 1860.

Pausch, Georges, *Journal of Captain Pausch, Chief of Hanau Artillery during the Burgoyne Campaign.* Translated and edited by William L. Stone. Albany: Munsell's Sons, 1890.

Riedesel, Friedrich von, *Memoirs and Letters and Journals of Major General Riedesel During His Residence in America, 2 vols.* Edited by William L. Stone. Albany: Munsell's Sons, 1868.

Riedesel, Friederike, *Baroness von Riedesel and the American Revolution, Journal and Correspondence of a Tour of Duty 1776-1783.* Edited by Marvin L. Brown, Jr. Chapel Hill, N.C.: University of North Carolina Press, 1965.

Roberts, Kenneth, ed., *March To Quebec, Journals of the Members of Arnold's Expedition.* Garden City, N.Y.: Doubleday, 1947.

Scheer, George F., and Hugh F. Rankin, *Rebels and Redcoats.* Cleveland: World Publishing Co., 1957.

Thacher, James, *A Military Journal During the American Revolutionary War, from 1775-1783.* Boston: Cottons & Barnard, 1827.

Washington, George, *The Writings of George Washington, v. IV.* Edited by Jared Sparks. Boston: Russell, Odiorne and Metcalf, 1834.

Watson, Winslow C., ed., *Men and Times of the Revolution, or Memoirs of Elkanah Watson.* New York: Dana, 1856.

Wheeler, Richard, *Voices of 1776.* New York: Crowell, 1972.

Willett, William M., *A Narrative of the Military Actions of Colonel Marinus Willett.* New York: New York Times and Arno Press,

1969.

Wright, Esmond, *The Fire of Liberty*. London, England: The Folio Society, 1983.

Secondary Works

Alden, John R., *The American Revolution 1775-1783*. New York: Harper, 1954.

Alden, John R., *A History of the American Revolution*. New York: Knopf, 1969.

Allen, Freeman H., "St. Leger's Invasion and the Battle of Oriskany," New York State Historical Association *Proceedings*, v. 12, 1913.

Anderson, Troyer Steele, *The Command of the Howe Brothers During the American Revolution*. New York: Oxford University Press, 1936.

Atwood, Rodney, *The Hessians, Mercenaries from Hessen-Kassel in the American Revolution*. Cambridge, England: Cambridge University Press, 1980.

Bakeless, John, *Turncoats, Traitors and Heroes*. Philadelphia: Lippincott, 1959.

Bancroft, George, *History of the United States of America, v. 4*. New York: Appleton, 1893.

Bellico, Russell P., *Sails and Steam in the Mountains, A Maritime and Military History of Lake George and Lake Champlain*. Fleischmanns, N.Y.: Purple Mountain Press, 1992.

Bennett, Clarence E., *Advance and Retreat to Saratoga in the American Revolution, The American Offensive and the Burgoyne Campaign*. Boston: Gregg Press, 1972.

Bird, Harrison, *Attack on Quebec, The American Invasion of Canada, 1775*. New York: Oxford University Press, 1968.

Bird, Harrison, *March to Saratoga, General Burgoyne and the American Campaign, 1777*. New York: Oxford University Press, 1963.

Blumenthal, Walter Hart, *Women Camp Followers of the American*

Revolution. Philadelphia: George S. MacManus Co., 1952.

Bowie, Lucie Leigh, "The German Prisoners in the American Revolution," *Maryland Historical Magazine*, v. XL, 1945.

Bowman, Allen, *The Morale of the American Revolutionary Army.* Port Washington, N.Y.: Kennikat Press, 1964.

Bowman, Larry G., *Captive Americans: Prisoners During the American Revolution.* Athens, Ohio: Ohio University Press, 1976.

Bush, Martin H., *Revolutionary Enigma, A Reappraisal of General Philip Schuyler of New York.* Port Washington, N.Y.: Ira J. Friedman, 1969.

Carrington, Henry B., *Battles of the American Revolution, 1775-1781, Including Battle Maps and Charts of the American Revolution.* New York: Promontory Press, 1973.

Chidsey, Donald Barr, *The War in the North.* New York: Crown, 1967.

Coakley, Robert W., and Stetson Conn, *The War of the American Revolution.* Washington, D.C.: Center of Military History, U.S. Army, 1975.

Codman, John, *Arnold's Expedition to Quebec.* New York: MacMillan, 1902.

Cortesi, Lawrence, "The Tragic Romance of Jane McCrae," *American History Illustrated*, v. XX, no. 2, April 1985.

Cumming, William P., and Hugh Rankin, *The Fate of a Nation, The American Revolution through Contemporary Eyes.* London, England: Phaidon Press, 1975.

Dabney, William M., *After Saratoga: The Story of the Convention Army.* Albuquerque: University of New Mexico Press, 1954.

Dandridge, Danske, *American Prisoners of the Revolution.* Baltimore: Genealogical Publishing Co., 1967.

Davis, Burke, *George Washington and the American Revolution.* New York: Random House, 1975.

Davis, Kenneth S., "In the name of the Great Jehovah and the Continental Congress!" *American Heritage*, v. XIV, no. 6, October 1963.

Eelking, Max von, *The German Allies in the American Revolution,*

1776-1783. Baltimore: Genealogical Publishing Co., 1969.

Fleming, Thomas J., "The Enigma of General Howe," *American Heritage*, v. XV, no. 2, February, 1964.

Flexner, James Thomas, *George Washington in the Revolution.* Boston: Little, Brown, 1965. Volume 4 of a 5 volume set.

Flood, Charles Bracelen, *Rise, And Fight Again, Perilous Times Along the Road to Independence.* New York: Dodd, Mead, 1976.

Freeman, Douglas Southall, *George Washington, A Biography. Volume 4: Leader of the Revolution.* New York: Scribner's Sons, 1951.

French, Allen, *The First Year Of The American Revolution.* Cambridge, Mass.: Riverside Press, 1934.

French, Allen, *Taking of Ticonderoga in 1775: the British Story.* Cambridge, Mass.: Harvard University Press, 1928.

Furneaux, Rupert, *The Battle of Saratoga.* New York: Stein and Day, 1971.

Gruber, Ira D., *The Howe Brothers and the American Revolution.* New York: Atheneum, 1972.

Haiman, Miecislaus, *Kosciuszko in the American Revolution.* Boston: Gregg Press, 1972.

Hamilton, Edward P., *Fort Ticonderoga, Key to a Continent.* Boston: Little, Brown, 1964.

Hargreaves, Reginald, *The Bloodybacks, The British Serviceman in North America and the Carribbean 1655-1783.* New York: Walker and Co., 1968.

Hargreaves, Reginald, "Burgoyne and America's Destiny," *American Heritage*, v. VII, no. 4, June 1956.

Hatch, Robert McConnell, *Thrust For Canada, the American Attempt on Quebec in 1775-1776.* Boston: Houghton Mifflin, 1979.

Hibbert, Christopher, *Redcoats and Rebels, The American Revolution Through British Eyes.* New York: Norton, 1990.

Higginbotham, Don, *The War of American Independence, Military Attitudes, Policies, and Practice, 1763-1789.* New York: MacMillan, 1971.

Holden, James Austin, "Influence of the Death of Jane McCrea on Burgoyne's Campaign," *New York State Historical Association Proceedings*, v. 12, 1913.

Hubbard, Timothy William, "Battle At Valcour Island: Benedict Arnold As Hero," *American Heritage*, v. XVII, no. 6, October, 1966.

Huddleston, F. J., *Gentleman Johnny Burgoyne*. London, England: Jonathan Cape, 1928.

Hughes, Rupert, *George Washington*. Three volumes. New York: William Morrow Co., 1930.

Jensen, Merrill, *The Founding of a Nation, A History of the American Revolution, 1763-1776*. New York: Oxford University Press, 1968.

Kidder, Frederic, *History of the First New Hampshire Regiment in the War of the Revolution*. Albany: Joel Munsell, 1868.

Krueger, John W., "Troop Life at the Champlain Valley Forts during the American Revolution," *The Bulletin of the Fort Ticonderoga Museum*, v. 4, no. 3, Summer 1982.

Lancaster, Bruce, *From Lexington to Liberty, The Story of the American Revolution*. Garden City, N.Y.: Doubleday, 1955.

Lowell, Edward J., *The Hessians and the other German Auxiliaries of Great Britain in the Revolutionary War*. New York: Harper Brothers, 1884.

MacGregor, Bruce, "A Failure to Communicate, The British & Saratoga," *American History Illustrated*, v. XX, no. 6, October 1985.

Martin, James Kirby, "'A Most Undisciplined, Profligate Crew': Protest and Defiance in the Continental Ranks, 1776-1783." In *Arms and Independence, The Military Character of the American Revolution*. Edited by Ronald Hoffman and Peter J. Albert. Charlottesville, Va.: University Press of Virginia, 1984.

Matthews, A. D. Sons, *Dedication of the Prison Ship Martyrs Monument, Nov. 14, 1908*.

Mauldin, Bill, *Mud & Guts, A look at the common soldier of the American Revolution*. Division of Publications, National Park Service, U.S. Department of the Interior, 1978.

Metzger, Charles H., *The Prisoners in the American Revolution*. Chicago: Loyola University Press, 1971.

Middlekauff, Robert, *The Glorious Cause, The American Revolution, 1763-1789.* New York: Oxford University Press, 1982.

Miller, John C., *Triumph of Freedom 1775-1783.* Boston: Little, Brown, 1948.

Mitchell, Joseph B., *Discipline and Bayonets, The Armies and Leaders in the War of the American Revolution.* New York: Putnam's Sons, 1967.

Montross, Lynn, *Rag, Tag and Bobtail, The Story of the Continental Army 1775-1783.* New York: Harper & Brothers, 1952.

Moore, Howard Parker, *A Life of General John Stark.* New York: H. P. Moore, 1949.

Morrison, Samuel E., *The Oxford History of the American People.* New York: Oxford University Press, 1965.

Neilson, Charles, *Burgoyne's Campaign.* Port Washington, N.Y.: Kennikat Press, 1970.

Nelson, Paul David, "Legacy of Controversy: Gates, Schuyler and Arnold at Saratoga 1777." In *Military Analysis of the Revolutionary War,* edited by the American Military Institute. Millwood, N.Y.: KTO Press, 1977.

Nelson, Paul David, *General Horatio Gates.* Baton Rouge, LA: Louisiana State University Press, 1976.

Nickerson, Hoffman, *The Turning Point of the Revolution, Or Burgoyne in America.* Port Washington, N.Y.: Kennikat Press, 1967.

Pancake, John S., *1777, Year of the Hangman.* University, Alabama: University of Alabama Press, 1977.

Palmer, Dave Richard, *The Way of the Fox, American Strategy in the War for America 1775-1783.* Westport, Conn.: Greenwood Press, 1975.

Pearson, Michael, *Those Damned Rebels: The American Revolution As Seen Through British Eyes.* New York: Putnam's Sons, 1972.

Peckham, Howard H., *The War For Independence, A Military History.* Chicago: University of Chicago Press, 1958.

Randall, Willard Sterne, *Benedict Arnold, Patriot and Traitor.* New

York: William Morrow, 1990.

Rawson, Jonathan, *1776, A Day-by-Day Story*. New York: Frederick A. Stokes Co, 1927.

Roberts, Robert B., *New York's Forts in the Revolution*. Rutherford, N.J.: Fairleigh Dickinson University Press, 1980.

Robson, Eric, *The American Revolution In Its Political and Military Aspects*. New York: Norton, 1966.

Rossie, Jonathan Gregory, *The Politics of Command in the American Revolution*. Syracuse, N.Y.: Syracuse University Press, 1975.

Royster, Charles, *A Revolutionary People at War, The Continental Army and American Character, 1775-1783*. New York: Norton, 1979.

Scott, John Anthony, *Trumpet of a Prophecy, Revolutionary America 1763-1783*. New York: Knopf, 1969.

Shy, John, *A People Numerous And Armed, Reflections on the Military Struggle for American Independence*. New York: Oxford University Press, 1976.

Smith, George, *An Universal Military Dictionary, A Copious Explanation of the Technical Terms &c. used in the Equipment, Machinery, Movements and Military Operations of an Army*. Ottawa, Ontario: Museum Restoration Service, 1969.

Smith, Justin H., *Our Struggle For The Fourteenth Colony, Canada and the American Revolution*. Two volumes. New York: Putnam's Sons, 1907.

Smith, Page, *A New Age Now Begins, A People's History of the American Revolution*. New York: McGraw-Hill, 1976.

Stanley, George F.G., *Canada Invaded 1775-1776*. Toronto, Ontario: Hakkert, 1973. Number 8 in the Canadian War Museum historical publications.

Stone, William L., *The Campaign of Lieut. Gen. John Burgoyne and the Expedition of Lieut. Col. Barry St. Leger*. New York: Da Capo Press, 1970.

Stone, William L., *Visits to the Saratoga Battle-Grounds, 1780-1880*. Albany: Joel Munsell's Sons, 1895.

Sweetman, John, *Saratoga, 1777.* New York: Hippocrene Books, 1973.

Tharp, Louise Hall, *The Baroness and the General.* Boston: Little, Brown, 1962.

Trevelyan, George Otto, *The American Revolution.* New York: McKay, 1964.

Tucker, Glenn, *Mad Anthony Wayne and the New Nation.* Harrisburg, Penn.: Stackpole Books, 1973.

Tuckerman, Bayard, *Life of General Philip Schuyler.* Freeport, N.Y.: Books for Libraries Press, 1969.

Underdal, Stanley J., ed., *Military History of the American Revolution, The Proceedings of the 6th Military History Symposium U.S. Air Force Academy 10-11 October 1974.* Washington, D.C.: Office of Air Force History, Headquarters USAF and U.S. Air Force Academy, 1976.

Upham, George B., "Burgoyne's Great Mistake," *New England Quarterly*, v. 3, October 1930.

Ward, Christopher L., *The War of the Revolution.* New York: MacMillan, 1952.

Wheeler, Joseph L., and Mabel A. Wheeler, *The Mount Independence-Hubbardton 1776 Military Road.* Benson, Vermont: J. L. Wheeler, 1968.

Williams, John, *The Battle of Hubbardton, The American Rebels Stem the Tide.* Montpelier, Vermont: Vermont Division for Historic Preservation, 1988.